Security Operations in the 21st Century

Canadian Perspectives on the Comprehensive Approach

Edited by Michael Rostek and Peter Gizewski

QCIR
QUEEN'S CENTRE FOR INTERNATIONAL RELATIONS

McGill-Queen's University Press
Montreal & Kingston • London • Ithaca

SCHOOL OF
Queen's
UNIVERSITY
Policy Studies

Publications Unit
Robert Sutherland Hall
138 Union Street
Kingston, ON, Canada
K7L 3N6
www.queensu.ca/sps/

The preferred citation for this book is:
Rostek, M., and P. Gizewski, eds. 2011. *Security Operations in the 21st Century: Canadian Perspectives on the Comprehensive Approach.* Montreal and Kingston: Queen's Policy Studies Series, McGill-Queen's University Press.

Library and Archives Canada Cataloguing in Publication

   Security operations in the 21st century : Canadian perspectives on the comprehensive approach / edited by Michael Rostek and Peter Gizewski.

Co-published by: School of Policy Studies and McGill-Queen's University Press.

Based on papers presented at the Canadian Perspectives on the Comprehensive Approach Conference held at Queen's University, Kingston, Ont., from April 15-16, 2010.
Includes bibliographical references.
ISBN 978-1-55339-351-1

   1. National security—Canada—History—21st century. I. Rostek, M. A. (Michael A.), 1961- II. Gizewski, Peter III. Queen's University (Kingston, Ont.). Centre for International Relations IV. Queen's University (Kingston, Ont.). School of Policy Studies

UA600.S43 2011   355'.033071

C2011-901297-9

TABLE OF CONTENTS

List of Figures vii

Preface, *Michel Rentenaar* ix

Acknowledgement xi

Abbreviations xiii

INTRODUCTION
Security Operations and the Comprehensive Approach,
Kim Richard Nossal 1

PART I: (RE-)DISCOVERING THE COMPREHENSIVE
APPROACH

Chapter 1: Discovering the Comprehensive Approach,
Peter Gizewski 13

Chapter 2: Discovering Effective Civil-Military Cooperation:
Insights from the NGO-CF Relationship, *Laura C. Ball and
Angela Febbraro* 25

Chapter 3: International Development of the Comprehensive
Approach, *Caroline Vavro and Richard Roy* 35

PART II: NON-GOVERNMENTAL PERSPECTIVES

Chapter 4: Comprehensive Approach and Fragile States:
Non-Governmental Organizations' Roles in Fragile Situations,
Nipa Banerjee 49

Chapter 5: Comprehensive Approach: A View from
South of the Border, *Beth Ellen Cole* 59

Chapter 6: We Share the Same Space, Not the Same Purpose: The Comprehensive Approach and Médecins sans Frontières, *Marilyn McHarg and Kevin Coppock* 67

PART III: COMPREHENSIVE APPROACH TODAY – INTERNATIONAL OPERATIONS

Chapter 7: The Joint, Interagency, Multi-national and Public (JIMP) Environment: Military Operations in a Crowded Battle-space, *Jim Simms* 75

Chapter 8: Comprehensive Approach: Towards a Strategic Doctrine, *START Secretariat* 87

Chapter 9: Civil-Military Coordination: Canada's Experience in Kandahar, 2005-2009, *Gavin Buchan* 97

Chapter 10: The Role of Development in a Comprehensive Approach, *Michael Koros and Xiang He* 109

Chapter 11: Military Considerations in Assisting Failed States, *Richard Roy* 121

PART IV: COMPREHENSIVE APPROACH TODAY – DOMESTIC OPERATIONS

Chapter 12: Comprehensive Approach, Domestic Operations: Integrated Border Enforcement Teams, *Todd Hataley* 135

Chapter 13: Canada's Northern Strategy: A Case Study in Horizontal Management, *John Kozij and Sylvia Bogusis* 149

Chapter 14: Family Relations: A Preliminary Analysis of the Use of the Comprehensive Approach at the Vancouver 2010 Winter Olympics, *Bernard Brister* 165

PART V: MAKING THE COMPREHENSIVE APPROACH WORK

Chapter 15: Religious Leader Engagement and the Comprehensive Approach: An Enhanced Capability for Operational Chaplains as Whole of Government Partners, *Steve Moore* 179

Chapter 16: A Trainer's Perspective on the Comprehensive Approach, *Steve Fritz-Millett* 193

Chapter 17: Interagency Training for the Canadian Comprehensive Mission in Afghanistan, *Megan Thompson, Angela Febbraro, and Anne-Renée Blais* 203

Chapter 18: The Relationship Between Non-Governmental
Organizations and the Canadian Forces, *Tara Holton,
Angela Febbraro, Emily-Ana Filardo, Marissa Barnes,
Brenda Fraser, and Rachel Spiece* 215

Chapter 19: The Comprehensive Approach: An Emergent
International Norm?, *Michael Rostek*...227

CONCLUSION, *Christian Leuprecht*...237

Notes 249

References...259

Contributors...279

LIST OF FIGURES

Figure 1: Strategic Framework for Stabilization and
Reconstruction...63

Figure 2: JIMP Visualized...78

Figure 3: RC (S) Representation of Stakeholders in 2008
Provided by Chief of Staff RC (S) 2 May 2008 83

Figure 4: RC (S) Operational Framework 84

Figure 5: Circumpolar Map 151

Figure 6: Ayles Ice Shelf..152

Figure 7: Arctic Marine Area 153

Figure 8: Canada's Icebreaker, Louis S. St-Laurent, Works with
US Coast Guard Cutter Healy 156

Figure 9: Governance Structure for the *Northern Strategy*......157

Figure 10: Canada's Northern Strategy 158

Figure 11: Religious Leader Engagement 187

Figure 12: Schematic of Joint Interagency Multinational
Public Concept...188

Figure 13: McKinsey 7-s 196

Figure 14: Schematic Representation of Common Interest
between Two Organizations 199

Figure 15: Type of Interaction...200

Figure 16: Primary Negotiation Strategies 201

PREFACE

Michel Rentenaar

Opening a newspaper with coverage of places like Iraq or Afghanistan, one often gets the impression that we win the wars, but tend to lose the peace. Now obviously the world is a little more complicated than that, but there is some truth to that statement. Indeed our armies are better trained, better equipped, and even better fed than the average insurgent. In direct combat, we therefore tend to win the kinetic fight in the short run. However, present-day security challenges both at home and abroad are very complex and therefore demand what is called a comprehensive approach.

There are many names floating around. Some call it a comprehensive approach, others an integrated or whole-of-government approach, and again others a 3D approach (defence, diplomacy, and development). I would say, "in the end rain is wet": this is not about definitions; this is about a different mindset to stability operations and crisis management.

Let us look at what the military does well. First of all, they obey orders (which is very nice, because otherwise we would have a coup d'état – I rather like democratic and civilian control over our military). Secondly, they are the best planners in the world. Don't ever ask diplomats (I am one myself) to plan how to get half a million people with their equipment from one place to the other. Thirdly, they have an excellent can-do mentality (don't give me problems, give me solutions, fix it!). All of these are remarkable strengths of our militaries. There are, however, also things that the military does not excel in. On average, they are not the greatest experts on politics, governance, and development, on tribal relations, and on root causes of conflict. For that one needs some specific civilian know-how.

The mindset that present-day challenges demand a comprehensive approach whereby military and civilians deconflict and where possible work together on security, governance, and development is recognized by our governments. In fact, there is no development without security, but, equally so, there is no lasting security without development and re-building of good governance. For NATO, this is laid down in the Strategic Concept that was recently agreed at the Lisbon summit (the UN and the EU have similar policy declarations).

But the debates about comprehensive approach (in Brussels, New York, or Ottawa) are not just held on a diplomatic level or in academic circles. Much experience about what works and what does not has been gained at the tactical field level in the Balkans, in Iraq, and in Afghanistan. In fact, you will find many such good examples in this book in front of you, including domestic applications. Within NATO, we are working on incorporating lessons learned from the field, on concept and doctrine development, on training and exercises with international community actors (IOs and NGOs), and on reforming our organization to be capable of covering the full spectrum of crisis management. On a personal note, I myself enjoyed and learned an awful lot from working together with British and American civil affairs teams during my two tours as a political advisor in Iraq and from, e.g., the Canadian Provincial Reconstruction Team in Kandahar during my time as civilian representative of the adja-cent Task Force Uruzgan. Seldom have I been more jealous of someone's job title than when I interacted closely with the Representative of Canada in Kandahar (the RoCK).

Let me end by quoting the NATO SCR in Afghanistan: "the com-prehensive approach is no guarantee for success of the mission, but the absence of it is a guarantee for failure." In my own words: military can-do and specific civilian know-how give us a pretty good shot.

Michel Rentenaar
Civil-Military Interface Advisor
NATO's Supreme Headquarters, Allied Powers in Europe

ACKNOWLEDGEMENT

The editors would like to acknowledge Mr. Regan Reshke, CD, PEng, OLS/OLIP, DCLD Science Advisor, for his substantial work on this project. Indeed, this book could not have been completed without his exceptional dedication, knowledge, and contributions to the effort.

ABBREVIATIONS

3D	Defence, Diplomacy, Development
3D PLUS	Defence, Diplomacy, Development and Commerce
3D+C	Defence, Diplomacy, Development and Commerce
ABCA	American, British, Canadian, Australian, and New Zealand Armies' Program
ADM	Assistant Deputy Minister
AIA	Apply a Model – Identify Interests – Adopt a Strategy
ANA	Afghan National Army
AU	African Union
BEST	Border Enforcement Security Task Force
CA	Comprehensive Approach
CANADEM	Canada "Experts Mobilized"
CanNor	Canadian Northern Economic Development Agency
CAPRA	Clients, Acquiring and Analyzing Information, Partnerships, Response, Assessment
CAS	Complex Adaptive Systems
CBSA	Canadian Border Services Agency
CCOA	Cabinet Committee on Afghanistan
CEDAW	Convention on the Elimination of All Forms of Discrimination Against Women
CEFCOM	Canadian Expeditionary Force Command
CF	Canadian Forces
CFD	Chief of Force Development
CIDA	Canadian International Development Agency
CIMIC	Civil-military cooperation
CoE	Centre of Excellence
COIN	Counter-Insurgency

Comd	Commander
CoPs	Communities of Practice
CRC	UN Convention on the Rights of the Child
CSC	Corrections Services Canada
CSIS	Center for Strategic and International Studies
CSIS	Canadian Security Intelligence Service
CSTC-A	Combined Security Transition Command-Afghanistan
DART	Disaster Assistance Response Team
DDR	Disarmament, Development, and Reconstruction
DEVAD	Development Advisor
DFAIT	Department of Foreign Affairs and International Trade
DFID	Department for International Development
DITF	Darfur Integrated Task Force
DLCD	Directorate of Land Concepts and Designs
DND	Department of National Defence
DRDC (CORA)	Defence Research and Development Canada, Centre for Operational Research and Analysis
EBAO	Effects Based Approach to Operations
EMBC	Emergency Measures British Columbia
EU	European Union
EX MG	EXERCISE MAPLE GUARDIAN
FCCMIC	Future Comprehensive Civil Military Interaction Concept
FCO	Foreign and Commonwealth Office
FLOCARK	Features, Lanes, Objectives, Canalizing Terrain, Avenues of Approach, Rating of Approaches, Key Terrain/Vital Ground
G29	Group of Twenty Nine
G8	Group of Eight
GoC	Government of Canada
HC	Humanitarian Coordinator
HD	Human Dimension
HIDTA	High Intensity Drug Trafficking Area
HoM	Head of Mission
IA	Integrated Approach
IBET	Integrated Border Enforcement Teams
ICE	United States Immigration and Customs Enforcement
ICRC	International Committee for the Red Cross

IEDs	Improvised Explosive Devices
IJMT	International Joint Management Team
IM	Integrated Mission
IMET	Integrated Market Enforcement Teams
IMPP	Integrated Mission Planning Process
INAC	Indian and Northern Affairs Canada
INSET	Integrated National Security Enforcement Teams
IOC	International Olympic Committee
IOs	International Organizations
IPS	International Policy Statement
IPSO	The Integrated Public Safety Organization
IPS	International Policy Statement
ISAF	International Security Assistance Force
ISR	Intelligence Surveillance and Reconnaissance
ISST	Interdepartmental Strategic Support Team
ISU	Integrated Security Unit
JDP	Joint Doctrine Publication
JIMP	Joint, Interagency, Multi-National and Public
JIPB	Joint Intelligence Preparation of the Battlefield
JMAC	Joint Mission Assessment Centre
JOC	Joint Operations Centres
JTF	Joint Task Force
JTF-A	Joint Task Force Afghanistan
KAP	Kandahar Action Plan
KLE	Key Leader Engagement
LICUS	Low Income Countries under Stress
LJMT	Local Joint Management Team.
LOAC	Law of Armed Conflict
LOs	Liaison Officers
MDGs	Millennium Development Goals
MNE	Multi-National Experiment
MNLA	Malayan National Liberation Army
MOD	Ministry of Defence
MSET	Marine Security Enforcement Teams
MSF	Médecins Sans Frontières
NAO	Northern Affairs Organization
NATO	North Atlantic Treaty Organization
NEO	Non-Combatant Evacuation Operation
NGO	Non-Governmental Organization
NSA	National Security Advisor

NSID	National Security, International Relationship and Development
ODA	Official Development Assistance
OECD	Organisation for Economic Co-operation and Development
OECD DAC	Organisation for Economic Co-operation and Development – Development Assistance Committee
OGA	Other Government Agencies
OGD	Other Government Departments
OPP	Operational Planning Process
PCO	Privy Council Office
PMESII	Political, Military, Economic, Social, Infrastructure and Information.
PMESII – PT	Political, Military, Economic, Social, Information and Infrastructure – Physical Terrain and Time
POLAD	Political Advisor
PRT	Provincial Reconstruction Team
PS	Public Safety Canada
PSO	Peace Support Operations
PVO	Public Volunteer Organization
QIP	Quick Impact Project
R22R	Royal 22 Regiment
RC	Resident Coordinator
RC (S)	Regional Command Southern Afghanistan
RCMP	Royal Canadian Mounted Police
RLE	Religious Leader Engagement
RoCK	Representative of Canada in Kandahar
SCR	Senior Civilian Representative
S/CRS	Office of the Coordinator of Reconstruction and Stabilization
SFT	Speech from the Throne
SME	Subject Matter Expert
SOC	Strategic Operating Concept
SOP	Standard Operating Procedure
SRSG	Special Representative of the Secretary General
SSR	Security System Reform
STABAD	Stability Advisor
START	Stabilization and Reconstruction Task Force
SU	Stabilization Unit
SWNCC	State-War-Navy Coordinating Committee
TTPs	Tactics, Techniques and Procedures

UK	United Kingdom
UN	United Nations
UNAMA	United Nations Mission in Afghanistan
UNCLOS	United Nations Convention on the Law of the Sea
UNCT	UN Country Team
UN-DESA	United Nations – Department of Economic and Social Affairs
UNDP	United Nations Development Program
UNFIL	United Nations Interim Force in Lebanon
UNGA	United Nations General Assembly
UNHCR	United Nations High Commissioner for Refugees
UNICEF	United Nations Children's Fund
US	United States
US JFCOM	United States Joint Forces Command
USAFRICOM	United States Africa Command
USAID	United States Agency for International Development
USSOUTHCOM	United States Southern Command
VANOC	Vancouver Olympic Committee
WHO	World Health Organization
WoG	Whole-of-Government

INTRODUCTION:
SECURITY OPERATIONS AND
THE COMPREHENSIVE APPROACH

KIM RICHARD NOSSAL

The proliferation of stabilization missions in the post-Cold War period radically transformed the way in which governments organized themselves for the challenges of bringing security to conflict situations and engaging in post-conflict reconstruction. A succession of multilateral missions in the former Yugoslavia, Sierra Leone, Haiti, Timor Leste, and especially Afghanistan led to a wholesale reconsideration of the way in which government departments with very different mandates operated in the same policy space. As the line between war-fighting and post-conflict peace support operations became increasingly blurred, there emerged a growing recognition that a more coordinated and holistic approach to security operations was needed. In particular, foreign policy planners sought to ensure that the operations of the armed forces, the foreign ministry, the development assistance agency, and other government agencies involved in stabilization missions, such as national police forces, were less fragmented and discrete. But it was also recognized that both the non-governmental and the private sectors were crucial players in the success of stabilization missions. Adding to the complexity has been the role of the international media in shaping global perceptions of local conflicts.

Efforts to find ways of involving all these actors in a comprehensive and holistic way in security operations were reflected in the development of ideas such as the "3D" approach – diplomacy, development, and defence – and the "whole-of-government" approach that sought to

Security Operations in the 21st Century: Canadian Perspectives on the Comprehensive Approach, ed. M. Rostek and P. Gizewski. Montreal and Kingston: Queen's Policy Studies Series, McGill-Queen's University Press.

coordinate the efforts of all government departments that contributed to security operations. These early ideas about how best to organize stabilization operations developed into what has come to be known as the Comprehensive Approach or CA. The idea of a "comprehensive approach" to security operations first emerged in the mid-2000s in the United States and Britain, catalyzed by the operations in Iraq. Since then, we have seen the idea of developing a Comprehensive Approach to create sustainable conditions for peace in security zones by employing multiple different resources, capabilities, and expertise in a concerted effort expanded to include issues of domestic security. It also spread across the western alliance. In Canada, for example, we have seen increased interest in the Comprehensive Approach concept by the Department of Foreign Affairs and International Trade (DFAIT), the Canadian International Development Agency (CIDA), the Department of National Defence (DND), and other Canadian government departments.

For all the work that has been done on developing a Comprehensive Approach to security operations, there are still important questions about the meaning of the concept, its utility, and how best to apply it. This volume, edited by Michael Rostek and Peter Gizewski, seeks to explore these issues, expand our understanding of this approach, and ultimately to contribute to the creation of a more effective and enduring Comprehensive Approach. The chapters in this volume provide insights from scholars, policy analysts, and government officials presented at a conference held in Kingston, Ontario, in April 2010 and sponsored by Queen's University's Centre for International and Defence Policy, the Defence and Security Research Institute at the Royal Military College of Canada, and their partners in the Department of National Defence – the Directorate of Land Concepts and Designs and Director General Partnerships and Emerging Issues.

(Re-)Discovering the Comprehensive Approach

Although the Comprehensive Approach is rightly seen as a new approach to organizing for security operations, its emergence has been heavily dependent on a slow evolution of ideas. Peter Gizewski explores the historical origins of the Comprehensive Approach and argues that while many of the ideas upon which the concept is based are hardly new, the development of the comprehensive approach reflects a marked evolution in thinking about organizational interaction, cooperation, and coordination. Indeed, Gizewski concludes that if such trends continue, the results, both for meeting future security challenges and for the identities of the organizations involved, may well be revolutionary.

Most analysts of the Comprehensive Approach argue that the continued development of the concept depends deeply on breaking down the barriers which can impede the creation of constructive relation-ships between organizations. Laura Ball and Angela Febbraro examine the growing relationship between the military and non-governmental organizations (NGOs) in an era that has been marked by the growing prominence of humanitarian operations. However, because NGOs and national military organizations have considerable differences in their structures and goals, considerable obstacles to progress can be created. Ball and Febbraro examine the tensions which such differences can pro-duce as well as possible means of surmounting them. In particular, they discuss how carefully constructed programs aimed at mutual education and training may provide a particularly effective means of ensuring the creation of a more constructive relationship between the military and NGOs.

As the concept has spread, considerable work has been done on developing it. Caroline Vavro and Richard Roy survey current efforts of the North Atlantic Treaty Organization (NATO) and the United Nations (UN), as well as the programs of Britain and the United States. They note that while such efforts differ somewhat in terms of detail, all confront a number of common challenges and obstacles, including concerns over what is seen as excessive military influence in the development of the Comprehensive Approach and how to establish inter-organizational trust and best practices.

Non-Governmental Perspectives

There is widespread recognition that the participation of NGOs is an important aspect of the Comprehensive Approach; however, it is not always clear how to ensure their participation in practice. Nipa Banerjee examines the issues confronted by fragile states in violent conflict and the potential of NGOs in a Comprehensive Approach to address the security and development challenges often essential to peace building. Banerjee observes that notwithstanding the CA's promise, recent experience reveals a failure to get the best value out of the approach. In Afghanistan, for example, she demonstrates that there has been a lack of coordination at a number of levels. Quick impact development projects have often fallen short in winning "hearts and minds" in the communities they are intended to serve. And a Comprehensive Approach has not necessarily resulted in achieving improved security – either real or perceived – among the Afghan people. She suggests that NGO participation in a CA context has actually often subverted their true potential, since their work is frequently conducted in a context that prioritizes support for counter-insurgency as opposed to longer-term societal and developmental needs. This not only risks tarnishing their image, but does little for the ultimate goals of stability and peace-building in fragile states.

Banerjee nonetheless concludes that NGOs have considerable potential to contribute to security operations. They have greater political objectivity; they enjoy better access to marginalized groups; they are closer to the grassroots; they have experience not only in delivering basic services, but also in providing some protection against human rights violations. All of these capacities provide NGOs with special advantages in mobilizing self-help capacities in the people. Such functions can and should form part of a comprehensive approach, even when the NGOs are delivering such necessary services, not essentially in coordination with the donor agencies, but functioning in parallel as valued contact partners for the civil population. To these ends, Banerjee suggests that a "synchronized" effort may be the best means of attaining objectives within a Comprehensive Approach. Unlike cooperation, which implies a process of active engagement at the operational level, this would enable partners to autonomously act within their own mandates to address common challenges. As such, the ability of NGOs to effectively meet the challenges of fragile states would not only be better ensured, it would increase.

Beth Cole echoes Banerjee's belief that inclusion of civilian agencies and NGOs is essential to an effective comprehensive approach. In the US case, Cole notes that efforts have been afoot to build a foundation for civilian doctrine, planning, lessons learned, training, education, and exercises for the multiplicity of civilian agencies trying to achieve success on the ground. In fact, such work has already helped to ensure that the civilian contribution has become less ad hoc and more organized over time. Nevertheless, considerable work remains to be done – particularly if civilian organizations are to realistically match the effectiveness of their military counterparts in the field.

Further, even if greater capacity to pursue a comprehensive approach is achieved, not all participants may be willing to embrace such an approach. In some cases, interaction with other actors may well work to compromise an organization's credibility and effectiveness. Marilyn McHarg and Kevin Coppock underline this point from their perspective within Médecins Sans Frontières (MSF), whose mandate is to provide emergency medical help to people caught in armed conflicts and natural disasters. But, as McHarg and Coppock note, in the comprehensive approach aid is a crucial tool for stabilization and counter-insurgency objectives; however, this runs counter to MSF's need to adopt an independent, neutral, and impartial orientation in pursuing its mandate. In such circumstances, coordination and cooperation with other players would not only be unwise, but counterproductive, since it would go against the identity and purpose of the organization itself. Consequently, McHarg and Coppock conclude that in some security operations, the best that can be hoped for is coexistence rather than active cooperation. Such a relationship would allow the CA to proceed, while ensuring the existence of the humanitarian space required for MSF to perform its key missions.

Comprehensive Approach Today – International Operations

Jim Simms examines the human terrain in Afghanistan and the adaptation by the Canadian Forces of the whole-of-government approach. The "Joint, Interagency, Multinational, Public" (JIMP) concept seeks to describe the players in an operating environment. In the case of armed conflict, JIMP is a means by which to make sense of the crowded battle-space within which the military operates. In Afghanistan, that battle-space is indeed complex, and the organizations involved wide-ranging. Accordingly, military forces must develop modalities to understand and use that human environment to their advantage. He shows that one way that Regional Command South was able to do this was to create the Partner's Coordination Board, a high-level information-sharing arrangement, and a Civilian Planning Cell.

The problem of failed and failing states and their associated dangers (e.g., irregular warfare, transnational terror, humanitarian emergencies) has generated especially strong support for the development of more comprehensive approaches to operations, particularly in Canada. The establishment of the Stabilization and Reconstruction Task Force (START) is especially notable. Members of the START Secretariat examine a number of the mechanisms created by the Canadian government in support of such an approach. Created to be DFAIT's "one-stop shop" for policy expertise on fragile states, it has already played an important role in Canada's mission in Afghanistan, the crisis in Lebanon in 2006, and the Haiti earthquake in 2010.

The Canadian experience with civil military coordination provides another example of the commitment to a comprehensive approach. Gavin Buchan examines Canada's experience in Kandahar and notes that the synchronization of civil and military activities was hardly a foregone conclusion. In fact it underwent a significant evolution. While the goal may well have been clear from the outset, a number of factors impeded its implementation, including differing departmental approaches to command, the lack of civilian headquarters in Kandahar, and an interdepartmental process ill-suited to rapid decision-making. Only with the passage of time were such problems addressed, most notably through creation of coordinative mechanism, the Representative of Canada in Kandahar (RoCK). The purpose was to locate in a single official a coordinator for the disparate civilian elements deployed to Kandahar, a counterpart for Commander Joint Task Force–Afghanistan (JTF-A) on civil military coordination issues, and a degree of "mission command" on the civilian side, so that a greater proportion of military and civilian coordination could take place intheatre.

Canada's experience in Kandahar leads Buchan to suggest that the key lessons for consideration when mounting future "whole-of-government" missions include: ensuring that there is a unity of civilian leadership;

creating a culture of mission command among civilian departments as well as within the military; and paying greater attention to joint civilian-military planning.

Michael Koros and Xiang He explore the role of development in Canada's Comprehensive Approach. Noting the growing number of studies which argue in favour of integrating knowledge and experience in addressing poverty reduction and the challenges of development, they explore how Canada has pursued such work in the context of a CA and identify a number of principles that are key for ensuring an integrated approach to addressing such challenges. Several of their observations are particularly relevant from a development perspective. They note that successful strategies must encourage and reinforce local ownership. They must help build legitimate local institutions. They must reflect the often differing needs and requirements of the women, men, and children in the affected state. Further, they must ensure equitable access, participation, and the sharing of benefits which derive from their implementation. Such principles reflect the often overlooked point that a successful CA – both in terms of development as well as security – must be premised on the ability to work *with* as opposed to simply *for* local populations if lasting progress is to be achieved. Koros and He also speak strongly to the importance of integrating diverse forms of knowledge and expertise in achieving any solution to the hardships that characterize failed and failing states.

Richard Roy underlines the growing importance of joined-up, integrated approaches to the problem of failed and failing states. For Roy, the challenges which such constructs pose are often impervious to the solutions of traditional linear planning and excessively quantitative methods used to solve problems. Instead, effective approaches must be based on a solid knowledge of societal networks, an understanding of principles of non-linearity and the development of a wide and varying knowledge base that can be efficiently marshalled and applied to problems when required. In effect, such challenges demand the development of an effective comprehensive approach. Canadian efforts to develop such an approach are increasingly evident – most notably with the publication in July 2009 of the inter-departmental study "Sustaining Canada's Engagement in Acutely Fragile and Conflict-Affected Situations." It is also apparent in the growing role of the military as a key advocate for the CA – in effect acting much like a norm entrepreneur in encouraging adoption and further development of the CA. In fact, Roy assesses a number of recent cases which demonstrate the military's application of CA-type principles and practices in a variety of situations abroad. Still, Roy underlines the fact that such engagements are never solely a military enterprise. In fact, while the military may be a key enabler of the CA, complexity demands mobilizing all possible actors to contribute to both defining the problem confronted and to executing the programs designed to ameliorate it. In this regard, continued refinement of the CA is essential.

Comprehensive Approach Today – Domestic Operations

While the Comprehensive Approach developed in the context of international security operations, its precepts can also be applied to domestic operations. Todd Hataley explores the development of Integrated Border Enforcement Teams (IBETs) by the Royal Canadian Mounted Police as a form of CA-type operations. The incorporation of a multi-agency approach for ensuring security within the domestic environment is not a new concept: police agencies have worked with partner agencies and community groups, to increase effectiveness and the ultimate goal of creating a safer domestic environment for decades. But the IBET experience reflects a marked evolution from law enforcement frameworks based on cross-border cooperation to shared enforcement and increasingly to shared jurisdiction. The teams were developed to bring together partner agencies in the US and Canada dealing with the specific problem of cross-border drug criminality (initially defined as trafficking), and expanded to include other cross-border criminal activities such as the illegal movement of people, weapons, money, and cigarettes. The practical result is that for the first time, dedicated teams of law enforcement officials from both sides of the US-Canada border share intelligence, resources, and set investigational and enforcement priorities as an integrated and international unit. Hataley underlines the fact that such programs remain at a relatively early stage of development and issues such as trust, leadership, mandate, and sovereignty must be addressed in order to provide the necessary guidelines for such units to effectively fulfill their shared objectives.

In a related vein, John Kozij and Sylvia Bogusis examine the development of Canada's Northern Strategy and the engagement of a range of government departments in a coordinated, integrated approach to the North. Indian and Northern Affairs Canada (INAC) worked collectively with a number of federal departments, including many colleagues from the Department of National Defence, to bring the Northern Strategy together. Kozij and Bogusis argue that a number of factors were responsible for galvanizing a comprehensive strategy for Canada's North. These factors included environmental changes, the growing economies of air and marine traffic, growing economic potential of northern resources. But perhaps the most important factor was the active and sustained leadership of the prime minister. Without Stephen Harper's consistent support and interest there would not have been as much impetus for the degree of interdepartmental collaboration. In short, the pursuit of a comprehensive approach requires a "champion" to more fully ensure its success.

Bernard Brister looks at the multiagency effort undertaken to provide security at the Vancouver 2010 Winter Olympics. While domestic Canadian application of a comprehensive approach is not a new phenomenon, the planning and execution of the security strategy for the Vancouver Games is seen by many as unique in both scope and size, and by virtue of its deliberate nature. The Integrated Security Unit (ISU) created for the Games involved the participation of over 300 agencies from three levels of government, two countries, the Olympic organizations, and a multitude of sports federations charged with the oversight of the conduct of each of the events. Moreover, the security plan involving more than 140 government agencies and 13,000 security personnel has been touted as the largest, most comprehensive domestic security operation in Canadian history. Brister notes that the security apparatus that was created for the Games worked very well – at least at the tactical level. Inter-agency working relationships established through the interactions of agencies' staffs at the ISU gradually improved and the flow of information and active participation in the cooperative resolution of security issues associated with the Games steadily increased and became faster and more efficient.

Such success owed both to the limited nature of challenges confronted and the ad hoc inter-agency cooperation procedures that developed at the tactical and personal level. However, Brister concludes that it is not clear whether the trust, cooperation, and interagency effectiveness achieved at the Games will result in any substantial institutional change or learning over the longer run. If past experience is any indication, Brister warns that issues of both bureaucratic hubris and organizational tribalism may well work to dilute – or even lose – many of the "CA successes" of Vancouver 2010 as recommended "lessons" move up institutional chains and confront ever-more bureaucratic resistance from senior officials intent on preserving the status quo.

Making the Comprehensive Approach Work

The concluding section shifts attention from an examination of the Comprehensive Approach as currently practiced to an exploration of a number of means for helping to ensure its more effective implementation and practice in future.

Steven Moore examines the potential benefits of leveraging the talents, expertise and status of key leaders. Key leader engagement – "the conduct of a deliberate and focused meeting with a person of significant importance in order to achieve a desired effect" – may hold promise for more effective CA strategies. Particularly intriguing is the engagement of religious leaders in conflict zones. Not only does analysis of the contemporary security environment indicate that religious factors are frequently a source of grievance and violent conflict in many regions of the world, but also a potential means through which to facilitate effective and lasting conflict resolution. Moore notes that religious communities are often vital centres of gravity within indigenous populations, and religious leaders have a capacity to shape moral opinion in the public domain. Given their profile among the people, local religious leaders could serve as a crucial resource in resolving conflict, particularly through such initiatives involving military chaplains working constructively with local religious leaders in conflict zones.

A Comprehensive Approach implies the importance of planning. Noting that advocates of the CA and related concepts require toolsets and metrics capable of ensuring the optimization of the implementation and performance of the approach, Stephen Fritz-Millett explores the case for the adoption of a tool known as "Apply Model–Identify Interests–Adopt a Strategy" (AIA). Fritz-Millett takes the reader through the model, and applies it to the mission in Afghanistan. Such a tool, Fritz-Millet argues, could be used to provide the Canadian Forces (CF) with an intentional, methodical, and holistic approach to understanding civilian actors and their interests in the mission. The result could well be an enhanced level of understanding of areas of potential co-operation and just as importantly, areas of potential friction between the CF and those organizations inhabiting the environment in which a CA is underway.

Another frequently cited means for moving toward a more effective CA is through provision of education and training activities. Megan Thompson, Angela Febbraro, and Anne-Renée Blais examine the interagency training of personnel preparing for deployment to Canada's mission in Afghanistan. From a survey of participants in a CF education and training course designed for those deploying to Afghanistan, including personnel from other government departments, they report that the training helped them to establish useful relationships with the CF (and other) personnel with whom they would be working in theatre. At the same time, however, perceptions of the training experience as it related to working with members of the Afghan population were less positive: fully half of the comments indicated a lack of interaction in this regard and the need for more information on the roles and responsibilities of other government departments and on Afghan culture.

The need to better understand the relationship between NGOs and the CF has become ever-more apparent since the end of the Cold War. The changing nature of international conflict has resulted in militaries increasingly taking on roles in humanitarian relief and development, a field traditionally belonging to civilian organizations. When civilian and military personnel are concurrently involved in providing humanitarian aid in areas of crisis, there is an increased risk of tension. Tara Holton and her colleagues examine the relationship between NGO workers and the CF, attempting to illuminate it in terms of what currently is working and how to make it work better in future, particularly in terms of collaborative efforts in-theatre. The responses they received indicate that while there may well be some meeting of the minds between groups regarding broad goals and the necessity for interaction, there are clearly significant differences which can work to block constructive interactions and collaboration. Still, a carefully constructed program of training and education, along with the development of cultures of mutual compromise, respect, and self-assessment may help surmount some of these obstacles. So too may the creation of programmes aimed at enhancing the role of civil-military cooperation (CIMIC) liaison in the CF.

The recommendations of Holton et al. hint at the fact that the successful adoption of a comprehensive approach will require development of new normative understandings concerning how agencies interact with one another in addressing security challenges. In this regard, active and sustained communication and assimilation of the CA philosophy and its practices is essential. Michael Rostek considers the extent to which the CA in fact does represent an emerging norm in the international system. Examining the evolutionary cycle through which all norms emerge, Rostek contends that the CA is in fact at the emergent stage of the norm lifecycle. This is supported in the Canadian context not only by the work that a number of key norm entrepreneurs have played in supporting the approach, but also by its growing inclusion in statements of policy and by evidence of its gradual institutionalization in a number of forms (both national and international). Such development is a cause for cautious optimism. Indeed, Rostek notes that while the CA has yet to reach a crucial "tipping point" in gaining the critical mass of support required to progress toward complete normative development, evidence thus far suggests that it does seem headed in that direction.

Finally, Christian Leuprecht not only offers a summation of a number of the key themes raised by the contributors, but also provides some critical commentary regarding the approach as a whole and the challenges it faces.

Conclusion

The Comprehensive Approach represents an effort to deal with the increasing complexity of security operations in the contemporary period, both international operations in the case of stabilization missions and domestic operations that require the involvement of numerous agencies and actors. The approach grows naturally out of earlier policy ideas designed to deal with the contemporary requirement for inter-agency cooperation in the field, such as the 3D and whole-of-government approaches. The research presented in this volume suggests that considerable progress has been made in applying this approach in Canadian practice. But it also poses some of the key questions that will have to be considered if the approach is to remain relevant in the future.

PART I
(RE-)DISCOVERING
THE COMPREHENSIVE
APPROACH

Chapter 1

DISCOVERING THE COMPREHENSIVE APPROACH

PETER GIZEWSKI

Introduction

In today's security environment, durable and sustainable responses to security challenges – both at home and abroad – are unlikely to be achieved through the efforts of any single agency or organization. In a world where instability, crisis and conflict often require addressing a myriad of ethnic, religious, ideological and material drivers, many analysts argue that an ability to bring to bear all instruments of national – and coalition – power and influence (e.g., diplomatic, economic, military, informational) on a problem in a timely, coordinated fashion is increasingly essential to achieving effective results. So too is an ability to address and, if possible, constructively engage the views and reactions of the public – both domestic and international – as operations unfold.

Recognition of the need to practice a more coherent, holistic approach to security operations has become ever more evident – both in Canada and elsewhere (OECD, 2006; Friis and Jarmyr, 2008; Rintakoski and Autti, 2008; Jakobsen, 2008). In fact, officials in Canada and a number of other states (e.g., the United States, the United Kingdom, other NATO allies) are increasingly calling for the adoption of a more "Comprehensive Approach" (CA) to operations. Such an approach would involve a more integrated, cooperative, and coordinated orientation to both policy and campaign planning that would draw upon a range of diplomatic, defence, development, and commercial resources as well as a range of players (both official and private) in efforts to address the key security issues of the day

Security Operations in the 21st Century: Canadian Perspectives on the Comprehensive Approach, ed. M. Rostek and P. Gizewski. Montreal and Kingston: Queen's Policy Studies Series, McGill-Queen's University Press.

(Leslie, Gizewski, and Rostek, 2008). The result, advocates claim, would be more effective responses to the challenges confronted.

The basic ideas underlying such an approach are hardly unique. In fact, recent study confirms that elements of the CA have existed for many years (Hrychuk and Gizewski, 2008). That said, formal articulation and concerted efforts to develop and implement the concept is a relatively recent phenomenon. So too is the strong and growing interest in its institutionalization. What accounts for this rise in interest and activity? What issues surround the CA's acceptance, implementation and practice? Moreover, what are the implications of an established, effective CA for its practitioners and the manner in which security challenges are addressed?

The following chapter addresses these questions in an effort not only to better illuminate the character of the CA itself, but also its current status and future prospects. To these ends, it describes the essential elements of the CA and some of its historical antecedents. It then goes on to examine the factors leading to the growing currency of such thinking as a means of addressing security challenges and the forces underlying it. In particular, it notes that growing interest in a CA is largely a function of the evolving security environment – an environment which has increased both the need for such an approach and, at the same time, the capacity to practice it (particularly given developments in information and communication technologies). Surveying current initiatives aimed at developing the approach, the chapter concludes by noting that the CA represents a marked evolution in the development of organizational interaction and collaboration which – given time – may well yield revolutionary results in future approaches to security challenges.

The Comprehensive Approach: Key Elements

Definitions of the CA vary. While some see the approach as a means of interacting with a myriad of national and international entities to resolve security challenges, others have used the term to refer primarily to whole of government and/or interagency coordination (Friis and Jarmyr, 2008, 4-6). Still others have loosely employed it to refer to simple coordination mechanisms at the tactical level (Roy, 2009).

Yet all descriptions and definitions have several basic characteristics in common. All for instance, view such an approach as a means of achieving greater awareness and interaction with other agencies and organizations. All see the CA as an essential means of facilitating greater organizational cooperation – and ideally collaboration – in attaining security objectives. And all view such interaction and the information, understanding and organizational synergies that can be gained from use of the approach as a means of enhancing the prospects for sound decision-making and ultimately, more coherent, integrated and effective responses to security challenges (i.e., to attain greater "strategic effect").

Growing consensus as to the elements which an effective CA would entail is equally clear. In this regard, a "fully functional" CA would feature *proactive engagement* between actors (if possible ahead of a crisis), so as to ensure more coordinated approaches and nuanced responses to complex situations. It would reflect s*hared understanding* between parties, whether military or civilian; thus optimizing the effectiveness of partner capabilities, distinct professional, technical and cultural disciplines, and discrete values and perceptions. It would feature *outcome based thinking* – with participants involved in operations focusing on what is required to deliver the desired end state when planning and conducting activities. Moreover, it would be characterized by a culture of *collaborative working*, generated through personal contact, human networking and mutual trust. Indeed, such understanding is critical for building the institutional familiarity between participants necessary for the effective function of the approach.

Advocates of the CA argue that its implementation would promise considerable benefits. With all actions based upon agreed principles and collaborative processes, greater organizational efficiencies would be obtained, and traditional organizational stovepipes overcome through enhanced synergies. Information sharing between organizations would be enhanced. Strategic framing of issues and campaign planning would be improved. A degree of organizational awareness, interaction, integration and coherence would emerge when addressing security threats rarely – if ever – before seen. Beyond this, the CA could even work to ensure a greater level of legitimacy – both domestically and internationally – for those security operations undertaken (Friis and Jarmyr, 2008, 3).

Precursors: Theory and Practice

Still, much of the basic logic underlying the CA has existed for decades – if not centuries. The concept of grand strategy offers case in point. Much like the CA, grand strategy calls for the marshalling of a diverse range of resources (e.g., economic, diplomatic, military, and legal-judicial) to accomplish a specified national end. Indeed, as Colin Gray notes, it involves the "purposeful employment of all instruments of power available to a security community" (Gray, 2007, 283). Stephan Metz is more precise still, defining grand strategy as "the integrated use of power resources in pursuit of national objectives" (Metz, 2008).

Counter-insurgency doctrine (COIN), with its strong emphasis on prevailing in irregular conflicts less by the use of military might than by winning the allegiance of an indigenous population through use of political, economic, civic and psychological actions does much the same – a fact reflected in its characterization by some as "grand strategy in miniature" (Gray, 2008). Doctrines of civil-military cooperation (CIMIC) are also notable (NATO, 2003) – particularly given their acknowledgement and explicit endorsement of the importance which the development of constructive military-civilian linkages (e.g., liaison, coordination, joint planning) can hold as an essential means of enhancing mission effectiveness.

Beyond this, history reveals a variety of instances in which "precursors" to a modern CA were pursued by states as a means of addressing domestic and international challenges (although with varying degrees of success). The planning and implementation of the post-World War II reconstruction of Japan (1941-46), and the development and implementation of the Marshall Plan in Europe (1947-1951) stand out as particularly prominent cases of success.

In the former case, successful integration of the US Government's military and civilian assets led to the creation of a practical strategy for reform and reconstruction of occupied territory. Under the State-War-Navy Coordinating Committee (SWNCC) – civilian and military officials generated an effective interagency strategic and tactical approach which ensured the existence of a coherent set of objectives and a flexible action script for occupation when US forces arrived in August 1945. In fact, prompt adoption of the Committees key recommendations were central to the transformation of Japan from a pre-modern, semi-feudal nation into a modern democratic capitalist state. (Schaefer and Schaefer, 2008). The latter meanwhile, not only involved the sustained cooperation of military, diplomatic and trade personnel but also an active campaign aimed at explaining key aspects of the initiative to the US public and allies. The practical result was the creation of a foreign aid plan that provided the crucial step toward European reconstruction after WW II (Hrychuk and Gizewski, 2008, 5-6).

The Commonwealth campaign against Communist insurgents during the Malayan Emergency (1948-1960) similarly reflected aspects of CA logic. Especially noteworthy was the use of layered coordination committees. At all levels of government (national, state, and district levels), military and civil authority was assumed by a committee of military, police and civilian administration officials. This allowed intelligence from all sources to be rapidly evaluated and disseminated, and all anti-guerrilla measures to be coordinated. The result was an integrated political-military campaign which substantially contributed to victory over the Malayan National Liberation Army (MNLA) (i.e., the military arm of the Malayan Communist Party) (Thompson, 1966; Nagl, 2002).

Examples of inter-agency integration and collaboration were evident on the domestic front as well. In 1964, for instance, state and local bureaucracies effectively collaborated to maintain Alaska's viability as a state in the aftermath of the most severe earthquake ever registered in North America. Here, success derived in no small measure from US President Lyndon Johnson's creation of the Federal Reconstruction and Development Planning Commission for Alaska – a Cabinet-level agency that developed a Rehabilitation Strategy and managed implementation through an effective division of labour among those agencies most engaged in recovery efforts (Ink, 2008).

Until recently however, the vast majority of efforts to actively achieve greater organizational coordination and cooperation in security affairs were relatively sporadic and ad hoc in character. Generally prompted by a high sense of urgency, most were cobbled together quickly in response to immediate challenges and crises and featured makeshift institutional mechanisms, structures and processes. Many required the full and active support of top political leaders and bureaucrats. While effective organizational collaboration was occasionally achieved under these conditions, it was primarily inter-departmental and interagency in character. Moreover, most efforts were of relatively limited duration – with collaboration dwindling once crises subsided and key tasks and objectives were achieved. Truly concerted efforts to articulate an approach aimed at sustained organizational interaction and cooperation through the development of enduring practices, procedures and principles rarely – if ever – materialized.

Cold War Environment: Limited Incentives/ Limited Capabilities

Past limits on organizational/inter-agency interaction, cooperation and collaboration owed to a variety of factors. Yet a central obstacle was an international security context which – for the most part – provided neither the incentives (i.e., the need) nor the means (i.e., the capabilities) to effectively practice and indeed institutionalize a strong culture devoted to such an approach.

For centuries, international politics has been heavily driven by the primacy of the state and realist thinking. Security equated heavily – almost exclusively – with state interests, their preservation and their pursuit as defined by governmental decision makers. It was also strongly shaped by the "high politics" of inter-state armed conflict. This tended to privilege certain issues and organizations over others. It also limited the degree to which organizational collaboration and cooperation was valued and sought.

During the Cold War for instance, the US-Soviet military and ideological rivalry stood as *the* overriding preoccupation of most Western nations. And, the requirements of superpower deterrence and containment eclipsed all other issues as major security concerns. It also ensured the power of large military, intelligence and diplomatic bureaucracies – all with deeply entrenched mandates, interests and agendas (Allison, 1971; Halperin, 1974; Zegart, 1999). Such interests were not only actively pursued but judiciously guarded – a fact creating a strong organizational aversion to collaboration with others.[1] In the United States for example, while individual departments carried out those parts of policies directed by leaders in their primary areas of responsibility, collaborative work on tasks involving shared responsibilities was rare (e.g., Project on National Security Reform, 2008, iii; Locher, 2009, 79). Regularized interaction with non-governmental organizations was rarer still. Not only were such actors relatively few in number, but given the chief security preoccupations of the state – they were generally limited in terms of their perceived policy relevance and hence, their ability to achieve influence within official circles.[2]

A lack of societal interconnectedness could only heighten obstacles to interaction and collaboration. Absent today's information and communication technologies, opportunities and capacities to organize and to network quickly, regularly and economically were less available (e.g., Ferguson, 2010; Ramo, 2009, 15-6). The fact that possibilities for low-cost global travel were also far fewer than they are today compounded such obstacles. Accordingly, awareness of organizations beyond government tended to be more limited and the ability to interact regularly with others – far more constrained. Beyond this, lower global interconnectedness tended to ensure that many events in other parts of the world were more contained and viewed as less consequential both in terms of their salience and impact. Their potential effects were less of a concern. Once again, the perceived need to identify and tap new organizational resources to act in such cases could only suffer.

Such realities, along with the achievement of a rough stability in the superpower relationship nevertheless helped serve to ensure that for the most part, the bureaucratic status quo remained relatively intact for decades. As such, while occasional cases of concerted organizational interaction, collaboration and cooperation were evident, drastic revision of existing, still largely stove-piped practices and procedures was neither pursued by governments in a forceful, sustained manner, nor viewed as particularly pressing.

Post-Cold War Environment: New Demands/ New Capabilities

The years following the Cold War's end in effect altered this reality; dramatically changing the calculus surrounding both the need and the capacity to engage in greater organizational interaction, cooperation and collaboration in security affairs. Increasingly, concerns over bipolar, state-on-state confrontation and superpower deterrence were eclipsed by a range of new security challenges including: the danger of attack from transnational terror groups, political instability and civil wars arising within fragile and failed states, ethnic and sectarian violence, and the destabilizing societal effects of organized crime and such forces as resource depletion, and global climate change (see for instance, United

States, National Intelligence Council, 2008; United Kingdom, Ministry of Defence, 2010).

Such challenges often emanated less from strong state entities than from a lack of effective governance. They could involve a wider range of issues and actors than ever before. And their importance could be magnified by the process of ongoing and ever greater globalization, particularly in the form of cascading information and communication technology. Indeed, such forces along with growing migration flows generated by ever greater accessibility to low cost travel generated greater interconnectedness globally (Katz and Aakus, 2002). They increased the ability of previously disparate and marginalized individuals, groups and movements to organize and influence events (both for better and worse) (Ostrum and Dolesak, 2003; Keck and Sikkink, 1998). And they heightened prospects that even local turmoil and instability – along with the character of national and international responses to it – could generate not only regional but global concerns and consequences. Increasingly, far off crises could effect global economies, disrupt international trade and commerce, trigger inter-state rivalries, shape public opinion and impact the political standing and legitimacy of far off governments (Watts, 2003, 301; Ramo, 2009, 35-6).

At the same time, notions of human security began to compete with national security as an important consideration in global affairs. Particularly in the West, the security and well-being of individuals within societies was increasingly accorded a status of equal if not greater significance than the well-being of the state (Boutros-Ghali, 1992; UNDP, 1994). Meanwhile, the number of domestic and international actors seen as key to addressing the security challenges – proliferated (Ramo, 2009, 35).

Incentives for approaches less focused on the use of military power alone, less on state than human security and less on deterring states and overrunning governments than stabilizing and reconstructing them correspondingly increased. So too did a growing realization of the ever greater need for more integrated, coordinated responses which would engage a wider range of issues and a broader range of participants in developing effective approaches to the challenges confronted (Patrick and Brown, 2007; Locher, 2009).[3]

Meanwhile, exponential advances in information and communication technologies offered ever-more capacity to fashion and pursue such responses. Such innovations and their spread made it increasingly possible to network quickly, regularly and efficiently with a wide variety of organizations (Diani and McAdam, 2003). Beyond this, they heightened the need to do so. Given the fact that globalized communications offered near-instantaneous information about far-off events, not only could public demands for government action increase but also popular scrutiny of the actions taken. In an ever-more "wired" world, responses to security and other challenges could – and do –increasingly effect perceptions of government legitimacy.[4]

Institutionalizing Interaction: Toward the Comprehensive Approach

Such an environment not only bred demands for greater organizational collaboration and cooperation in addressing security challenges, but strongly suggested a need to elaborate and extend it. Indeed, it has produced both a growing need as well as an increasing ability to practice a more comprehensive approach to security operations. In this regard, an ever-more varied range of challenges and threats has called for an approach capable of drawing upon all available resources in an effective, efficient and timely manner. At the same time, the proliferation of new players and actors, along with the growing connectivity of modern information and communication technologies offers ever more capacity to realize it.

Reflections of the changing mindset have been evident in references to Defence, Diplomacy, Development and Commerce (3D+C), as well as Whole of Government (WOG), Comprehensive Crisis Management and Interagency Approaches. Yet growing recognition that a *truly* inclusive and effective response to contemporary security challenges could involve entities well beyond official government departments and agencies has increasingly generated interest in and support for the term CA – both within governments and beyond.

In essence, the CA marks a direct response to the realities of the changed security environment. Indeed, the concept seeks to address the challenges it poses – offering a less stove-piped, more inclusive means by which interaction and if necessary, cooperation and collaboration between organizations (and even between government organizations and elements of the public) can be more effectively achieved in support of enhanced security (Gizewski and Rostek, 2007).[5] In fact, its very articulation and pursuit signals a marked progression in thinking about how governments must approach security challenges in the contemporary international system.

The approach has received growing endorsement both nationally and internationally. And a growing level of activity is increasingly devoted to the development of the CA. Not only does this include efforts aimed at the CA's further conceptual elaboration, but at developing programs aimed at educating and training both military and civilian personnel in application of the ideas and practices it advances. Initiatives are afoot to identify as well as develop the enabling technologies, organizational structures and processes most suitable to its effective practice. And researchers are also engaged in projects aimed ensuring the proper organizational mindset upon which the approach depends – identifying the psychological requirements essential to building nurturing and extending trust and more effective interaction, coordination and cooperation within and between organizations (Gallant, Reding, and Gizewski, 2010).

More notable still is the fact that efforts to apply more integrated and "CA-like" approaches to security operations are increasingly apparent as well. In this regard, the application of such principles and practices has been increasingly evident in ongoing operations in Iraq, in Afghanistan and in Haiti. The concept is somewhat mirrored in the integrated operational planning process of the United Nations (UN). It has gained official standing and growing currency within NATO. And it has increasingly informed thinking in the development and practices of a number of operational military commands. In this regard, the civilian command, interagency modalities and "soft power" mandate of US Africa Command (USAFRICOM) is exemplary. So too is the "collaborative approach" of US Southern Command (e.g., USSOUTHCOM).

To be sure, the idea continues to confront a number of obstacles. Devising practices and procedures capable of ensuring an ability to work with a range of organizations, each with its own culture, mindset, agendas and goals is no easy task. Indeed, such efforts continue to confront issues of cultural and professional bias, problems of information sharing, legal/jurisdictional issues, constraints stemming from resource asymmetries between organizations, and concerns related to the protection of organizational credibility and essence (Kapstein, 2010). Lack of clarity in mission definition and goals can be equally, if not more problematic – impeding the degree to which such an approach can be organized and applied so that component players can rationally and effectively work together to achieve desired outcomes. Nor, despite some anecdotal evidence indicating the CA's value to operations, is it entirely clear how some of the benefits claimed for it can be validly and reliably measured and assessed (Gizewski and Rostek, 2007, 42-3; Leslie, Gizewski, and Rostek, 2008, 8).

Not surprisingly, and despite growing endorsement of the approach in principle, full acceptance and institutionalization of the CA has yet to be achieved. Bureaucratic incentives to promote and engage in the approach remain on the whole, underdeveloped, and resources devoted to the broad implementation of a CA continue to be relatively limited. Beyond this, the level of buy-in and active support from key political leaders and senior governmental officials is uneven.

Given that the approach itself remains at a relatively early stage in its overall development however, progress thus far must still be considered noteworthy. Not only has the CA generated intense discussion and debate, but widespread interest both nationally and internationally from a variety of institutions. It has prompted a varied and growing agenda of scientific investigation and experimentation. Most importantly, it has resulted in a growing shift in attitudes – within both official and unofficial circles – regarding the manner in which security operations should be conducted.

In particular, it has resulted in a clear acknowledgement that today's security challenges require a more institutionalized, less stove-piped and more inclusive, multidimensional approach in order to be effective.

Future Prospects: A New Norm for Security Operations?

The degree to which the obstacles facing full adoption of the CA can be overcome remains unclear. In the event that present challenges are surmounted however, continued pursuit of the CA agenda may hold out the possibility for more substantial and far-reaching change in the years ahead. In fact, full development and implementation of such thinking could – over time – work to usher in a fundamental change in the manner in which organizations view one another and how they interact to address problems and challenges.

In this regard, evidence suggests that the CA is already generating a subtle but nonetheless significant shift in organizational mindsets regarding how operations are viewed and conducted. In the case of allied militaries for instance, growing familiarity with the concept has been accompanied by a move away from viewing other organizations as simply resources to be used in support of the demands of the military mission in favour of an appreciation of the need of the military itself to more fully integrate in support of the broader objectives of the mission as a whole – objectives which must often include integration of the goals and viewpoints of a range of other players[6] (Djik, 2010).

Should the CA become more widely accepted and institutionalized, the prospect of organizations engaging in further shifts in thinking cannot be ruled out. Indeed, the regularized interaction with other organizations that adoption of the CA would involve and the "give and take" that this generally entails could work to expand organizational perspectives, sensitizing organizations to new ways of viewing security and its pursuit. This could effect not only thought and planning – but action. In time, it may even work to broaden organizational identities and mandates. The result may well be the creation of a new norm governing how future security operations are conducted (Gizewski and Rostek, 2009, 36-8)

Conclusion

Interest in the development of the CA is widespread and growing. Yet many of the basic ideas underlying the approach are not entirely new. Not only have elements of the approach long existed, but efforts to practice a more "CA-like" approach to operations are clearly evident throughout history. Overall, such practice was primarily ad hoc and sporadic in character, limited in the scope of organizational interaction both sought and achieved, and heavily dependent on the initiative of key leaders for their success. In fact, such efforts took place in a security context which provided neither the incentive nor the capabilities needed to support a more institutionalized, regularized form of organizational interaction.

Changes in the security environment following the end of the Cold War have nonetheless increased both the need for such an approach as well as the capacities to implement and practice it. Such forces by and large account not only for the articulation of the CA, but growing efforts aimed at its development and implementation.

The approach has sought to jettison the largely ad hoc and piecemeal practices of the past in favour of a far less stove-piped and more inclusive means of conducting security operations. And while full acceptance and implementation of a CA has yet to be achieved, its development thus far is impressive. Indeed, even in its present stage of development, the CA marks an evolution in thought and action regarding the manner in which security is pursued in the contemporary international environment. To the extent that further acceptance and institutionalization of the approach occurs, its long term impacts could well be profound. Fully implemented, the CA could, over time, work to generate new understandings of the role of a range of organizations (both official and unofficial) in security – broadening the manner in which they view security issues and their role in addressing them.

Chapter 2

DISCOVERING EFFECTIVE CIVIL-MILITARY COOPERATION: INSIGHTS FROM THE NGO-CF RELATIONSHIP

LAURA C. BALL AND ANGELA FEBBRARO

Historical Antecedents of the Comprehensive Approach

In the post-Cold War era (1989/1991[7]–present), Western militaries have experienced a dramatic shift in the nature of the conflicts in which they have been involved (Francois, 1995; Iribarnegaray, 2002). The collapse of the Soviet Union left a vastly different geopolitical power structure in its wake, along with a rise in nationalism (often along ethnic lines), religious extremism, regional conflicts, state disruptions, and humanitarian crises (LeBlanc, 2007). In this new security environment, successful military operations often require effective collaboration between a variety of diplomatic, economic, development, and military instruments of power and influence (Gizewski and Rostek, 2007). Recognition of this new requirement has inspired what is now referred to as the "comprehensive approach" to operations; however, there are some important antecedents to this approach, as expressed in these terms. For instance, as Leslie, Gizewski, and Rostek (2008) have described, the comprehensive approach to operations derives heavily from "whole-of-government" and "3D + C" (i.e., defence, diplomacy, development, and commerce) philosophies calling for closer collaboration between various agencies in achieving policy objectives, and as discussed in Canada's recent defence and international policy statements (see also Gizewski and Rostek, 2007). In fact, a comprehensive

Security Operations in the 21st Century: Canadian Perspectives on the Comprehensive Approach, ed. M. Rostek and P. Gizewski. Montreal and Kingston: Queen's Policy Studies Series, McGill-Queen's University Press.

approach involves developing a capacity to interact with a variety of players in a cooperative, constructive manner. For the Canadian Forces (CF), movement toward a "JIMP-capable" Land Force represents one means of implementing or operationalizing a comprehensive approach to operations. In essence, the term Joint, Interagency, Multinational and Public (JIMP) is a descriptor that identifies the various categories of players that constitute the broad environment in which military operations take place (Leslie, Gizewski, and Rostek, 2008).[8]

Thus, as Leslie, Gizewski, and Rostek (2008) have pointed out, CF interest in a comprehensive, whole-of-government, or JIMP-enabled approach is not without precedent; and indeed, efforts to practice such an approach are currently underway, such as in Afghanistan. Consistent with the requirements of this new security environment, new forms of military organization, such as provincial reconstruction teams (PRTs) and Disaster Assistance Response Teams (DART), have emerged in recent years. Canadian PRTs, which consist of military and civilian components, were first established in early 2003, and the first DART mission occurred in 1996 (Gizewski and Rostek, 2007). However, the ideas underpinning the comprehensive approach, or JIMP, are reflected in structures and practices with even longer histories than these relatively new institutional forms (Gizewski and Rostek, 2007). The Joint and Multinational *military* aspects of JIMP have had long histories and are well established in national and international military structures, respectively, and while the Interagency and Public *civilian* components may pose greater challenges for the military, the antecedents of these components may be seen in past civil-military cooperation (CIMIC) practice. Ever since civil affairs units were established within the United States (US) military during World War II, CIMIC has been considered a force multiplier for commanders. A reserve function with the Canadian Land Force, CIMIC, although military-centric, provides an institutionalized foundation from which the JIMP concept, and especially the Interagency and Public components, can evolve (see also Gizewski and Rostek, 2007, 62-63).

Similarly, we can find other antecedents of the comprehensive approach if we consider historical analyses. For example, Hrychuk and Gizewski (2008) documented the use of comprehensive-type approaches relevant to the Marshall Plan, as well as in diverse operations such as those carried out in Lebanon/the Dominican Republic, Cambodia, Bosnia and Kosovo. In particular, the Marshall Plan, also known as the European Recovery Plan, is cited as an excellent example of successful "postwar cooperation and development" on a large scale (Hrychuk and Gizewski, 2008, 5). Initiated in 1947, the Marshall Plan involved the US government providing aid towards European recovery after World War II; that is, after military forces had ended the war and remained to hold the peace in order to enable economic recovery (Hrychuk and Gizewski,

2008). One of the distinguishing features of the plan's implementation was that it received strong endorsement from a number of different components (initially government, but subsequently the broader public, as well). This core agreement among important players about the goals of the plan is cited as one of the key factors in its success (Hrychuk and Gizewski, 2008). In addition, Hrychuk and Gizewski (2008) identified common problems that occurred in a range of historical comprehensive or "JIMP-like" situations, including: inadequate coordination at the pre-planning and planning stages of missions; problems resulting from inadequate understanding of the complexities of each diverse player; and failure to develop and use concrete and established mechanisms and processes rather than ad hoc measures.

Historical analyses of past operations correctly point out the JIMP-like nature of past campaigns (Hrychuk and Gizewski, 2008). However, as Brown and Adams (2010) have argued, there is also a very real danger in underemphasizing the radical shifts (cultural, structural, and otherwise) that would need to occur in order to achieve full JIMP capability. As will be discussed, perhaps one of the clearest examples of the need for such radical shifts can be seen in the NGO-military relationship.

Increasing Role of the Military in Humanitarian Operations

Within the new security environment, not only is there a broader range of players than was the case in the past; militaries themselves are taking on a broader range of non-traditional, non-war-fighting functions, such as reconstruction and development projects, in order to address the new and increasingly complex challenges. Indeed, since the end of the Cold War, there has been an increasing trend towards military participation in humanitarian aid operations, as the number of humanitarian crises and victims in need of relief aid has risen (Francois, 1995). Such operations have typically occurred in "failed states" or developing countries; examples include Bosnia, Haiti, Sudan, and Rwanda (Francois, 1995; Natsios, 1996). Collectively, such operations represent an attempt to counter a new frontier in conflict: complex humanitarian emergencies.

What is meant by complex humanitarian emergencies? These situations are defined by the following five characteristics:

> ... [i] deterioration or complete collapse of central government authority; [ii] ethnic or religious conflict and widespread human rights abuses; [iii] episodic food insecurity, frequently deteriorating into mass starvation; [iv] macroeconomic collapse involving hyperinflation, massive unemployment and net decreases in GNP [Gross National Product]; and [v] mass population movements of displaced people and refugees escaping conflict or searching for food. (Natsios, 1996, 67)

Over the course of the last 15 to 20 years, humanitarian emergencies, as well as peacekeeping operations with humanitarian goals, have rapidly become the primary responsibility of the United Nations (UN) and many international forces (Francois, 1995). The UN notes that there have been 63 peacekeeping missions since 1945; however, only 18 of these began before the end of the Cold War. In 2009 alone, the UN was engaged in a total of 16 active missions (United Nations, 2009). In conducting such missions, and as mentioned above, militaries are now expected to take on new and diverse roles and responsibilities, including supervising ceasefires, demining projects, the return of refugees, the design and supervision of social reforms (administrative or otherwise), economic reconstruction, and verification of human rights (Iribarnegaray, 2002). This has not only required militaries around the world to become more proficient in dealing with civilians, but it has also provided the space for them to come into contact with NGOs.

This chapter outlines, in broad strokes, the nature of the military's relationship with NGOs, with particular attention to the experiences of the Canadian military with such organizations within the last two decades. We examine how tensions in this *civil-military relationship* stemming from a variety of sources, such as differences in organizational structure and culture, as well as stereotypes of both the military and NGOs, may influence interactions and the possibility for collaboration. The NGO-military relationship will also be examined within the context of theory on cooperation and coordination, as well as social-psychological theorizing on intergroup relations, with an aim towards making suggestions for mutual training and education.[9]

"Cooperation, Coordination, or Something Else?"

Given that contact between the military and many NGOs seems unavoidable in the current global context, the question becomes one of *how* they work together, rather than *if*.[10] In other words, how is the military-NGO relationship defined? As Christopher Ankerson asked, are we looking at "cooperation, coordination, or something else?" (2004, 1).

Coordination involves working together in a hierarchical relationship – the balance of power exists mainly with one party (Ankerson, 2004). According to Ankerson (2004), the power within the NGO-military relationship resides largely with the military, due to their substantial access to resources. In addition, the military already operates within a *hierarchical culture*, in which they value a chain of command and tend to adopt a more authoritarian style of leadership (Scheltinga, Rietjens, de Boer and Wilderom, 2005). In contrast, NGOs typically exhibit a *clan culture*, which is characterized by a flattened, consensus-based decision-making structure (Scheltinga, Rietjens, de Boer and Wilderom, 2005). Beyond a two-party situation, a coordinated effort could also be enacted through the use of a third party. This would commonly be the role of the UN, as the UN already coordinates multi-player international military missions, as well as operating NGO-like bodies such as the UN High Commissioner for Refugees (UNHCR), the World Food Bank, and the United Nations Children's Fund (UNICEF).

Cooperation, in contrast to coordination, has been conceived of as a relationship in which two parties share the balance of power equally and have an equal stake in the project (Ankerson, 2004). This style of partnership is closer to the clan culture characteristic of NGOs. Cooperation, sometimes referred to as an *integrated approach*, is seen by some theorists as the ideal goal for the NGO-military relationship (e.g., Byman, 2001; Eriksson, 2000; Williams, 1998). But is this a tenable suggestion? Research by anthropologist Donna Winslow (2002) suggests that there may be challenges in achieving this goal.[11]

Tensions in the NGO-Military Relationship

Winslow (2002) found that despite increased contact, the NGO-military relationship remains difficult for both parties. She identified five primary sources of tension in this partnership: 1) organizational structure and culture; 2) tasks and ways of accomplishing them; 3) definitions of success and time frames; 4) abilities to exert influence and control information; and 5) control of resources. Each will be discussed in turn.

Organizational Structure and Culture

Organizational structure and culture is probably the most important aspect when discussing NGOs, the military, and their ability to work together (Winslow, 2002). NGOs and the military differ on numerous fundamental levels in terms of their organizational structure and culture. As was mentioned earlier, from a structural standpoint, militaries are organized hierarchically and tend to be characterized by an authoritarian and centralized decision-making style. On the other hand, NGOs tend to have a diffuse, flattened hierarchy, and decision making tends to be consensus-based and decentralized (Scheltinga, Rietjens, de Boer and Wilderom, 2005; Williams, 1998; Winslow, 2002). This is, of course, an over-generalization, as militaries differ across nation and time, and NGOs differ widely in their practices and configuration.

Such differences in organizational structure and culture, as well as in organizational mandates, can often leave both parties unable to understand one another. According to Miller (1999), NGOs also tend to be skeptical of the "blurring of lines" between the two parties, which humanitarian operations encourage. NGOs tend to feel that the purpose of a military is to prepare for and engage in war, whereas NGOs often see themselves as cleaning up after the crises they view as caused by military intervention (Miller, 1999). Military personnel, on the other hand, tend to view relief workers as dismissive of authority, as "hotheaded and un-disciplined" (Dallaire, 2003, 299), and as only interested in opportunities for media attention (Dallaire, 2003; Miller, 1999; Pollick, 2000; Winslow, 2002). Essentially, as one relief worker stated in an interview with Laura Miller, in regard to the US military in Somalia: "Both of us come from very strong cultures, and both think we're right and know how to do things best" (1999, 192).

There are also differences in the composition of these organizations. Militaries tend to consist mostly of young men, typically between the ages of 19 and 22 (Winslow, 2002). In addition, their peace operations units are usually uniracial. In contrast to this, NGO and UN field staff members tend to be women, typically ranging in age from their 20s to their 40s, and who typically have diverse ethnic backgrounds (Miller, 1999; Williams, 1998; Winslow, 2002). These "demographic differences may help to perpetuate a distance between the two populations" (Miller, 1999, 192). Even within the military, some of these differences may play out, as subtle barriers still exist for military women (Winslow and Dunn, 2002). Thus, if male military members do not fully accept the presence or leadership of women within their own ranks, then they may not fully embrace the idea of working along-side predominately female NGOs.

Tasks and Ways of Accomplishing Them

NGOs and the military may agree that humanitarian aid and reconstruc-tion projects need to occur, but that is where the similarity often ends. As Winslow (2002) explains, their respective definitions of *how* and *why* these projects should occur are not entirely commensurate. Militaries are typically involved in "quick impact projects" (QIPs), which are con-struction or reconstruction projects designed to assist the community. For example: "In Bosnia, the Canadians rebuilt a hospital wing, set up a dental clinic, built a woodshed for a school, cut and delivered wood to the elderly, etc." (Winslow, 2002, 8). These sorts of projects are designed to be completed quickly and efficiently, in order to win the "hearts and minds," or trust and confidence, of the local population, as well as to gain valuable intelligence (see also Longhurst, 2006-2007).

NGOs, on the other hand, engage in the same types of projects, al-though less so in an attempt to gain information (Winslow, 2002). They tend to create few boundaries between themselves and the local popula-tion, and often incorporate local cultural practices into projects. These projects tend to be long-term and to rely on community participation. Thus, it might be said that a major difference between NGOs and the military is that the military does its projects *for* the community, while NGOs do the projects *with* the community (Winslow, 2002).

Definitions of Success and Time Frames

As indicated earlier, NGOs and the military tend to differ in what they consider to be a successful venture, and how long this should take. In general, militaries tend to establish short-term goals and definitions of success – for example, civil security – which may be established in a matter of hours, days or months, whereas NGOs tend to define success in terms of long-term social and economic development, which typically takes years or decades to achieve (Winslow, 2002). In terms of reconstruction projects, the military may consider a project a success if they were able to finish the project quickly and with an efficient use of resources, and if they were able to gain some intelligence through their interactions with the community in the process. For NGOs, on the other hand, teaching the community to become more sustainable and self-sufficient would be considered a major success. Involving the community in this way may not be efficient in the short term, but may become so in the long term: "Community involvement in reconstruction not only fosters responsibility for that community, it can ultimately lead to community ownership of the process thereby facilitating a smooth transition to autonomy" (Iribarnegaray, 2002, 14).

An additional factor that influences the time frame in which projects are carried out is the length of time spent in the field (Winslow, 2002). The average Canadian soldier has a rotation of 6 to 9 months, whereas a relief or development worker often provides their services for at least 12 months and sometimes several years. The length of military rotations also determines the scope of the projects they can commit to: short-term is usually the only viable option (Winslow, 2002; see also Longhurst, 2006-2007).

Abilities to Exert Influence and Control Information

For both the military and NGOs, the media, as a vehicle for exerting influence and controlling information, is extremely important. For NGOs, media attention-seeking is of the utmost importance, as it often determines the funds they have available to conduct relief and development work. As Dana Eyre has noted, "to understand an NGO, one must understand the three major influences specific to that organization: its funding stream, its organizational mandate, and its pattern of political and media involvement" (1998, 16). However, the pursuit of media attention has also become a source of tension between NGOs and the military, as the military has sometimes found this pursuit to be "irritating" and "distasteful" (Pollick, 2000, 60). The military has sometimes seen the competitiveness that it can breed between NGOs: "In reality, this often comes down to competition for media coverage: the group with the best TV and press coverage tends to get better financing" (Pollick, 2000, 60). Clearly, funds are of paramount importance. Accepting funds from donors, which may be facilitated through media attention, may allow NGOs to remain independent and neutral and, at least in theory, unaffected by international or government politics. But where do NGOs' funds come from? Gordenker and Weiss (1996) provided an analysis of many of the major NGOs, and showed that at least 90 percent of their funds stem from the governments of wealthy nations. Also, these funds may come with strings: "all NGOs and foundation donors operate under some governmental, donor-imposed or doctrinal restrictions" (32). Depending on the circumstances, such restrictions may limit or complicate NGO independence, neutrality, or impartiality.

This is not to say that the military does not also value media attention. In fact, some in the CF have come to realize the importance of media relationships. Dallaire has stated that the media is now as useful to military aims as any force that can be deployed: "The media was the weapon I used to strike the conscience of the world and try to prod the international community into action" (2003, 333).

Also at issue when considering the ability to control information is the problem of information sharing (Winslow, 2002). As noted above, relief and development workers are often in the field much longer than are military personnel, and thus may be more likely than military members to form relationships with the local community. As a consequence, members of NGOs are often privy to a great deal of information that could be useful to the military. However, due to their principle of neutrality, NGOs may be unwilling to share that information with the military. In addition, both militaries and NGOs may have security concerns in regard to information sharing (Winslow, 2002). Thus, the issue of information sharing is complex and may be contentious for both sides.

Control of Resources

A final point of tension in the NGO-military relationship is, once again, tied to the issue of funds. The military has access to and controls many resources, including vehicles and aircraft, which would make humanitarian missions easier for NGOs (Winslow, 2002). This is a double-edged sword, with NGOs falling on either side. On the one hand, military involvement can help facilitate the transportation of refugees, medical aid, relief, and food supplies. Military presence may also provide protection, and contribute to a general "atmosphere of security" (Dallaire, 2003). In fact, this aspect is so crucial that NGOs have, at times, called for increased military intervention for the purposes of obtaining protection (Miller, 1999). On the other hand, some NGOs have resisted military protection as it may compromise their neutrality and independence, and thus place them at greater physical risk (Winslow, 2002).

Moving Forward

We have seen, based on the work of Winslow and others, that the NGO-military relationship has been marked by tension and misunderstanding. We have also seen that these tensions may be exacerbated by stereotypes and assumptions on both sides: for example, military members may perceive NGO workers as "flaky do-gooders," whereas NGO members may perceive military members as "authoritarian" or "arrogant" "boys with toys" (Winslow, 2002). However, steps are being taken by the CF in order to resolve some of these tensions. As one example, since 1996, the CF has fostered a professional relationship with one of the largest international NGOs, CARE, which has a Canadian chapter (Benthall, 1993; CARE Canada, 2009; CARE International, 2009). CARE Canada has helped the CF to train their CIMIC operators.

In general, military members tend to feel positively about their interactions with NGOs during their training, and often express the desire for more collaborative training possibilities. These would include having relief and development workers come together with the military for joint exercises, and having joint conferences where each group can speak to and learn from the other. For example, relief workers who are engaging in agricultural work could benefit from military training in demining procedures (i.e., the removal of land mines in agricultural areas; Miller, 1999). NGOs, on the other hand, tend to remain skeptical of the value of these joint interactions, fearing that they will compromise their independence and neutrality.

It is certainly possible that joint training and conferences conducted while in Canada may reduce some of the tension between NGOs and the military, while at the same time provide some common ground for communication. However, once in theatre, in some situations, if NGOs are seen as cooperating with the military, then they may be at an increased risk for danger. However, perhaps this need not be an all or nothing relationship. As Janice Stein (2001) has argued, the geopolitical landscape has changed so much, that it may no longer be ethical to remain neutral: "Neutrality is appropriate in a neutral environment, but the environments of complex emergencies are generally predatory rather than neutral" (33).

Apart from the issue of neutrality, however, effective cooperation may be understood as an issue of power relations, as Ankerson (2004) has described in the context of theory on coordination and cooperation. Likewise, we suggest, invoking social-psychological theory (e.g., Aronson, Bridgeman, and Geffner, 1978; Cook, 1985), that the NGO-military relationship may be framed as a problem of *intergroup relations*, in which power relations play an important role. As such, equal status (or other aspects of power, such as access to resources or numerical superiority), as well as interdependence and shared or common goals, may be key to effective cooperation between groups. At this time in history, the NGO-military relationship is probably best described in terms of coordination, as a hierarchical working relationship, and it is usually the military that holds the balance of power (e.g., in terms of resources; Ankerson, 2004). However, also important in collaboration are broad (super-ordinate) common goals, such as commitment to peace and stability, which many NGOs and the military may share (Winslow, 2002). And in fact, on a more mundane level, NGOs and the military may have a great deal in common: They both tend to have a hardworking "can-do" attitude, they both often work in dangerous and austere conditions, and they both share a willingness to work among the suffering, the dying, and the dead (Winslow, 2002). These similarities may provide a common ground for building communication, coordination, or even cooperation; they may help NGOs and the military view each other more positively; and they may even encourage friendship ties that can be critical for successful intergroup relations (see also Pettigrew, 1998). Also important to effective collaboration is that proactive coordination between the military and NGOs (as well as between the military and government agencies and international organizations) occurs *before* a crisis emerges (Olson and Gregorian, 2007).

However, if the negotiation of power relationships is key to the success of the NGO-military relationship, or indeed any intergroup relationship, then how might this negotiation be possible? Although an in-depth exploration of this topic is beyond the scope of this chapter, we may begin to discern an answer. On balance, both NGOs and the military must be seen as "equal partners." However, rather than requiring that the power relationship between NGOs and the military be equal in every case, or even that a coordinating third-party, like the UN, might oversee or ensure an equal power relationship between the two parties, we suggest that the power dynamics in the NGO-military relationship may shift, depending on the context. An equal power relationship, and general cooperation, can be fostered through joint training prior to deployment. However, in theatre, one party may act as a coordinator (or the leader), and assume the balance of power, in an area where they have greater expertise, experience, or capability (e.g., the military in the area of security/protection; NGOs in the area of humanitarian work). In this way, the power may continually shift between parties, but mutual understanding, trust and respect for each other's contributions can guide this otherwise hierarchical relationship towards effective cooperation, *on balance*. Furthermore, such shifting power dynamics, as well as mutual respect, trust and understanding, may guide effective collaboration not only between NGOs and the military, but within a comprehensive approach in general.

Chapter 3

INTERNATIONAL DEVELOPMENT OF THE COMPREHENSIVE APPROACH

CAROLINE VAVRO AND RICHARD ROY

Introduction

Paradigms shift slowly. Once established, a paradigm – how we see and interpret the world – changes slowly until it is seemingly suddenly replaced by a new one. That build up to the tipping point, where the new paradigm suddenly gains wide acceptance, takes time, rigorous research and careful examination (Kuhn, 1996). We presently seem to be edging down this path of acceptance with the comprehensive approach (CA). There is an interesting allure to this new concept. It promises greater efficiencies and effectiveness, always welcomed when constrained by scarce strategic resources. The seeds of moving beyond narrow departmental perspectives to more fully integrated national strategies are contained within the Comprehensive Approach. As a construct, CA moves beyond the unrealistic expectations of linear planning to permit better framing and analysis of complex problems, issues and crises. Despite being under development for over five years much struggle continues with the basic definition and underpinnings of the concept. While there is a plethora of initiatives designed to study this concept, more work is required. Nonetheless, progress seems inevitable.

For all the attention presently afforded it, is the comprehensive approach really relevant? There does seem to be a historical case to be made that when assistance in troubled states is closely coordinated that the likelihood of ultimate success improves. As frequently pointed out today, part of the success in the Malayan Emergency was attributable to the

Security Operations in the 21st Century: Canadian Perspectives on the Comprehensive Approach, ed. M. Rostek and P. Gizewski. Montreal and Kingston: Queen's Policy Studies Series, McGill-Queen's University Press.

detail, central coordination at all levels of the administration of all plans and activities expected to counter the Communist terrorists. Mirroring the procedures, organizations and tactics from Malaya, the British repeated their success, albeit much less pleasantly, in Kenya (Anderson, 2006). Inter-allied structures, coordinating everything from food to fuel, were important keys to the Allied victories in both World Wars. Even as far back as the Boer War, the British military pursued the commandos while the civil component concentrated on post-war reconstruction plans. The accompanying resurgent interest in counter-insurgency that accompanied the campaigns in Iraq and Afghanistan has lead to a re-examination of the mechanisms necessary to achieve broad based coordination and synchronization in these and past complex campaigns. Granted, this approach does not apply only to these cases but also in the strikingly similar peace enforcement missions such as Bosnia and Kosovo. With the flood of actors invading the modern operational space, the implementation more harmonized, de-conflicted and synchronized programming would most assuredly benefit the recipients. There is therefore a significant relevance and great value in developing this concept further.

The following is an overview of the work which selected major actors have carried out in advancing their versions of the comprehensive approach. It will start by outlining the measures and activities of two key international organizations: the North Atlantic Treaty Organization (NATO) and the United Nations (UN). This will be followed by a description of the programs of the two leading nations developing the concept – Britain and the United States (US) – highlighting common challenges and obstacles. The chapter concludes by pointing to the importance of further development of the comprehensive approach.

The North Atlantic Treaty Organization (NATO)

NATO has devoted considerable effort towards developing their version of the comprehensive approach. The study of this concept was initiated by the Danes in 2005 when they brought their Comprehensive Planning and Assessment techniques forward into the NATO fora (Stepputat, 2009, 15). Since then, the progress in developing this concept has been carefully marked at every subsequent NATO summit with constant pronouncements on its status. For instance, at the 2006 Riga Summit the initial identification of the importance of the concept and initial direction on how to proceed with it were given. At Bucharest 2008, the comprehensive approach was endorsed and direction given to implement an Action Plan – a set of pragmatic proposals to develop and implement NATO's contribution to the comprehensive approach. At Strasbourg/Kehl in 2009, the progress on the Action Plan was assessed and further updates directed. The Action Plan is the principle mechanisms used to develop the concept in NATO and is structurally represented by the establishment of

Comprehensive Approach Action Team. This team was fixed on seeking pragmatic solutions vice wrestling with the more challenging issue of defining exactly what constituted the concept. This definitional aspect is recognized as an enormous challenge given the collective consensus aspect of NATO work. It is clear though that the organization recognizes its importance. As recently as the Chief of Transformation's Conference in December 2009, a great deal of the conference agenda was dedicated to issues relating to the comprehensive approach. The Conference's final report included recommendations to emphasize the importance of education to improving its use, promoting the concept in military-to-military engagement and seeking ways to make non-governmental organizations into more willing partners in NATO activities (NATO, 2009, 7-13).

Perhaps NATO has made its greatest progress in including aspects of the CA in its revision of its planning methodologies. NATO has recently revised its planning methodologies but this does not guarantee acceptance by other actors and does carry some risk. For instance, a shallow re-write of the NATO strategic planning processes was used as a tool for collective strategic planning in the US Joint Forces Command (US JFCOM) led Multi-National Experiment 5 (MNE 5).[12] This completely ignored valid and relevant existing models for international strategic coordination already in use for missions like Bosnia, Kosovo and elsewhere (Whitfield, 2007). The new NATO model may have applicability but should not be an exclusive model nor an imposed replacement for the planning methodologies of potential partners. A second stumbling block may be how closely wed the new methodology is to the effects based approach to operations (EBAO). This planning philosophy is presented at times in an over zealously manner to civilian partners and suffers from the assumption that second, third or even fourth order effects can be predicted in the complex operating environment of today which calls into question the underlying validity of this model.[13] The early and easy equating of the comprehensive approach as simply adding civil aspects to EBAO, the assumption that NATO "had" the answer, lent little credibility to this effort in outside circles. Nonetheless, the recognition of the need to adjust planning and take a more holistic view bodes well for the development of the CA.

Additionally, there are two serious issues in NATO's approach that must be considered. The first is role definition, a matter which was being hotly debated as the New Strategic Concept is being developed. Will NATO be expeditionary or not? The noncommittal view of many NATO nations toward being expeditionary and their unwillingness to take on the hurdles associated with developing these capabilities challenge the Alliance's ability to streamline itself for future missions like Afghanistan. While the CA is important in either case the interaction with external actors will be measurably different depending on where NATO forces will deploy. Second, despite the aspirations of some nations, NATO remains primarily a military alliance. This is not bad in itself. Throughout the early 1990s the US frequently lead interventions and then transitioned the mission over to UN forces, a role NATO could now usefully fill. Its struggles in Afghanistan reflect its military-centric reality. From a purely military perspective, constructing a consistent vision of victory, a narrative to define success, has been troublesome. In the case of Afghanistan, there have been marked improvements since the appointment of General A. McChrystal; however, the watch words for staff planners in the International Security Assistance Force (ISAF) remain *caveat emptor*. Many contingents remain riddled with national caveats that the ability to weld NATO forces together and craft sustainable, functional campaign plans remains and enormous challenge and make NATO's operation very similar to UN ones. Despite the appointment of a senior NATO civil representative in Afghanistan, NATO and ISAF do not truly possess a civil side, lack civil expertise across a wide range of functional areas and do not possess any direct control over non-NATO civilians operating in Afghanistan. Further, there is a common mantra now in circulation that given the military nature of many Provincial Reconstruction Teams, NATO should be accorded the position to coordinate development across Afghanistan. This may be an instance of mis-applying the reconstruction lesson from Iraq.[14] Given the normal and existing bi-lateral nature of development assistance between contributing nations and the Government of Afghanistan, the presence of the normal development representatives, and the complete lack of familiarity with the finer points of development policy and theory amongst the bulk of the NATO staff, this proposal is badly flawed at best. When many nations remain unwilling to commit their soldiers to combat it is unlikely there will be much enthusiasm to let unqualified officers commit millions of dollars of development assistance from those bearing the brunt of the fight. There is no doubt that NATO will be a key partner within the CA within its proper role, functional areas and expertise. NATO needs to appreciate what its partners can do and allow them the space carry out their missions.

The United Nations (UN)

Since the end of the Cold War, the UN has been fully confronted with the challenge of integration due to both its greatly increased operational tempo and the advent of more complex peace support operations (Government of Canada, Department of National Defence, 2006). Striving to improve its internal integration, the UN has sought to transform itself from an institution that solely issued Security Council mandates as instructions to deploying military forces to an organization that practices a more holistic approach to operations. This has forced the UN to grapple with major institutional shifts on an incremental and continuous basis. The key milestones within the UN system as it has adopted its integrated approach – its version of the comprehensive approach – included in the *Brahimi Report* (2000). This approach included the establishment of the Peace Building Commission and associated mechanisms in 2006, the Secretary General's *Decision on Integration* (UN Interoffice Memorandum, 2008), and the development and fielding of the Integrated Mission Planning Process (IMPP) between 2006 and 2009. All these initiatives have sought to improve the coordination between elements deploying temporarily under Security Council mandates, the UN mission, and UN elements with longer term presence in conflict areas, the UN Country Team (UNCT). On this journey the UN identified the following under-lying issues that indicated the requirement for this greater integration: no one agency or actor can establish a sustainable peace on their own; there was great overlap between many of the aspects of peacekeeping and peace building; and that UN's ends were best served by a coherent, linked strategy in country.

Recognizing its utility, the UN has diligently been working its integrated approach, long before it was discovered and re-labelled by others. Many of its new norms for integration can be seen at UN Headquarters. This includes structural components such as the Department of Peacekeeping Operations / Department of Field Support establishing the Joint Mission Analysis Centre and Joint Operations Command and from a process perspective, there is evidence in the Consolidated Appeals Process. There are system wide initiatives to deliver greater integration in the field too. Part of this involves more clearly defining the role and powers of the Special Representative of the Secretary General (SRSG) and the relationship with the Deputy SRSG, the Resident Coordinator (RC) and / or the Humanitarian Coordinator (HC). Studies have been conducted to define and delineate the levels of integration desired: full, partial or limited. Within the context of planning a mission the UN can now state the general expectation for the degree of collaboration and integration it expects. The Integrated Mission (IM) approach refers to a specific mission design in which the UN mission and the UNCT are structural linked to form a single entity. The Integrated Approach (IA) means there will be a strategic partnership between them regardless whether they are structur-ally integrated. At its core much of the UN effort remains focused on the degree of coordination of all its elements in a country.

Despite the bright prospects of better UN mission coordination there remain some growing pains. First, it can take a long time to establish a UN mission as national responses, both to the plan and to the resources requested, condition when its can be launched. Leadership teams often have to devote much of their initial energies to ensure the mission co-alesces and may lack familiarity with the country to which they are being deployed. Given time, and the assistance of the UNCT, the mission should increase in effectiveness. Second, funding mechanisms for the UN mission and the UNCT are sharply different. This may hinder synchronization and delivery of projects that complement each other efforts as budgetary cycles may be ponderous and not sufficiently agile to respond to urgencies in country. Finally, as a relatively new norm, particularly the IMPP, many groups within the UN are only just becoming familiar with the procedures, becoming less fearful of them and determining their proper place within them. Excellent lessons in integration are evident from the field. As counter-insurgents often point to Malaya as a valuable example (Hack, 2009, 383-414).UN integration disciples may soon be pointing to the last few years of the United Nations Interim Force in Lebanon (UNFIL) and other such missions as they further develop their concept.[15]

Britain

There is little doubt that Britain has been a global leader in the development of the CA but identifying who is leading the national effort is difficult. It is an unfortunate habit in Western militaries to point to doctrine publications within other defence institutions and presume they have wide acceptance within other parts of that nation's government, such has been the case with the United Kingdom Ministry of Defence's Joint Discussion Note 4/05 – *The Comprehensive Approach* (Director General Joint Doctrine and Concepts, 2006). Dr. Andrew Dorman's (2007) rejoinder article *The Comprehensive Approach: Nice Idea but is it Real?* that explained how little influence or weight was attached to this discussion note by other members of government is less well known. Similarly, the doctrinal seepage that occurs from British military work into the hallways of NATO and the European Union, based on a desire to limit repetitive nugatory work, demands some care as to not misinterpret these efforts for broad based acceptance in these intuitions of a military-introduced initiative (United Kingdom Ministry of Defence, 2010). More broadly, at the national level former Prime Minister Tony Blair's Join-up Government initiatives speak to the unifying principles and parameters that make a comprehensive approach effective. There is recognition within the United Kingdom of the need for key government departments to be better aligned for the management of foreign deployments. While dialogue obviously existed, closer focus on national security strategy is now being provided by a Cabinet subcommittee – the Ministerial Committee – National Security, International Relationship and Development (NSID) highlighting that the UK has initiated the study of the comprehensive approach across a broad range of national institutions.

The United Kingdom has embedded the comprehensive approach into its practices through organization, funding, training and study. Organizationally, the UK established the Stability Unit. It is co-owned by the Department for International Development (DFID), the Foreign and Commonwealth Office (FCO) and the Ministry of Defence (MOD). Its core responsibilities include co-ordinating and supporting cross government stabilisation planning and execution; ensuring the rapid and integrated delivery of targeted expertise in a cross-government approach; and leading on stabilisation lesson-learning and assisting with implementation. The Unit has spent considerable effort in examining in detail "what stability means," collecting lessons learned in the immediate operational environment and then ensuring that information is widely disseminated. They have contributed greatly to the understanding of the policy and pragmatics of the coordination necessary in situations where stabilisation is a core focus.[16] With regards to funding, the UK established common funding pools, the Conflict Prevention Pools, a joined-up government initiative. The aim of the pools was "helping them (the relevant departments) increase the impact of what they do through better coordination and common strategies." To access funds, the applicants submit their requests to a panel consisting of all members of the departmental partners. This bidding on shared, common funds helped ensure greater dialogue in project planning and implementation plus more joined-up projects (United Kingdom, Foreign and Commonwealth Office, 2003). Training opportunities were also important to promote the utility of working together in a comprehensive fashion. This ranged from massed exercises like Joint Venture 2008 to many other smaller initiatives. These common events show value in enhancing cross institutional familiarity and trust. Finally, study and analysis have played a role too. Newer UK doctrine manuals, like Joint Doctrine Publication (JDP) 3-40 *Security and Stabilisation: The Military Contribution* (UK Ministry of Defence – Assistant Chief of Defence Staff – Development, Concepts, and Doctrine, (2009) and the series of JDPs on campaigning and planning, now have a more nuanced perspectives on the military's role with respect to the other actors in an operational area. Even the United Kingdom House of Commons Defence Committee (2010) recently completed a detailed study of the utility of the concept – *Comprehensive Approach: The Point of War Is Not Just to Win but Make a Better Peace*.

The United States

Though often thought of trailing the field, the United States is actual closer to the leading edge in developing the comprehensive approach concept. This is due in part to its long and sustained effort to improve interagency coordination, a fixation of the US military since the discovery of its importance in the 1994 intervention in Haiti (Hamblet and Kline, 2000, 92-7). The US military's recognition of the importance of this issue is evident in the ever widening influence it has upon their joint doctrine. From the other actors' role and task baseline as outlined in Joint Publication 3-08, *Interagency, Intergovernmental Organization, and Nongovernment Organization Coordination During Joint Operations* (2006), a re-issue of a useful 1996 manual, to the current release of a series of handbooks on military support to stabilisation by the Joint Warfighting Center,[17] most, if not all, US joint doctrine manuals touch on the importance of the co-ordination with other actors to conduct modern, successful campaigns. The import of understanding the other actors in the battlespace is equally reflected in important works like the United States Institute of Peace's *Guide for Participants in Peace, Stability and Relief Operation* (2007). While much of the initial impetus for this work was the greater exposure and involvement of the US in post-Cold War peacekeeping missions, the cur-rent importance is attached to the resurgence of the need to be able to wage effective counter-insurgency. This type of warfare requires a broader, more integrated collective effort both in-country and at home which even continues into reconstruction and stabilization. This emphasis on the im-portance of collaboration is outlined in the National Security Presidential Directive 44 *Management of Interagency Efforts Concerning Reconstruction and Stabilization Operations* and is equally reflected in the *Quadrennial Defense Reviews* of 2006 and 2010. Operations in Iraq and Afghanistan, having prompted greater study of how to achieve success in irregular warfare, are keeping the importance of interagency cooperation in view (United States, Department of State, 2009).

The desire to improve interagency coordination is demonstrated in how the US has structured and established various organizations, in how military doctrine is being developed and on operations. The establishment of the Office of the Coordinator of Reconstruction and Stabilization (S/CRS) revealed the importance afforded centralized coordination necessary in addressing stabilization and reconstruction issues. The core mission of the S/CRS is to lead, coordinate and institutionalize US government civilian capacity to prevent or prepare for post-conflict situations (United States, Department of State, 2010). Additionally S/CRS has worked to develop doctrine and concepts for whole-of-government reconstruction and stabilization efforts as well as developing a framework to aid in strategic planning, the *Interagency Conflict Assessment Framework* (United States Reconstruction and Stabilization Policy Coordinating Committee, 2008). Preparing deployable civil elements remains a key goal of the organization. Elsewhere, many US combatant commands have trialed interagency initiatives. The command most fully integrated appears to be US SOUTHCOM, perhaps because its geographic responsibilities are so close to the continental US (Lawner, Kaster, and Matthews, 2010, 22-31). It has far reaching, closely intertwined programs and operations involving various military components, as well as the US Coast Guard and elements from several other federal agencies. Its integration of diverse elements is further facilitated by a specific directorate, the Partnering Directorate, establish specifically to develop and monitor interagency dynamics.[18] The broader perspective of the comprehensive approach can also be seen in how the US military has prepared recent key doctrine manuals. In the case of both FM 3-24 *Counter-insurgency* and FM 3-07 *Stability Operations* extensive consultation across government as well as with an extremely wide audience of other actors occurred as these manuals were being drafted (United States Institute of Peace, 2009). Finally, a new mindset has been evident on operations. As the US has explored the implications of counter-insurgency, irregular warfare and conflict prevention the inputs, advice and opinions of other actors have been actively sought. Recently, for the disaster in Haiti, the US military provided direct liaison officer to USAID and to the humanitarian leads on the ground to assist in their planning. In Port-au-Prince this facilitated the humanitarian commun-ities' ability to plan for and deliver food aid during a 14 day surge while US military forces focus on supporting these efforts with the necessary security. It has become apparent that the US is making great strides towards operating in a more holistic fashion which can be viewed as a comprehensive approach.

Hurdles to the CA

Through the evidence presented above, it is apparent that progress is being made in the development and the implementation of the comprehensive approach. Many organizations, institutions and nations, all bounded by their own cultural norms and perspectives, are seeking to effect greater coherence and coordination in order to achieve greater efficiency and effectiveness on modern operations. In the development of this concept practically all have experienced similar difficulties in advancing it.

One of the first problems in advancing this concept has been an overt perception that this was purely a military initiative or demands a military lead. This problem is associated with the amount of resources militaries have massed to study the concept. That some of the initial work done on the concept began in the military community is true; a reflection of the recognition of the importance of coordinating multiple actors in modern counter-insurgency, stability operations and even peacekeeping. This urgent exploration within militaries brought a mass of researchers to the issue and a subsequent explosion of papers and studies especially as this mode of collaboration is seen as vital to success. An avalanche of information seekers has tended to overwhelm the more limited staffs of the partners and other actors whose opinions and participation are so actively sought in these initiatives. Similarly, mass leads to the second issue particularly on operations, gap filling. Military forces are primarily deployed to provide security but what exactly does this mean and how is it delivered? If there is a perception that something vital in theatre is not being done that has a bearing on security it is common for militaries to fill that void. Militaries normally have excess or redundant capacity, a function of the constitution of their war-fighting organization. This al-lows for them to react rapidly to fill identified urgent requirements based on presumed operational necessity albeit perhaps not to the scope and extent a regular practitioner of the discipline in question could. While it may offend some organization's culture – in some case because the need was not first discovered by them – the worry that the development of this concept was initiated in militaries should be irrelevant. First, on operations, militaries have long standing requirements to interact with a multitude of actors; a brief examination of peacekeeping literature easily demonstrates this. It should be no surprise that militaries recognize the value in coordination and interaction with these wider communities and seek dialogue with them. Second, based on political decisions to assist a failed state, all national resources dedicated towards that effort are best integrated to the furthest extent possible and practical. So regardless where this initiative originated, it has national strategic value.

A second impediment occurs due to trust and domination issues. Groups form better when they face common, urgent external problems. Trust is the key to group dynamics. Trust forms based on the general interactions within the group and the perceived credibility of others within the group. It is reinforced, making a more cohesive and effective team, when there is mutual respect and respect for institutional differences between group members. Trust builds when others are treated fairly, their positions and institutions are respected and the overall objectives of the group are supported – this means not just "talking the talk" but "walking the walk." But what does working together really mean? There will always be different organizational norms and incentives. There will be different perspectives on what needs to be solved and how. There will be difficulties determining who will decide what needs to be done and setting timelines. Trust is difficult enough to nurture and maintain, it is especially so when dominance issues arise. If military partners become overbearing about who is ultimately in charge or overly fixated on unity of command it can rapidly decompose. The reality is that if multiple partners are undertaking many actions within their own functional domains that may equally contribute to success, few , if any, will be or need to be under military command or control. Unity of effort, based on a negotiated common strategic vision, may be the best that can be hoped for. It must be recognized that there will always be a free-rider problem in modern operations – organizations that will be present but not participate in the collective efforts but still accrue benefits from them. However, overplaying the military's command and control dictum, especially for areas well outside of military expertise, serves little purpose. As this concept is more fully developed, the exploration of how partners can interact usefully at the strategic and operational level will continue to be important.

A final hurdle is the dividing line between daily practice and preparing for the future. Many partners and practitioners, whether operational deployed or bureaucratically entrenched, are more worried about the immediacy of the here and now, not potential future improvement. Depending on the networks they operate within, many profess to be executing the comprehensive approach on a daily basis. For them it is an existing, functioning philosophy. The problem with this attitude is that it denies the need to codify or examine or improve on the process for future benefit. It denies making the processes and techniques widely available for education and training and somewhat presumes current practices are the best ones. Codifying and clarifying the comprehensive approach concept is important for a number of reasons. First, while it can be improved by capturing best practices from operations there must be a benchmark to measure against. Once benchmarked, improvements will be more easily identifiable within institutions, across inter-partner working processes and even in the conceptualization and strategizing for how best to intervene in particular situations (e.g., disaster response, non-combatant evacuations, humanitarian intervention). Second, training together, both more fully and more often, will promote both operational competencies and a greater general awareness of the roles and responsibilities of other partners thus easing the transition to operational effectiveness once individuals or groups are deployed. This common training needs to be informed by a common concept. Finally, by elaborating the concept more completely organizations can better craft their own roadmaps to manage their way forward towards being more capable and effective team members so they can remain operationally and strategically relevant.

Conclusion

There is a great amount of effort being devoted to develop and improve on the CA concept in a multitude of international organizations and in a multitude of capitals. Many are working hard to conceive, design and build the capabilities required within this concept. But who is it for? Is it primarily useful for ensuring the "needy" are well aided by coherent, consistent and well-organized programs and campaigns in an assisted state? Is it primarily useful for affording Western interveners a tool to ensure they can de-conflict their combined efforts? Or is it primarily useful to ensure the careful spending of strategic resources in the support of national interests? Not surprisingly, the concept has utility in all these applications and more. It would serve Canada's interest well to further the model and develop our own concept while concurrently monitoring and assisting the development efforts of potential future partners.

PART II
NON-GOVERNMENTAL
PERSPECTIVES

Chapter 4

COMPREHENSIVE APPROACH AND FRAGILE STATES: NON-GOVERNMENTAL ORGANIZATIONS' ROLES IN FRAGILE SITUATIONS

NIPA BANERJEE

The Comprehensive Approach (CA) normally and traditionally implies an integrated and coordinated approach to security, development and peacekeeping. Such an approach is often simply explained as a division of labour and, when required, cooperation between aid workers and international military forces. Under ordinary non-conflict emergency situations, comprehensive civil-military coordination transpires into emergency response and humanitarian work by relief agencies under protection of armed soldiers; and under certain circumstances, joint work by aid workers and military forces in refugee camps and health clinics, often for urgent provision of food, water and sanitation. In brief, CA, in simplistic terms, implies integrated missions of civilian and military workers during and after emergency situations; and often under the auspices of the UN agencies.

But in the modern days of active conflict and post-conflict fragile situations, peace operations have taken heightened forms of complexity, which makes the familiar and traditional image of civil-military team coordination/cooperation too simplistic to address the security and peace building needs. In contemporary situations, many of the emergencies arise out of violent conflict; and the principles and methods of how

Security Operations in the 21st Century: Canadian Perspectives on the Comprehensive Approach, ed. M. Rostek and P. Gizewski. Montreal and Kingston: Queen's Policy Studies Series, McGill-Queen's University Press.

civilian and military agencies work in conflict or post-conflict fragile areas are not only different but are often contradictory generating tensions, despite the common interest of the agencies in helping the affected population. Additionally, the dynamics of the Comprehensive Approach have radically changed due to the infusion of a larger number of actors, governmental, and non-governmental, increasing the complexity of the integrated missions.

This article focus on the challenges that active conflict and post-conflict fragile states encounter. It evaluates the need for: multi-dimensional comprehensive assistance; challenges and opportunities posed by comprehensive approaches in fragile situations; and finally, the potential of one of the major actors in the Comprehensive Approach – Non-Governmental Organizations (NGOs) – to address the needs of security and development for the purpose of peace building.

Challenges Faced by Fragile States in Active Conflict and Post-Conflict Contexts

Fragile states are the focus of both government and non-governmental development cooperation. More than one-third of Official Development Assistance (ODA) is spent annually on fragile and conflict-affected countries, to help them "transit" out of conflicts to paths of sustainable development, promote national ownership of such development and help them deliver essential services to the citizens i.e., the basic services of human security, life sustenance and welfare. But aid does not always flow promptly and effectively to help the process of transition. What are the causes of the lack of progress despite the high level of commitment and what lessons can be learned from the work that has been carried out in fragile states so far?

The lack of development progress in fragile states is attributable to more than simply economic and financial crisis. Experience in the past few years has shown that beyond alleviating suffering in the short term, little substantial progress has been made to date in most of these countries. In the absence of well functioning political and social institutions, extremely complex challenges continue to occur.

Fragile states are designated as Low Income Countries under Stress (LICUS) by the World Bank. The LICUS are performing inadequately in achieving real economic growth, reduction of poverty and the promotion human development. Often they experience violent conflicts, including terrorist threats. Inadequate real economic growth results in failure to significantly invest in the provision of basic public services expected by the citizens of all legitimate states.

The inability of fragile states to perform basic public service functions arises from factors such as the weakness or low capacity of state institutions, absence of political will, and/or commitment of state authorities to deliver. On occasion, a combination of these factors contribute to inadequate delivery of services. Regardless of the reasons for the failure of states to deliver services, the residual effect is an erosion of societal support and confidence. This in turn, undermines government legitimacy and authority among the citizenry. The impact of such discontent gives rise to social, political and economic tensions, precipitating violent conflict, loss of state control, and, ultimately, state failure.

Multi-Dimensional Problems Necessitating Comprehensive Approaches

When conflicts are violent, not only is societal security endangered, but there is potential to affect global security, making the international community's interventions vital. Given the multi-dimensional problems inherent to fragile states – continued poverty and human security issues emanating from rule of law and government deficiencies – the international community's response must be multi-dimensional and comprehensive. The most utilitarian Comprehensive Approach should use reconstruction and development as the primary means of expanding the central government's authority across the country thus providing a security dividend for the population.

In the contemporary context, security building is part and parcel of an all encompassing approach to peace making, peace building, peace keeping, and combat or counter insurgency operations. The security-development nexus is at the base of such an all embracing approach and translates into a Comprehensive Approach. Such an approach is comprised of a range of elements including defense, development, and diplomacy and a wider network of actors assisting in delivering such elements.

The question remains, how successful have integrated or comprehensive approaches been at meeting the security, development and peace challenges confronting fragile states?

Assessment of the Comprehensive Approach in Security Building and Stabilization

It should be noted that the concept of the Comprehensive Approach is relatively new. Civil-military coordination was traditionally used for emergency responses. Then the term "3-D Approach," comprising Defense, Development and Diplomacy actions, became popular. In the course of time, this concept further developed to include other actors evolving into the "Whole of Government Approach." This approach de-emphasized the notion of purely military solutions to conflict. The latest step in the naming of the concept is the Comprehensive Approach. These terms have been used in various forms in addressing the problems of conflict and post-conflict in fragile states, such as Afghanistan.

Allegiance of local populations is critical to establishing legitimacy for central governments. Key to achieving such credibility is the winning of hearts and minds through the delivery of social and human security services, justice, and the rule of law to the citizenry. Often lacking, such capacities must be built into government institutions at all levels: central, provincial, district and village if state building is to be realized.

The important issue to note is that winning the hearts and minds of the people *is essential* for security and stability, moreover the "win" must not only be for the troop contributing countries, their militaries or for international NGOs, but most importantly for local governments and the citizens they represent. In brief, what we need to ensure is that development aid leads to higher levels of legitimacy of the local government. We must also consider whether development aid is resulting in more positive attitudes towards the international actors and whether development aid is leading to increased security. The effectiveness of the Comprehensive Approach and the role of NGOs or civilians must be assessed in this context.

Key Actors

Actors implicated in the Comprehensive approach are as follows: the government at all levels in the country of operation; the population of the host country; international government partners and their outlets of delivery of defence, development and diplomacy (departments of Foreign Affairs, National Defence and ODA agencies); and, the international and national non-governmental organizations are the major actors in any Comprehensive Approach scheme.

Deficiencies of the Comprehensive Approach: Past and Current

At each evolutionary step noted above, strategic planning deficiencies resulted in a lessened application of a broad spectrum approach. Major deficiencies identified were: lack of coordination at various levels; absence of coordination between ministries and agencies of the fragile state itself; absence of adequate coordination of the international community with the host government; lack of coordination between various international government partners; weak coordination and cooperation between each western country's departments of foreign affairs, national defense and ODA agency; and inadequate buy-in of the NGOs. Reticence by the NGO community to extend cooperation emanates from concerns for autonomy and independence, principles relating to the maxim "do no harm to the recipient states." These coordination and cooperation deficiencies have made contemporary security operations less comprehensive than desirable. The Comprehensive Approach thus far suffers from malnutrition.

Research in fragile states suggests that civil-military collaboration and civilian and reconstruction oriented activities may aid in facilitating tactical level entry for the military assisting the acquisition of local knowledge and connections. However, these studies also highlight the strategic limitations of using foreign aid as a political and military tool for countering terrorism or insurgencies and promoting stability and security.

Small-scale and scattered Quick Impact Projects (QIPs), promoted under the Comprehensive Approach mechanism did little to win hearts and minds in the longer term or permanently change perceptions of the military or the troop contributing nations in the communities where the projects are implemented.

Studies show that Comprehensive Approach does not necessarily result in improved perception of security in the people or in reality improves security. Indeed there is little evidence that projects, embracing comprehensive concepts, have contributed to improved security by addressing the perceived underlying causes of terrorism and violent extremism. There is no evidence that civil-military reconstruction and aid activities win the hearts and minds of the people or increase the state legitimacy required to counter violence. As said earlier, in order to achieve the allegiance of the people, the government must be "seen" to deliver services – not contributing militaries or even NGOs.

Moreover, evidence indicates that civilian teams do not necessarily have the requisite skills and knowledge to work with local communities. They are not often adequately prepared before deployment nor provided with consistent support while in the field. Short term rotations result in relationships and projects lacking in continuity.

To be successful, the Comprehensive Approach must first meet Afghan priorities. In this context, the central objective of forging greater cooperation between military and civil (including NGOs) actors is shoring-up the fragile country's recovery and development process in order to win wider political support for the government. Unfortunately, the civil-military integration, originally conceived as a key component of security and peace keeping strategy has been increasingly geared towards countering insurgency rather than towards longer term development agendas.

CA Impact on Humanitarian Assistance and Aid

Given the issues discussed above about the requirements for stabilization and development of fragile states and their governments' legitimacy and state building, the effectiveness of NGOs role should assess the degree to which development aid leads to: higher levels of legitimacy of the government; more positive attitudes towards the international actors; and, increased security.

Traditionally, NGOs provide humanitarian assistance in war zones to support the civilian population. But NGOs argue that in order to gain appropriate access to war zones and create the humanitarian space necessary to deliver assistance safely, the principles of neutrality, impartiality[19] and independence are essential. NGOs argue that these principles are compromised as humanitarian intervention is increasingly politicized and militarized. This acts to the detriment of the delivery of both humanitarian assistance and long-term development aid.

The Comprehensive Approach, in effect, changes the nature of both humanitarian assistance and aid. Both "humanitarian assistance" for immediate relief of vulnerable population in war zones and "aid for longer term development" are abused when appropriated for winning wars or serving political interests of troops contributing countries.

The assumption that aid is an important soft power stabilization tool leads to billions of dollars of aid investment in conflict or post-conflict regions. Large portions of aid are channelled to unstable regions, where troops of aid-giving countries are located. Increased integration of humanitarian assistance into military and political strategies has had negative impact on secure delivery of services by the NGOs to the vulnerable population in the insecure zones.

Concurrently, the Comprehensive Approach in fragile states has changed the nature of longer term aid. Aid for development is no longer based on priorities of development need and principles of effective delivery (aid effectiveness principles). Rather, it is used as a strategy to appease communities and win the hearts and minds of the civilian population for foreign troops' protection.

CA Partnerships and the Resulting Impact on the Nature and Objectives of Aid

For the combination of political, military and development measures to foster security, peace and good governance under a Comprehensive Approach, a partnership of equals must imbue a true spirit of cooperation. The reality is that defense often outmatches diplomacy, and definitely development. NGOs argue that military components dominate the Comprehensive Approach and tend to increasingly utilize aid as a means to gain security benefits and troop protection. Thus aid is less focused on the needs of the population and the development priorities of the fragile state clients. Under the Comprehensive Approach, relief and reconstruction work is used to legitimize military presence. Diversion of major portions of aid and reconstruction funds to the provinces is a clear reflection of the intent to utilize aid resources for troop protection and/or promote security rather than address development objectives.

This approach of channelling funds to unstable and insecure provinces for troop protection and greater visibility of troop-contributing countries, (as John Manley wanted for Canada in Afghanistan) is problematic. Development funding in these regions often fails to positively impact people's lives in a timely fashion. NGOs perceive military personnel as insufficiently trained for conducting development tasks. Delayed and often unsuccessful aid efforts generate negative civilian perceptions of aid and development efforts. Hence, the objective of winning hearts and minds, even for troop protection, fails.

As noted above, under the Comprehensive Approach as employed thus far, the military has engaged in relief and reconstruction work to legitimize their presence. Given that aid is utilized for promotion of security as opposed to development, a large portion of ODA funds are channelled through military or civil military units, such as the Provincial Reconstruction Teams or PRTs rather than through more traditional humanitarian and development agencies. Delivery of aid projects by the military leads people to believe that the assistance is part of a military strategy in the war on terror. Such attitudes contribute to blurring of lines between military and civilian actors which increase the risk for aid workers. The perception of aid workers' association with political and military processes can become deeply ingrained in the minds of local belligerents, which increase risks for aid workers. The security situation poses a threat to NGOs in some fragile states, and the lack of security is now so prevalent that many NGOs are no longer able to deliver services.

The cost of operations are unusually high in some fragile states. Security management for NGOs is time consuming and equipment costs are high. With little spare funding available for security, risks to NGOs and non-profit organizations increase. So too do the risks that projects will fail. In such circumstances, project supervision is inadequate, particularly in remote and insecure areas; progress of activities is poor, performance and effectiveness measurement is inadequate and chances of corruption are higher. Consequently, NGOs question whether the high costs associated with security overshadow the benefits which development projects actually yield.

These factors drive NGOs to guard against humanitarian aid and development being subordinated to political and military interests. Use of aid to meet political and military interests of the troop-contributing countries in Afghanistan has resulted in increased insecurity for humanitarian workers. Consequently, a number of NGOs have moved away from the aid field, thus reducing humanitarian assistance. The result has been a reduction in development needs and priority based assistance, eroding trust in foreign aid among locals and foreign workers. As such, the concept of a Comprehensive Approach, has been badly discredited.

NGO Cooperation With Host Country Partners

NGO interest in avoiding the blurred lines between political/military aid and pure humanitarian and development assistance, are often criticized by those who consider them to be anti-government. Indeed they argue that such NGOs are prone to focus on parallel mechanisms of development programming which have the potential to undermine host government development efforts.

NGOs' humanitarian values and codes do not prevent them from working with host governments or ODA agencies of donor governments in the interest of peace building. The conditions to be met are that NGOs' values and goals are respected; the principle of aid allocation according to people's need is upheld; humanitarian motivations for assistance are guaranteed and aid effectiveness principles for producing quality results are ensured. In Afghanistan 80 percent of NGO activities are tied to government programs. NGO dominance risks disenfranchising many local organizations, which may shut down key government services. Yet, in the absence of the government's ability to deliver essential services, NGOs are compelled to provide necessary assistance on behalf of the government.

NGOs in the Context of Fragile States: Challenges and the Way Ahead

Despite NGO interests in working with host governments and citizens of fragile states, NGOs face considerable challenges that have yet to be resolved. This is true, in particular, with regard to the sustainability of development works. Because of protracted conflicts, fragile states often have no infrastructure and weak social capital. Social partners in the form of local NGOs are either non-existent or lack the necessary know-how to carry out complex projects. Transferring responsibility for projects to the local population is often problematic. To ensure that projects are adequately rooted in the society, innovative ideas and new approaches have to be developed.

As per the analyses provided above, NGO collaboration with PRT's in unstable provinces is problematic. Priority must be given to engaging the NGO community in such a manner so as to benefit from their expertise and skills in reconstruction and stabilizing endeavours.

Accordingly, the Comprehensive Approach must meet priorities of local populations. If security is the number one priority of a conflict affected country and the Comprehensive Approach is clearly able to address the main causes of conflict, then the people of Afghanistan will be supportive of deployment of development funds to promote security objectives. Citizens' support will encourage and lead NGOs to support and cooperate with the security promoting programs. Under such situations, NGOs can stimulate civil society's engagement in the development process and mitigate the influence of the insurgents. Cooperation of NGOs should be sought for development work on condition of not violating their humanitarian values, (impartiality, neutrality and independence).

NGOs experienced in the provision of emergency and/or humanitarian assistance relief can serve as the best instruments in post-conflict periods.

NGO expertise with grass roots development work is invaluable. Reduction of armed violence in the communities is an aspect of promoting community development. Armed violence most often manifests itself at regional, local and community levels. NGO involvement in community conflict resolution and community-based armed violence reduction would be of value. Coordinated work by NGOs in different ethnic communities could help form common platforms for addressing the root causes of ethnic tensions. Concerned civilian groups within local communities are known to partner in armed violence reduction programming and monitoring. NGOs have the capacity to promote advocacy and leadership roles in reducing such violence. NGO support in mobilizing host government work could also be instrumental. Thus, NGOs working under contract with the government should be encouraged. There is evidence that NGOs contracted by the government to deliver services achieve better and faster results than those funded directly by international ODA agencies.

With development agencies increasingly taxed in many fragile states, NGOs can play key roles in filling gaps either by acting separately or at times cooperating with the host government and international community. If a fragile state is commitmented to implementing reforms and engaging in dialogue with all actors, the reform agenda could be reinforced with the help of NGOs. Where effective governance is limited, NGOs could support the work of external donor agencies in state stabilization by generating capacity in local civil society so as to change society from within. In the case of fragile states, with very low capacity for implementing delivery of development services, program/project implementation by NGOs could prove essential. Under such circumstances, the government can reach the population via NGOs to satisfy the basic human needs of the people. Cooperation of the NGOs in provision of such services is a much required feature in a conflict or post-conflict area.

NGOs have specific skills and advantages which give them comparative advantage in making contributions in conflict areas where donor agencies or the state have little impact. Their political objectivity, better access to marginalized groups and proximity to the local population, experience in delivering basic services, and in protecting against human rights violations, give them unique advantages in mobilizing self help capacities. The potential exists for NGOs to partner as parallel organizations in the delivery of essential services to civilian populations.

Such functions would support the population while not jeopardizing NGOs' objectivity. The combination of fulfilling the parallel needs, which external donors are largely unable to address due to lack of experience, and at the same time long term perspectives, is essential in addressing the challenges confronting fragile states.

Conclusion

Rather than cooperation, a "synchronized" effort is more practical for attaining a unified effort under a Comprehensive Approach. Unlike cooperation, which implies a process of active engagement at the operational level, synchronized approaches enable partners to autonomously act within their own mandates to address common challenges.

Bearing in mind the specific skills and experiences that NGOs bring, and the risks involved in working in insecure environments, a three-pronged strategy is conceivable. By developing local skills, promoting advocacy potentials for peace building and adopting conflict preventive methods, a Comprehensive Approach can be employed by NGOs for improving the living conditions of the population. In the course of this approach, alternative local systems of order will be treated not as a security problem *per se,* but as part of a solution with NGO programs working in tandem with the international community's longer term programs.

Chapter 5

COMPREHENSIVE APPROACH: A VIEW FROM SOUTH OF THE BORDER

Beth Ellen Cole[20]

Following a multi-year effort to produce "doctrine" for the civilian side of the US government for stabilization and reconstruction missions, important lessons have emerged for those who endeavor to execute a joined-up, integrated comprehensive approach. The US Institute of Peace, an independent agency created by the US Congress to help build capacity for peace, with support from the US Army Peacekeeping and Stability Operations Institute, documented the experience of the multiplicity of actors involved in a comprehensive approach in a comprehensive manner for the first time.

This experience is presented in the form of a manual anchored by a framework of common end-states, necessary conditions, and approaches that arise from the conduct of dozens of missions. According to *Guiding Principles for Stabilization and Reconstruction* (US Institute of Peace and US Peacekeeping and Stability Operations Institute, 2009), a comprehensive approach is one that brings together specialized organizations to stabilize extremely dangerous environments while laying the foundations for a sustainable peace.

Doctrine is a term used frequently in this chapter, one not often discussed in the context of a comprehensive approach. For military forces, the meaning is familiar. For civilian institutions, a bit more description is required.

Security Operations in the 21st Century: Canadian Perspectives on the Comprehensive Approach, ed. M. Rostek and P. Gizewski. Montreal and Kingston: Queen's Policy Studies Series, McGill-Queen's University Press.

What Is Doctrine?

Doctrine provides a guide to action, not a set of rules. It strives to enshrine shared principles, to minimize ad-hocery and to facilitate synchronization. It is enduring until changed as the environment changes. This conceptual basis for action: has the following purposes: (i) it provides a common lexicon and definitions based on the experience of others; (ii) it analyzes experience and translates it into principles; (iii) it explains relationships; (iv) it links to other documents; and (v) it offers a guide for allocating resources. It always needs to be attuned to cultural considerations and the local context.

For the purposes of this chapter, a comprehensive approach is discussed with a few other specific boundaries in mind:

1.   The *type of mission* in which a comprehensive approach applies is one in which a country or region is moving from violent large-scale conflict to peace. It includes the presence of both peacekeeping and/ or peace enforcement troops and an array of civilian peace-building institutions with some form of international leadership and a mandate, preferably one from the United Nations.

2.   The *temporal dimension* of these missions, important to the understanding of when organizations lash up to implement a comprehensive approach, is not addressed here purposefully. Many institutions align their objectives according to particular phases or time spans of a mission, but any agreement on the precise time allocation for each eludes us. Moreover, most practiced hands know that these missions feature the absence of linearity, making phasing somewhat useful for planning and organization, but always subject to the peculiar challenges of specific environments. Therefore, the principles included here for the comprehensive approach cover the span of time from the moment the international community first recognizes the need for an intervention through to the time when the host nation can provide security and basic services to the host nation population. According to experience, a decade will pass before this achievement is in hand.

3.   The *focus* of the doctrine prepared by the US Institute of Peace (USIP) does not attempt to address the development challenges that take generations to overcome. Development agencies persist in their work long after peacekeeping and peace-building "forces" depart. The focus here is on that unique, perilous stage where everything must be viewed through the lens of conflict. Wherever necessary, we have tried to nest short-term, must-have objectives within longer-term development goals.

The Basic Organizational Requirements for a Comprehensive Approach

The US military gathers the experience of its members from operations, turns it into doctrine to guide its actions, and uses a "lessons learned" system to refresh that doctrine over time. A robust planning apparatus turns doctrine into concrete objectives, an education and training system prepares each soldier, and a web of support sees each member of the service through from deployment to return to home soil. This well-honed, time-tested, continually updated, and complex system is what gives the US President the confidence to look repeatedly to his military commanders to stabilize the most challenging environments known to humankind. The military devotes large resources to these requirements. The civilian side does not.

The absence of such a system on the civilian side hinders cooperation between civilian and military agencies. Without a system to knit together the civilian and military capabilities of the US and that of allies, such as Canada, the ability to execute any kind of comprehensive approach is impeded. Individual states have little chance of effectively linking to the non-governmental and regional and international institutions whose knowledge and skills form a critical part of any comprehensive approach when they are in internal disarray. Finally, and most importantly, the hinging of these actors to the political, economic, and social leaders in the host nation is a decidedly unformed, ad hoc process. It is truly a system-of-systems that needs to be built.

To realize the comprehensive approach, all the components of this system – for each state and each institution involved – would ideally be in place and allow each actor to lash up, as required and appropriate, with the other. Imagine if each institution created a lessons-learned process that enabled the sharing of information across the peace-building community. Dare to think that each mission actor might identify, train, and unleash planners who might, in turn, work on critical planning issues across organizations. A system-of-systems that can be joined up to create more powerful effects than any one individual entity is the desired result. This is what is needed to achieve any degree of coherence or coordination.

Unifying Strategic "Doctrine"

Yet, in this author's view, the system starts with strategic doctrine that describes what we are trying to achieve. Strategic doctrine that embodies the lessons from past experience and elevates best practices, that is revised periodically to reflect guidance emerging from current missions, and that is vetted across the peace-building community (including the host nations) is the foundation for a comprehensive approach. Official government agencies may tend to lament the seeming chaos of the non-governmental community that delivers life-saving humanitarian assistance, but they should read Sphere (Sphere Project, 2004) first. A first-class "doctrinal" manual that enshrines core principles in a humanitarian charter and minimum standards for each sector of assistance, Sphere provides an example for those who dream of a comprehensive approach. What are the minimum standards for the stabilization community? Why, after more than sixty missions spanning five decades, is there no comprehensive document that helps provide the common guidance and lexicon for a community which sends high ranking officials to endless international conferences to ponder the unsolved challenges of coordination?

Doctrine is not a panacea for the hard work of those who must execute the mosaic of inter-related tasks to achieve greater strategic outcomes. Sphere does not by itself lead to miracles of coordination in the humanitarian sector faced by mammoth challenges such as that in post-earthquake Haiti. Securing peace in Afghanistan may offer the equivalent of this tragedy for the peacebuilders. These complex operations pose the most daunting problem sets for the realization of a comprehensive approach. But there is simply no excuse for allowing newly minted members of the US Civilian Response Corps or those on Canadian rosters to go off into harm's way without some basic understanding of the experience of the past. The need is for a digest of experience that can be referred to again and again – and not from some lecturer's power point presentation or anecdotes from past mission lore.

Insightful, robustly rich lessons are recorded in the disparate file cabinets and computer servers of dozens and dozens of institutions. There are post-conflict guides on economic development, democracy and governance emerging from the US Agency for International Development (USAID). A trove of papers exist on document accountability and transparency approaches from the World Bank for effective economic governance. The ground-breaking reports on security sector reform from the Organization for Economic and Security Cooperation in Europe's Development Assistance Committee (OECD DAC) offer serious guidance. The frameworks that help tie states of the African Union together in the quest for peace and stability provide one way to organize strategy. These examples are a mere glimpse into the diamond mine of literature the "comprehensive community" has amassed (US Institute of Peace and US Peacekeeping and Stability Operations Institute, 2009, 196).

What emerges is a truly counter-intuitive realization. Far from the disunity among this community that is widely-reported, a review of institutional guidance (US Institute of Peace and US Peacekeeping and Stability Operations Institute, 2009, 223) suggests that a common strategic vision exists. Though a multiplicity of different terms to describe different goals masks this unity, the convergence about basic goals is striking.

The *Guiding Principles* manual offers a strategic framework for the first time to record and describe this common understanding. In every war-torn country, including Afghanistan, we have strived for 5 core end states: a safe and secure environment, the rule of law, stable governance, a sustainable economy and social well-being.

FIGURE 1: STRATEGIC FRAMEWORK FOR STABILIZATION AND RECONSTRUCTION

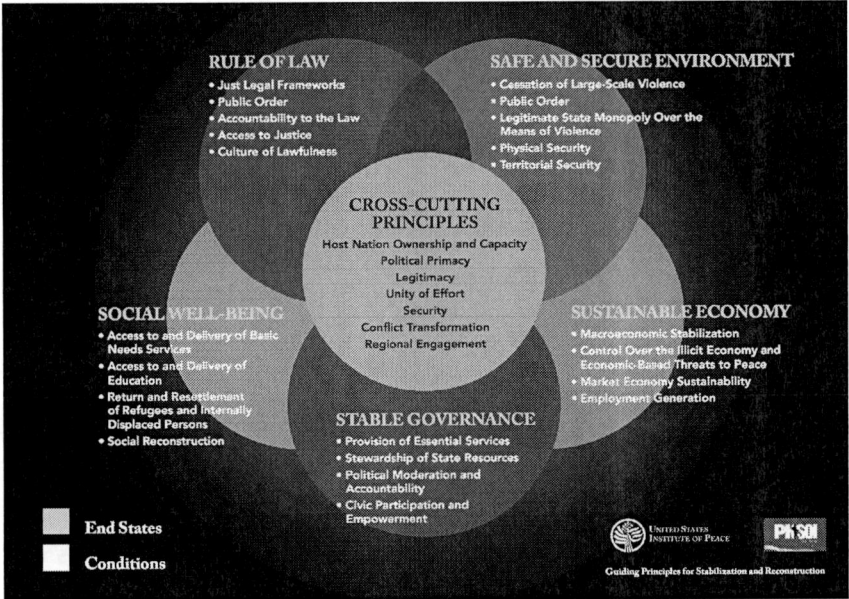

The humanitarian assistance community operates with a cluster approach. There are clusters for shelter, water, health and more. It allows the organizations, for example, that specialize in providing water, rehabilitating water systems, and working with host nation officials with responsibility for water supply management to lash up immediately with others in that cluster. This accelerates coordination and the delivery of assistance.

In every major state actor, within U.N. agencies, at the European Union, and other bodies, experts and capabilities dedicated to the rule of law exist. Where do they go to coordinate and lash up when a conflict is brewing that will result in a mission? We know that restoration of the rule of law, from experience, will be among the first priorities – like water. If we organize along this framework, rule of law contributors would be identified *before* a crisis. Rule of law contributors might even share best practices, conduct assessments and train together and deploy in some integrated manner.

But this is also not sufficient by itself. What is a safe and secure environment? What is rule of law? Where are the common definitions and terms? The review of major institutional guidance, conducted by the USIP team, permits a general description of each end-state. It also allows a generous response to the question of: what characterizes rule of law or stable governance in a stabilization environment? What conditions must be established to have stable governance or a sustainable economy or basic social well-being? What approaches have been utilized effectively? The manual attempts to answer these questions.

A set of 22 necessary conditions have been identified that should be met to achieve these end states. These *shared* "minimum standards" were developed based on a comprehensive review of the 500 core doctrinal documents for these operations.

One reason why the community has failed to embrace common "doctrine" is a belief that this would prevent a rational prioritization based on the unique characteristics of each conflict. A framework grounded in experience that offers a broad view of the inherent complexity of missions requiring a comprehensive approach allows the planner and the decision maker to prioritize from among some recurring and known ingredients for success. The application of the principles and the conditions in the *Guiding Principles* manual for Afghanistan demonstrates the utility of this strategic approach:[21]

The first is the primacy of politics and the need to *reach political settlements*, not only at the national level where crisis resides, but at regional and local levels as well. We must separate reconcilable insurgents and spoilers from those who refuse to forsake violence. The Afghan National Peace Jirga, held in Kabul in early June, is a manifestation of this need to forge a political settlement to help resolve the conflict.

Second, we cannot achieve success anywhere in Afghanistan without first establishing a safe and secure environment. *Physical security* for the population and key government, cultural, religious, and economic centers will require that international forces work closely with the local security forces to provide protection. The increase in the number of international forces in 2010 acknowledges this fundamental condition for peace.

Third, we must redouble efforts to achieve *a legitimate monopoly over the means of violence* – by Afghans for Afghans. The objective is not only to train and equip police and soldiers, but develop the professional and accountable leadership and management needed to oversee those forces. After years of missteps and inadequate resourcing of this part of the mission, the international community and the government of Afghanistan put their money and focus here. Success in meeting this condition will permit the responsible exit of foreign forces.

Fourth, we must prioritize *territorial security* by mitigating the threats over the Afghanistan-Pakistan border. Dealing with the border will require a higher level of engagement between the Afghan and Pakistani governments and their populations on each side of the border. A heightened diplomatic offensive on the part of many actors is ensuing to tackle this problem – between governments. USIP, for example, has also launched community level cross-border dialogues to promote bottom-up solutions to the insecurity of the border region.

Fifth, we need to continue to prioritize the identification and disruption of finance networks of the insurgents, organized crime and terrorist organizations fueling the fires in Afghanistan. This means shutting down foreign financing and disrupting the reliance on the narcotics trade. It means getting serious about the prosecution of corrupt officials and criminal elements who feed the conflict.

Sixth, improving *access to justice* for the population will require bolstering or rebuilding the informal mechanisms for dispute resolution that the insurgents are now replacing. Low-level disputes will ignite broader fighting if not tended to and resolved. Taliban justice substituting for Afghan justice is not acceptable. Supporting the development of the traditional justice system that provides the critical continuum from police to prosecutor to judge to corrections is as critical as building the Afghan army.

Seventh, we must help build the capacity of the government to deliver essential services to the population and to be seen as the primary deliverers. This is necessary to move the population away from the insurgents, who de-legitimize the government by providing these services themselves.

Eighth, stewardship of state resources means that essential services must be provided within a construct of accountable governance. Prioritizing support for sub-national institutions of governance – formal and informal – will be key to ensuring an entry point for services and to boosting the confidence of the population in governance. Ensuring that safeguards are in place for expenditure of public funds – including the participation of an active civil society – is key to meeting this condition.

The Civilian Imperative

In a stabilization and reconstruction environment, we need more than the military contribution. We must let soldiers be soldiers and help secure the population. We need the unique skills and knowledge that civilians bring to help the host nation government and its population build rule of law, stable governance, a sustainable economy and the fundamental conditions for social well-being which are also essential to securing stability. We should be oriented toward realistic definitions of these end states rather than exit or withdrawal dates in Afghanistan if we are to create, at a minimum, a stable bulwark against forces of extremism that seek our destruction. This is mainly a civilian, not a military responsibility.

Plugging the Civilian Gap

For the past six years or more, the United States Institute of Peace has been helping to build a foundation for civilian doctrine, planning, lessons learned, training, education and exercises for the multiplicity of civilian agencies trying to achieve success on the ground. The civilian contribution has become less ad hoc and more organized. If current predictions hold, the Quadrennial Diplomacy and Development Review, a first for the US Department of State and the US Agency for International Development, might just elevate and buttress organizational capabilities to deal with conflict on the civilian side. But there are miles to travel on this path before we can realistically match the effectiveness of the military instrument and begin to truly execute a comprehensive approach.

This same path is being traveled by many governments among their agencies and in many large regional and international institutions as well. Over a dozen state units or offices attempt to bring inter-ministerial capabilities together to work on the comprehensive approach. Some like Canada's Stability and Reconstruction Team (START), the US State Department's Office of the Coordinator for Reconstruction and Stabilization (SCRS); and the British Stabilization Unit are approaching five year anniversaries, and progress has been uneven in the delivery of capacity.

The UN's peacekeeping manual (United Nations, 2008) – developed with all of its partner agencies in the U.N. system – is their attempt at "doctrine," though important elements of the U.N. system were deliberately left out because the Department of Peacekeeping Operations did not have the writ to write for the other agencies. The Integrated Mission Planning Process (IMPP) is another attempt at forging a comprehensive approach among UN components. A best practices network has been formed and lessons are being shared. These efforts coupled with the state approaches above signal a new determination to work at integration.

Uniting civilian and military assets should start with overarching strategic doctrine that lays out what we are trying to achieve. This doctrine has to be based on experience. We have at least five decades of experience in places such as El Salvador, Cambodia, the Balkans, Rwanda, Haiti, East Timor, Sierra Leone and Liberia, to name a few. When we lay out what experience has shown, we can start to unite disparate actors behind a common framework. That is the first step to a comprehensive approach.

Chapter 6

WE SHARE THE SAME SPACE, NOT THE SAME PURPOSE: THE COMPREHENSIVE APPROACH AND MÉDECINS SANS FRONTIÈRES

MARILYN McHARG AND KEVIN COPPOCK

The comprehensive approach involves using aid as a tool for stabilization and counter-insurgency objectives. When it comes to non-governmental organizations' involvement in these objectives, the position of Médecins Sans Frontières (MSF) does not necessarily represent the position of other non-governmental organizations.

On the contrary, MSF's position is in the minority. Although other organizations are willing to coordinate within the comprehensive approach, MSF believes it is extremely important to differentiate its work from the comprehensive approach. It is crucial that MSF's view, unconventional for some, be well understood. Without that understanding, MSF does not have the capacity to distinguish itself, leaving it unable to provide care to people who otherwise go without.

MSF is a medical humanitarian organization focused on providing life-saving interventions for people facing humanitarian crisis. It provides medical aid to people who are most in need. It is very simple. It is very narrow. It's about treating patients.

MSF believes it has a duty to respond to others in the face of extreme human suffering. This tends to be where people are actively harming other people, often in war zones. In these settings, our purpose is to medically assist others in surviving war. MSF is not there to solve war or to build states.

Security Operations in the 21st Century: Canadian Perspectives on the Comprehensive Approach, ed. M. Rostek and P. Gizewski. Montreal and Kingston: Queen's Policy Studies Series, McGill-Queen's University Press.

To work toward solving war and building states is to take on military and political objectives that can run contrary to MSF objectives. The MSF charter pledges to provide medical care based on impartiality, neutrality and independence. These are the pillars of humanitarian assistance as described in the Geneva Conventions and the Protocol of 1977. They focus on treating those most in need, no matter who they are or where they come from.

Basing MSF's action on impartiality, neutrality, and independence insists that it does not take sides in a war.

When people are confronted with war, it is terrifying. Within the context of war, atrocities are committed; people are uprooted continuously by different factions, armies, and agendas. Often people don't know whom to trust. A space of "normalcy" is required for human survival, dignity, and humanity, regardless of allegiance.

Humanitarian assistance does not prioritize the politics of a situation, or take into consideration who is fighting whom. The priority, the focus, is on people caught in the crisis; it is on giving those people access to quality medical care. This is exactly what people in war zones need.

People need assurance that when a doctor vaccinates their children, delivers their babies, or heals their wounds, that doctor is not going to do anything other than treat them. Patients need to trust that their hospital beds are not traps where they might be arrested.

This assistance is a basic right under international humanitarian law.

MSF is currently delivering humanitarian assistance in almost 70 countries, with close to 28,000 staff. In 2008, as an example, its medical teams administered almost 9 million outpatient consultations and provided inpatient hospital care to 300,000 people.

They conducted more than 47,000 surgeries, delivered 100,000 babies, and treated 212,000 children for severe acute malnutrition.

More than half of this work has been in areas of armed conflict such as Somalia, Central African Republic, the Democratic Republic of the Congo, and Pakistan. In these crisis zones, our teams provide surgical care to war-wounded, treat malnourished children, run mass vaccination campaigns, and bring primary health care to remote rural communities where people would otherwise have no access to health care.

MSF practices impartiality and it does not discriminate. Because of this, MSF is better able to respond where medical and health needs are the greatest. Epidemiologic patterns do not follow front lines; disease transcends factional areas and does not respect borders. MSF must be true to its impartial and neutral approach (i.e., not discriminating based on ethnic, religious, political, national, or state interests). This provides the capacity to be ready and able to respond accordingly. This means *not* aligning with warring parties or being perceived as being aligned. Each party to the conflict must understand that MSF does not take sides.

Without attending to this, MSF puts itself at risk resulting in its inability to provide medical assistance, thereby saving fewer lives, and relieving fewer people of their suffering.

MSF's capacity to respond is achieved by different measures. First, it is essential for MSF to talk with all sides in a conflict. When MSF teams returned to Afghanistan in 2009, they negotiated with the International Security Assistance Force (ISAF), with the Afghan National Army (ANA), and with the Taliban. The reason for talking with each party was the same: this was about securing MSF's capacity to respond (i.e., negotiating access to those in need of assistance).

Such dialogue is not only crucial to accessing populations, it is essential in maintaining presence. MSF does not use deterrence. Nor does it rely upon the protection of compound walls, vehicles, etc. Instead, MSF strives to get verbal assurances of its acceptance. To garner that acceptance, MSF also runs quality, relevant programs that will be perceived positively by the communities where MSF works.

MSF believes that by carefully choosing project activities according to need, and by making its actions and interactions relevant, it is more likely to successfully negotiate access and secure its presence. It is not a guarantee, but it has allowed MSF to work in many different war zones over the last 40 years.

Interestingly, MSF has found it harder to achieve this acceptance in countries where Western militaries are present. MSF recognizes that this is simply based on the fact that we are from similar countries of origin. MSF claims of independence, no matter how true, are not perceived as such in these situations and are met with scepticism by forces opposed to Western militaries and by the Western military forces themselves.

This perceived lack of independence and impartiality is exacerbated when militaries and governments seek integrated approaches, and non-governmental organizations join in and focus their efforts in the regions aligned with these militaries, or participate in state-building initiatives. Rhetoric referring to non-governmental organizations as "force mulitpliers" and wars as "humanitarian interventions" add to the confusion and risk, legitimizing violence as a means of providing impartial humanitarian assistance. It is not just about what non-governmental organizations are called, but also about how non-governmental organizations define themselves through their words, actions, and funding practices. Impartial humanitarian action is about limiting the devastation, not legitimizing it.

Militarizing humanitarian action makes it a target, which in turn limits the access of those needing the aid most. In MSF's experience, it is negotiation that provides access to patients. The acceptance by all parties allows patients to more freely access MSF care. This is not to say that militaries or governments should not provide aid. On the contrary, in a number of settings they are responsible for doing so. What is needed is to differentiate the various types of aid and the objectives behind them to allow space for impartial humanitarian action.

MSF's motivation is not political, nor militarily focused. Yet while MSF is not targeting international or even national agendas, it is not naïve about the impact that it can have on political or military agendas, particularly in its external communications. Often, MSF is feeding into one agenda or another. It is not possible to avoid this impact in a war zone. These environments are hyper-politicized and any action will have an impact one way or another. It is important to recognize this, understand the potential impact, and be ready to respond accordingly. But such concerns cannot drive MSF's work, otherwise the patient will be de-prioritized and their life further threatened.

When MSF returned to Afghanistan in 2009, its teams found a very different environment from the one they left in 2004. During the war, parties to the conflict on all sides showed a shocking disrespect for healthcare workers and facilities. Hospitals, clinics and medical personnel were targeted by armed opposition groups like the Taliban. As well, according to our teams, the Afghan government and international forces repeatedly raided and occupied health structures. People no longer felt safe when they sought medical assistance. They no longer believed a hospital could provide impartial care. Because of this, MSF has had to re-establish trust from the ground up.

In the end, it is the ordinary people who are suffering. According to the UN, last year Afghanistan saw the highest number of civilian casualties in the war to date. Moreover a survey conducted for the International Committee of the Red Cross estimated more than half the population had little or no access to basic services. The reality is that the Afghan government and its allies – including the United Nations – are responsible to provide healthcare in areas they control, and this leaves hundreds of thousands of civilians with little or no access to any care at all.

It those people with high health needs and without access to health services that MSF must assist. Although MSF does not believe in a unity of purpose, it does believe in a mutual understanding with all warring parties. This allows for the delivery of impartial aid in order to contain the devastation of war on any side of the conflict. We do not share the same purpose, we share the same space, and with that we need to find ways of co-existing. In order to do this, gun free health premises are necessary; where there is no use of force against the facilities or arrests of patients while in our facilities.

Conclusion

Patients must have a right to freely access healthcare. It is MSF's duty to provide that health care. It is the duty of all militaries to ensure that lives of non-combatants are respected and that humanitarian agencies can provide impartial assistance to the victims of conflict. To this end, and in practicing a comprehensive approach, it is imperative that the humanitarian space be recognized and not co-opted. In the end, co-existence must be an accepted condition for MSF to function effectively within challenging and complex security environments.

PART III COMPREHENSIVE APPROACH TODAY – INTERNATIONAL OPERATIONS

Chapter 7

THE JOINT, INTERAGENCY, MULTI-NATIONAL AND PUBLIC (JIMP) ENVIRONMENT: MILITARY OPERATIONS IN A CROWDED BATTLE-SPACE

JIM SIMMS

Introduction

The Canadian Forces (CF) is in a dynamic period of operations most often characterized by our participation in the international community's engagement in Afghanistan. This participation serves to highlight a refocused policy of engaging the instruments of national power towards a common or shared goal. The delineation of how this policy is translated into a conceptual approach, what encompasses this approach and the doctrinal ramifications to this approach is not universal and would benefit from clearer and more concise language and, eventually, doctrine. Key to the employment of the CF in realizing government policy is the capacity to effectively meet the challenges posed by numerous and ever-more complex relationships. There are several terms used to describe these relationships or the interaction of military forces with other actors and stakeholders in any action in which the military may be engaged – be it domestic or international.

This paper posits that military operations take place in an environment that can be generally characterized as being (to different degrees each time) joint, interagency, multi-national and public (JIMP) (Gizewski and Rostek, 2007). An analysis of the JIMP environment will help "make sense

Security Operations in the 21st Century: Canadian Perspectives on the Comprehensive Approach, ed. M. Rostek and P. Gizewski. Montreal and Kingston: Queen's Policy Studies Series, McGill-Queen's University Press.

of the crowded battle space" by clearly showing the links between various classes of actors superimposed on the back drop of the master element of JIMP – the public. In the end, the military has little choice but to accept a crowding of the battle space so it behooves the CF to find solutions to optimize its actions within this crowded space. Specific examples will be introduced of how one organization – Regional Command Southern Afghanistan (RC (S)) – used structural or procedural approaches to adapt to the JIMP environment.

Policy and Approach

In Canada only the government can make public policy. Certainly departments are empowered to provide policy advice and recommendations. A conceptual approach is a very broad "strategy" that bridges policy and the dominant environmental considerations and provides some guidelines for how policy will need to be resourced and put into action. The environment includes those major considerations (analysis) that must be made with the resultant deductions that lead to concrete courses of action. Strategy is "the how" and can be viewed from a tactical, operational or strategic level.

In its conceptual development of the Army of Tomorrow the Canadian Army's Land Staff have developed a force employment concept summarized as adaptive dispersed operations. Dispersion can be in relation to time, space or purpose. For the rationale of this paper it is purpose dispersion that is most important. That is to say that "Land Force units and soldiers must be able to operate effectively – in either a supported or supporting role – in all whole of government campaign plan lines of operation" (Godefroy, 2007, 30). Here we can now see policy permeating the conceptual development of the way military forces must operate and this, in turn will lead to a further development and refinement of specific doctrine – encapsulated in the comprehensive approach. A comprehensive approach, then, is an approach that is mindful of the old and new players in the battle space. It is not an approach that attempts to define the role of the various actors but rather to understand the actors and improve mechanisms for coherence (or as a minimum de-confliction) of actions. As NATO notes in its *Future Comprehensive Civil-Military Interaction Concept (FCCMIC)*, there is a requirement "to move, when appropriate, from ad hoc actions by interested parties to more institutionalized and standardized relationships; thus the need to address insufficiency of formal mechanisms to promote, or even permit interaction between actors" (NATO, 2007, 2). It is these formal mechanisms that will be further explored later in the paper. As the Army notes, "outward-focused, integrated and multidisciplinary approaches must be the norm to address the complex problems and challenges posed by an increasingly multidimensional security environment" (Godefroy, 2007, 25).

There is a policy level that involves the whole of government towards complex security situations. There is also a broad concept for action entitled the comprehensive approach being explored and tried "on the ground." The question is: what is the environment in which the policy and the approach must be put into action?

The Security Environment

This approach of coordinated action (the comprehensive approach) needs to be agile and versatile enough to cater to a host of possibilities. For the CF this could be either domestic or expeditionary based. Arguably the "new" environment is characterized by an expanding list of actors, participants or stakeholders. How to cater to this crowded battle space is, therefore, one of the challenges of current and future operations. Thomas O'Connell, a former US Assistant Secretary of Defence for Special Operations and Low-Intensity Conflict, noted that we are "now dealing with many disparate and complex issues that require a large number of governmental agencies, different countries, numerous private companies and NGOs to achieve our goals." He further notes that "warfare is inherently inefficient because the environment is difficult to control and subject to the vagaries of human interactions" (O'Connell, 2007, 9). This environment has been presented as "multi-dimensional." Clearly the environment is characterized by new and pervasive human interactions – all of which result in the reaction/counteraction chain.

In fact the development work that led to the CF Strategic Operating Concept (SOC) noted that the "modern operating environment has increasingly become an interdependent, complex system of political, military, social, economic and physical elements, which is nowhere more evident than in failing states, and for the purpose of conducting operations can be considered the 'multidimensional battle space'" (Government of Canada Department of National Defence, 2004, 7). Noteworthy, is the fact that the first Canadian reference to the term JIMP appeared in this early draft of the Strategic Operating Concept (Government of Canada Department of National Defence, 2004). There has been a considerable amount of discussion as to what JIMP is and what it is not. One definition of JIMP refers to it as a framework of Joint, Interagency, Multinational, and Public actors who collaborate and cooperate at all levels of command to achieve shared objectives. Arguably, this suggests that there is a common consensus among the players on collaboration and cooperation. Furthermore it seems to suggest that all the players in any action can be, and want to be, identified. This is likely too simple an approach. Proposed definitions for the component parts or elements are suggested as follows:

- **Joint** – involving other national military elements and support organizations,

- **Interagency** – involving other government departments (OGDs) and agencies (OGAs) both domestic and foreign,
- **Multinational** – involving one or more allies or international coalition partners,
- **Public** – involving variety of elements including; domestic and international publics, non-governmental organizations (NGO), public volunteer organizations (PVO), private sector, media and commercial organizations (both domestic and foreign). (Gizewski and Rostek, 2007, 7)

For the purposes of this paper each of these JIMP components will be referred to as elements of operating environment. Not all CF operations are multi-national. In fact key operational activities such as the military response to the Oka crisis and routine fisheries patrols are purely national. However, there is some benefit in emphasizing the most difficult case scenario of a multiplicity of actors of all different sorts. Additionally, it is obvious that the public grouping is very broad – indeed, perhaps too broad. The blurring between public and private illustrates one such example of the complications. Suffice it to say that the large grouping underscores the importance of military forces to recognize the power of actors and stakeholders outside the militaries direct engagement and, often, coordination. When considered as a group the complete grouping of elements of JIMP might resemble a series of interactions as described below and previously suggested by CF Joint Concept Developers.

FIGURE 2: JIMP VISUALIZED

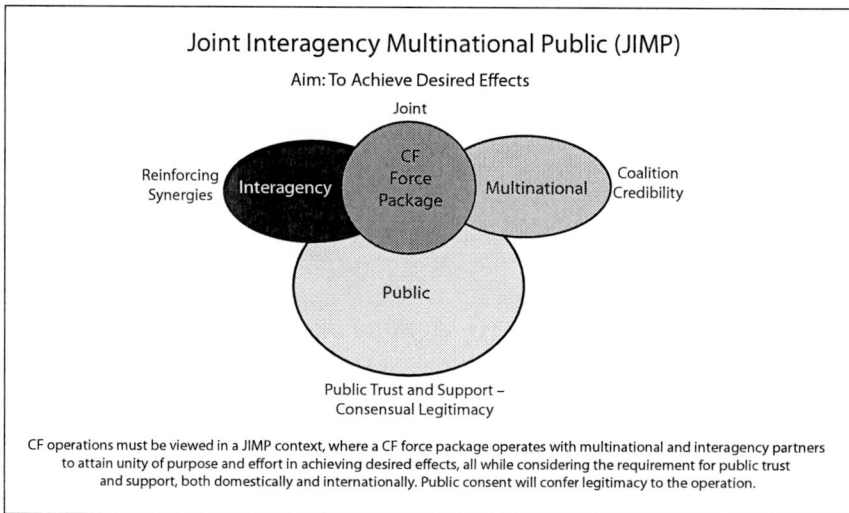

Joint Interagency Multinational Public (JIMP)

Aim: To Achieve Desired Effects

Joint

Reinforcing Synergies   Interagency   CF Force Package   Multinational   Coalition Credibility

Public

Public Trust and Support – Consensual Legitimacy

CF operations must be viewed in a JIMP context, where a CF force package operates with multinational and interagency partners to attain unity of purpose and effort in achieving desired effects, all while considering the requirement for public trust and support, both domestically and internationally. Public consent will confer legitimacy to the operation.

Source: Government of Canada Department of National Defence (2004, 16).

The Canadian Army currently defines JIMP as follows:

> A domestic and foreign collaborative framework involving military elements and support organizations, other government departments (OGDs) and agencies (OGAs), one or more allies or coalition partners, and a variety of public elements including non-governmental organizations (NGOs), public volunteer organizations (PVOs), the private sector, the media, commercial organizations and the citizenry, who cooperate at all levels of command to achieve shared objectives.[22]

This definition is problematic in the sense that reference to a "collaborative framework" suggests that there is wide spread agreement between these players on a framework objective and modalities. Some, however, do not support this statement.[23] In fact some would even suggest that based on the experiences in Iraq and Afghanistan that there should be a decoupling of such efforts as humanitarian from military objectives because competing goals obscure other objectives (Ward, 2008).

Given that JIMP is about the environment where military operations will be conducted and given that the comprehensive approach seeks to achieve a holistic, collaborative and cooperative approach beyond just the military campaign or action, then what will be the most challenging element of the JIMP construct and how might it be overcome? In order to answer this question the elements of JIMP must be explored. Certainly antecedents of the joint and multinational components exist in the continental staff system and this is well established doctrinally and has been operationalized. A precursor of interagency and, to a limited degree, the public component is civil-military cooperation (CIMIC). When the four elements are considered together, the public aspect becomes obvious as the antithesis to the culture of military structure and control. The military must accept that it will not have control but certainly influence over the public element of the JIMP environment and must develop strategies to overcome any limitation this may pose to achieving success in the comprehensive approach to operations.

What seems to be missing, however, is the "so what"? It seems to be of little value just to acknowledge that there is a requirement for greater interaction between military forces, other government departments, and inter-agency actors. It seems to be too obvious that the public element is important. We see this on a regular basis as citizens of Afghanistan and Iraq are killed as unfortunate outcomes of military action and we also see it as domestic public opinion puts pressure on political elites to act – one way or another. Some, such as Gizewski and Rostek (2007, 7), suggest that JIMP, or being JIMP compliant, is "one means of operationalizing a comprehensive CF approach to operations." By extension, this would also be operationalizing a whole-of-government approach. Frankly, a comprehensive approach is much more complicated than this and involves authorities, understanding, will, and resources. Where the concept of JIMP is key is in the understanding of the environment in which the key actors will interact or chose not to interact.

The JIMP Environment

JIMP is about the environment and is fundamental to a successful comprehensive approach regardless of whether thatd approach is widely accepted by the various stake holders. In essence it is about making sense of the crowded battle space. The more comprehensive the approach, the more complicated will be the environment and the need to understand it. Suffice it to say that, regardless of how comprehensive the approach, current military operations will – in some manner – be conducted in an environment that is joint, interagency, usually multinational and public. It should also be noted that the JIMP environment does not displace the importance of more traditional elements of the military environment such as enemy or terrain but is a tool to understand the other actors within the environment.

The JIMP environment is not new. Yet an enhanced understanding of its effect on the overall success of the comprehensive approach in realizing strategic intent, has gained importance. This environment should not be confused with the environment of geography (ground), air, space, etc. – in essence the "bubble." Rather it is a means by which to consider how the crowding of the battle space by the multitude of actors can be analyzed in a manner that will make some sense.

The JIMP environment is about people, organizations and relationships – building understanding, respect and trust. The environment is directly proportional to how comprehensive an approach is demanded or driven by policy. In the extreme, a comprehensive approach will demand that the CF, or any military force for that matter, cannot lead and must cultivate involvement by key non-military actors.

In a complex battle space the ability to understand, dissect and explore the environment is crucial. While no one solution will fit all situations it is desirable to develop a modality to fully consider all the factors that will provide a clear appreciation. One such way is to consider the key divisions. Not enough has been written about the JIMP[24] approach but, as explored above, JIMP is less an approach than a characterization of the environment. Each of these elements of the environment will have a different weight depending on a multitude of variables including the level considered (strategic, operational or tactical), the type of engagement on the spectrum of conflict and on the strength of the players involved.

Alluded to earlier, the environmental elements of joint and multinational are closely tied to the continental staff system. More than ever, countries are unlikely to "go it alone" even if they have the military wherewithal to do so. Canada's present and future involvement in operations is largely influenced by both NATO and by our interoperability programme with America, the United Kingdom, Australia and, to some degree, New Zealand. For the Canadian Army this interoperability is the subject of a well developed programme – commonly known as the American, British, Canadian, Australian, and New Zealand Armies' Program (ABCA). As noted earlier, Canada has been instrumental in shaping ABCA's forward vision – a vision that denotes the comprehensive approach driving the importance of the JIMP environment. As stated in its future concept:

> ...it should be borne in mind that military operations need to be part of a broader, coherent cross-government and internationalized response to tackle the causes of, and remove the threats to, ABCA partners. (ABCA, 2006, 2).

It is obvious that as NATO expands and as all international operations become even more coalition based, more attention needs to be afforded the joint and multi-national elements of JIMP. It will be the inter-agency synchronization piece and the public importance of the battle space that should garner much future analysis and exploration.

The Case of Afghanistan

Few would argue that, for Canada and its key Allies, Canadian action in Afghanistan is a veritable laboratory of the interactions of military forces and all the other actors and stakeholders in action in the current operating environment. In fact, against the backdrop of failed and failing states and the doctrine of the Responsibility to Protect, and given the expectation that counter-insurgency operations will be the norm for the near future, Afghanistan has become the analysis vehicle of choice. But is Afghanistan instructive for the purposes of examining the utility of doctrinal terms and concepts and in identifying modalities for operating in this defined JIMP environment?

The first task is to examine whether Afghanistan meets the definition of whole of government policy. The answer here would have to be yes. Introduced earlier, this issue was specifically addressed in the latest federal speech from the throne (Canada, House of Commons, 2007). Likewise, the mere formulation of the Manley Commission underlies the importance of the policy and the broad implications of that policy across government. This is reinforced by the recommendations of the report (Manley et al., 2008). Certainly the political ramifications of the report underlie the importance of the report and the government way ahead from a political and policy perspective (*National Post*, 2008).

The second task is to explore the approach to realizing the policy to establish whether it can be deemed a comprehensive approach or not. Here, it is instructive to review the report of the Chief of Review Services (2007) and the comments pertaining to this very subject. Additionally, upon examination of the initiatives of both the Department of Foreign Affairs and the Canadian International Development Agency we see that while there may be some terminology challenges there is indeed a comprehensive approach to realizing the whole of government intent. To determine how comprehensive this approach is, will require examination beyond the inter-agency Canadian piece. For this, an examination is made of the NATO Regional Command South Headquarters of the International Security Assistance Force (ISAF) mission. There are currently three key branches of this military organization (as well as a more traditional branch of Support functions): operations; stability and security reform; and re-construction and development. A fourth branch is being planned by the Chief of Staff designate in consultation with the Commander designate from the Netherlands. This will be a branch for governance and influence. The fact that operations are considered comprehensively across the spectrum of possible actions is one indication. Another would be the number of civilian advisors to the Commander and staff in this headquarters including: a stability advisor (STABAD); three political advisors (POLADs); a US Agency for International Development (USAID) advisor, a US State Department advisor; amongst others. From a Canadian national perspective, the appointment of a senior Department of Foreign Affairs and International Trade (DFAIT) representative in 2008 underscores the desire to bring a balanced approach to the demand for a comprehensive approach to all action in Afghanistan.

The third requirement is to determine whether the environment is largely characterized as JIMP. The answer is yes, from both a NATO/Coalition perspective and a Canadian National perspective. While land operations centric, the mission depends on aviation and air support – a large amount of that air support is provided by NATO naval forces. Add to this the Special Forces nature of much of the action and the special assets providing the Intelligence Surveillance and Reconnaissance (ISR) enabling function and this theatre of operation is without question joint. The interagency piece is obvious given the involvement of multiple government departments and agencies including Defence, DFAIT, CIDA, Correctional Services Canada and RCMP.[25]

The multinational environment is evident given the number of nations involved in the mission both from a military perspective and from a civilian perspective. Certainly in the Canadian area of interest there is a multinational aspect at every level including at the NATO Regional Headquarters South (RC (S)) where the command and control of the mission rotated between the UK, Canada and the Netherlands and then transitioned to the United States.[26] The Afghanistan mission public environment is undeniably the most complicated of the elements of the JIMP environment but, arguably, the most important. From a public perception point of view, the Afghanistan mission is critical – at home – to sustain national will, political intent and resources. From a host nation perspective, the public environment is even more critical. In fact, the centre of gravity for both the Taliban and for the NATO forces is the public support and certainly the public acceptance of the legitimacy and the capability of the Afghanistan government – federal, provincial and district – is a key criteria for mission success.

The number of actors involved in this particular battle space can be partly visualized as follows:

FIGURE 3: RC (S) REPRESENTATION OF STAKEHOLDERS IN 2008
PROVIDED BY CHIEF OF STAFF RC (S) 2 MAY 2008

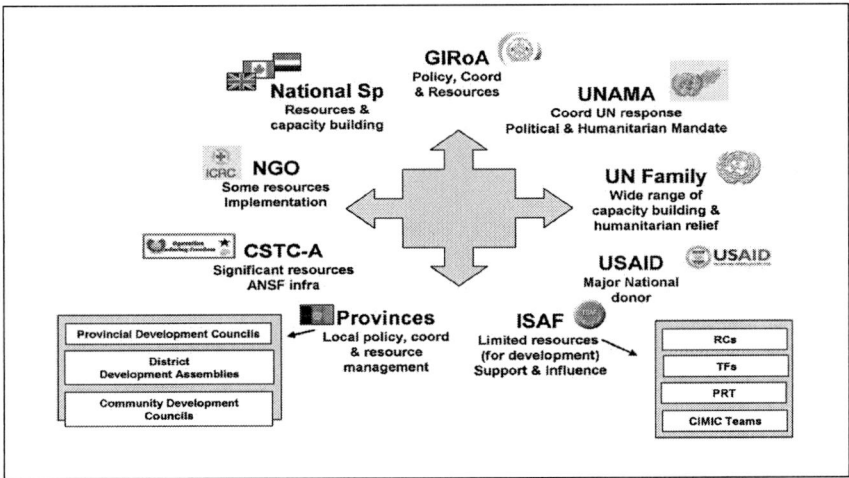

This representation illustrates that what happens in one set of inter-actions will have an effect on other interactions. For example, the NGO community is associated with broader international involvement with the local population. There are indigenous NGOs. When NGOs decide to pull out of a particular area because of the security risk, there is a cor-responding effect on the relationship between the local population and the NATO/ISAF military forces. What is not represented in this diagram is the indigenous public – the individual Afghan. At the end of the day it is about this element – certainly in the counter-insurgency battle space. Here everything must be considered for its impact on the public.

Certainly the operational framework of the mission for Regional Command South, as depicted on the following schematic, underscores the JIMP environment as it is obvious that multiple stakeholders are active at all steps even when there are tenuous security situations. The inter-related nature of the environment demands that a clear understanding of all JIMP elements and the effects that actions of one of the elements will have on the other is a key product of the estimate or analysis function.

FIGURE 4: RC (S) OPERATIONAL FRAMEWORK

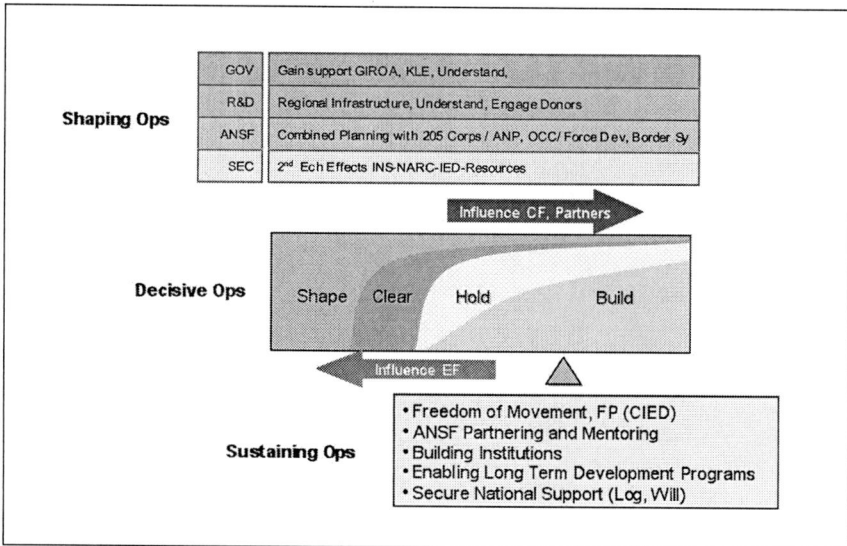

Furthermore, the Afghanistan model demonstrates a key point – while there is a direct correlation between the degree of comprehensiveness in the approach and the preponderance of JIMP actors, the fact remains that even in more kinetic focused approaches the environment will still be characterized as JIMP. Therefore the results of any action must be considered in line with the environment and the deductions that this analysis will bring. For example, it could be said that NATO forces in southern Afghanistan can use their considerable influence and resources to advance the government agenda (with action/focus at the provincial and district levels) in the right direction. This could be achieved through the influence of the task forces and, also, through the use of the Provincial Reconstruction Teams (military).

However, an analysis using the JIMP environment framework and considering the multiple and dynamic interactions of all the elements against the backdrop of the master element "public," might lead to the conclusion that ISAF driven re-construction and development outside the framework of effective Government sends the signal that the Afghan Government is not in control or is indifferent to the concerns of the population. This, in turn, might lead to a deduction that the government must be seen to be delivering public services and re-construction and development and might lead to changes in the scheme of manoeuvre of the military forces to ensure that governance is considered in all actions.

This underscores the requirement for military forces to develop modalities to embrace, understand and employ the JIMP environment to their advance or – at minimum – to mitigate any negative effects from uncontrolled JIMP elements. One way that RC South was able to do this in the 2008-2009 timeframe was through structural and procedural adaptations.

Regularly scheduled activities helped the military forces make sense of the crowded battle space or operations area and certainly some shared understanding if not shared intent. One of the key modalities as part of this new way of embracing JIMP was the formation of the Partner's Coordination Board. This high level information sharing arrangement met on a regular basis at the most senior level including the key military commanders, the key contributing nations senior civilian leaders, UN leaders, international organizations, and eventually Afghan officials such as the election officers. Within the purview of this organization a regional approach to supporting the six provinces in the South advancement of economic objectives was advanced. While there is undoubtedly an overlap with meeting the intent of the comprehensive approach in this example, the real reason for this and other procedural changes was to empower the military forces to operate in the JIMP environment with some success.

Besides procedural change, structural changes can enable military forces for success in the JIMP environment. In RC South there were many including the introduction of a Civilian Planning Cell with experienced developmental and governance staff to form part of structured and ad hoc planning teams. These persons were not solely there to provide advice on a military product, rather to be an integral part of the planning team. Likewise, a robust effects organization was put in place that had as part of its mandate, consideration of all stakeholders (JIMP elements). A part of this organization's mandate was the planning and synchronization of key leader engagement covering the range of JIMP elements.

Conclusion: A Strategy to Enhance Process

All the players in the international arena of action are examining ways to affect others. Sometimes, they work with a multitude of actors and, at times, simply need to understand the interactions and interests of all those in the arena. More actors and goals in this environment increases complexity. How does the military maximize its effectiveness and influence in this environment?

In the first instance, a conceptual model for analysis and further force development of concepts and capabilities is essential. The final analysis will show that a whole-of-government policy lends itself to a comprehensive approach to realizing intent. This comprehensive approach necessitates new analysis and reflection. This environment is largely Joint, Interagency, Multinational and Public. An appreciation and ongoing analysis of this environment will emphasize new planning processes, more common language, the requirement to assist others in building capacity and capabilities, the understanding and respect for mandates and authorities of partners and the need to create networks of people, processes and technologies.

Arguably the CF should not be the lead in the refinement of the comprehensive approach concept or the supporting and enabling concepts and, indeed, the development of non-military capabilities. However, given that the CF must embrace this concept, it behoves the CF to take a leading role. A fundamental part of this leading role will be to designate a Centre of Excellence (CoE) for CA development. Based on current mandates and possibilities this is best placed in the nascent CF Warfare Centre.

No one element of the JIMP environment should be taken for granted. The Afghanistan case illustrates that there remains many experiences pertaining to joint and multi-national elements and initiatives to be explored. Analysis in operations must aim at exploring interoperability aspects should be supported and encouraged. In their efforts to realize regional objectives within the JIMP environment, the modalities being developed, tried and exploited by the various stakeholders must be scrutinized. Finally, the "public" element will continue to be the dominant element of the environment. The influence of populations, national and host must be further explored. How to address such influence must be the subject of considerable analysis. In the final analysis, the JIMP environment must be embedded within training and professional military education in order for actions to be comprehensive and successful today and into the future.

Chapter 8

COMPREHENSIVE APPROACH: TOWARDS A STRATEGIC DOCTRINE

START Secretariat[27]

Introduction

Fragile and conflict-affected states are a defining feature of the current international peace and security environment. Over forty states can currently be characterized as fragile (OECD Development Assistance Committee, 2010), representing a population of some 1 billion and annual costs to the international system of some US$270 billion (Chauvet, Collier, and Hoeffler, 2007). These countries are among those most exposed and vulnerable to external and internal shocks. They are characterized by complex and context-specific blends of violence, criminality and corruption, widespread human deprivation and vulnerability – dynamics that often spill over national borders, with regional and global implications. Moreover, fragile states are generally less resilient than any other states when facing a major natural disaster, requiring international support to alleviate the population's suffering and to provide basic services.

In recent years, Canada has adopted more holistic policy instruments in recognition of the need to have a coherent response to security, humanitarian, and development challenges in fragile states. The unique context of Canada's engagement in Afghanistan is one clear example of this need. Today's complex security environment is seen as requiring a whole-of-government approach to international missions, bringing together military and civilian resources including and beyond diplomacy, development, and defence in a focused and coherent fashion. Government of Canada organizational structures are changing or being created to foster

Security Operations in the 21st Century: Canadian Perspectives on the Comprehensive Approach, ed. M. Rostek and P. Gizewski. Montreal and Kingston: Queen's Policy Studies Series, McGill-Queen's University Press.

and operationalize this philosophy. Work is ongoing to institutionalize and implement lessons learned over the past decade, and to continue to improve our whole-of-government responses to crises.

The Global Response

The international community is committed to addressing the complexity of state fragility and the security vulnerabilities it creates. In June 2010, G8 leaders and their partners agreed to work together to strengthen the international availability of civilian experts to support: (i) rule of law and security institutions, (ii) the capacities of key littoral states and regional organizations for maritime security, and (iii) international peace operations (Government of Canada, 2010, Annex II). The international community, including Canada, has also increasingly recognized that responding to state fragility and security vulnerabilities requires multi-faceted responses. A wide range of actors are called upon in fragile and conflict-affected states to:

- stabilize situations,
- protect civilians,
- provide humanitarian relief,
- advance peace processes and implement peace agreements,
- encourage reconciliation and investigate human rights violations,
- monitor and respond to the illegal movement of arms and natural resources,
- disarm and demobilize former combatants,
- facilitate security system reform and the rule of law, and
- initiate long-term development activities.

The unpredictability and highly context-specific nature of the relationship between governance, security, and development needs in a given country or region makes the integration of such efforts both essential and very difficult to sequence in advance of an engagement. Moreover, attempts to build coherent responses can be frustrated by the sheer number of actors involved, each of whom has his or her own timelines, priorities, strengths, and weaknesses. Attempts by the international community and local actors to build a coherent program of support are frustrated by the inevitable fluctuations in political will. These difficulties are particularly pronounced when individual institutions or networks, governments, and government bodies are working in isolation prior to engagement. The ability to address circumstances – such as state fragility and vulnerability to humanitarian crisis or conflict – requires the coordination of diplomatic, development, and security policy, both domestically for those states that choose to engage in a particular crisis, and multilaterally when those states find themselves pursuing common goals in the same country.

The international community has increasingly responded to this new reality by adjusting policy tools and developing new mechanisms to respond to crisis and fragility in an integrated way. With the UN Security Council mandating an increasing number of integrated missions – a system-wide UN response, subsuming security, political, and humanitarian aspects of crisis-management – the UN Secretariat has been ramping up its efforts to bring its vast array of resources together within a "3C" approach – coordinated, complementary, and coherent (Melkert, 2009). The issuance of guidelines and policy directives on integrated mission planning (see UN 2006 and UN Integrated Missions Planning Process, 2008), civil-military coordination (see UN Departments of Peacekeeping Operations and Field Support, 2010), and joint operations and mission assessment centres (JOC/JMAC) (see UN Departments of Peacekeeping Operations and Field Support, 2006), as well as the possibility of an expansion in the scope of work of the Peacebuilding Commission to engage at the immediate post-conflict stage, all attest to this growing trend. The Organisation for Economic Co-operation and Development (OECD) promotes coherence among donor agencies as one of its core principles of engagement in fragile states and has issued a series of Principles for Good International Engagement in Fragile States and Situations and Good Humanitarian Donorship Principles. The organization describes its commitment to policy coherence as a focus "on issues pertaining to the inter-linkages of growth, social and institutional policies including migration, trade, investment, and development cooperation and their joint impact on development and human security" (see *Towards Comprehensive Development Policies*, 2005). Building on its experiences working in a multidimensional environment in Afghanistan, NATO has declared its commitment to adopting a "comprehensive approach" to operations that recognises the need to work in concert with a wide array of partners, including the UN and the African and European Unions (NATO Bucharest Summit, 2008).

Canada is also adapting to new global circumstances. The establishment of the Stabilization and Reconstruction Task Force (START) within Foreign Affairs and International Trade Canada (DFAIT) is in direct response to the recognition that ad hoc and uncoordinated policy, program, and operational responses to complex international crises are insufficient and unsustainable. Created to be "one-stop shopping" within DFAIT for policy expertise on fragile states' issues and related integrated responses for the Government of Canada, START is underpinned by an operational capability to deliver targeted programming and an evolving capacity to deploy civilian experts when and where required. START is also intended to provide a platform for the coordination of government policy, programming, and operations in support of international crisis response, whether a natural disaster, a sudden-onset conflict situation, or efforts at conflict prevention, peace-building, and mediation where a whole-of-government effort is required. As START continues to mature, it is enhancing Canada's capacity to respond to the kinds of complex crises from which acutely fragile and conflict-affected states suffer, and has played an important role in Canada's responses to crises such as the situation in Afghanistan, the crisis in Lebanon, and the Haiti earthquake. Canada recognizes meanwhile that democratic systems of government are best equipped to advance long-term stability and prosperity. START and other DFAIT divisions work closely together to support projects to enhance the role citizens play in decision-making processes in countries undergoing a democratic crisis, in fragile states and in repressive contexts where there are windows of opportunity.

Other like-minded countries have also created specialized national units to address international crisis and state fragility. The US Office of the Coordinator for Reconstruction and Stabilization (S/CRS), within the State Department, is charged with integrating all relevant US resources and assets in conducting reconstruction and stabilization operations and coordinating US government expertise on early warning and conflict prevention activities. S/CRS also facilitates the management of planning and deployments of civilians by strengthening civil-military coordination, enhancing professional development through training and civil-military exercises, and building human resources. The UK Stabilization Unit (SU), jointly owned by the Department for International Development (DFID), the Foreign and Commonwealth Office (FCO), and the Ministry of Defence (MOD), provides specialist, targeted assistance in countries emerging from violent conflict where the UK is helping to achieve a stable environment. The main activities of the SU are: assessments and planning, deployments, and lessons learned. The SU provides a rapidly deployable civilian cadre that can work alongside military in countries emerging from violent conflict. Other countries, such as the Netherlands, Australia, and Denmark have created or are in the process of creating units with similar intent. The European Union has also adopted a multi-dimensional approach to crisis management that includes conflict prevention, police and military operations, peace-building, and reconstruction.

In addition to the creation of dedicated entities, significant effort is still required to encourage and sustain better harmonization of planning, policies, and programs at the national and international levels, and to secure resources. Regardless of the specific orientation that is taken – integrated missions, comprehensive approach, whole-of-government, 3C, etc. – it is clear that the challenges related to donor and civil-military coordination in fragile and conflict-affected situations persist.

Lessons Learned

While many lessons are often specific to context, it is possible to identify some patterns invaluable to institutional learning. In reflecting on recent

Canadian experiences, a number of key lessons have emerged that have been critical in informing Canada's approach to whole-of-government crisis response.

1. Integrated Analysis, Planning and Implementation and Review

While it is understood that coherent responses require whole-of-government or integrated approaches, we have come to learn what this actually calls for in practice. Truly comprehensive action requires integrated, whole-of-government effort through all phases: analysis, planning, implementation, and review. This involves building better systems and patterns of cooperation through joint training and exchanges, standard operating procedures to decrease a reliance on personality-driven cooperation, joint analysis based on shared intelligence, and promoting shared lessons through joint after-action reviews. Coordination, once a crisis has arisen or an operation launched, will never be as effective as it should be unless all stakeholders are working in an integrated fashion as a matter of course. The challenge from the perspective of government entities lies in coordinating horizontally the activities of multiple departments and agencies, which, given the need to maintain ministerial accountabilities, are structured vertically. Where there is military involvement, the challenge of integration becomes even more pronounced because of the convergence of very different civilian versus military institutional cultures, doctrines, processes, and priorities.

In the area of natural disaster response, for example, Canada has sought greater coherence and horizontal management capacity through the development of standard operating procedures (SOPs) which clarify the roles and responsibilities of all inter-departmental actors involved in a Canadian response. These SOPs also seek to promote greater coherence in decision-making around the appropriate use of civilian and military resources. In addition, the Government of Canada has Guidelines on Humanitarian Action and Civil-Military Coordination which outline areas where the Canadian Forces and humanitarian actors may need to cooperate. The Guidelines promote an integrated approach towards issues surrounding military involvement in humanitarian assistance and provide guidance on ensuring that respective operational imperatives do not come into conflict. The consistent application of the SOPs and Guidelines has led to a predictable, institutionalized process that has been the driving force behind Canada's response to natural disasters since 2005, including the Haitian earthquake of 12 January 2010. A joint, systematic process of gathering and mainstreaming lessons learned after each major disaster response has led to the refinement and improvement of the SOPs and brought a degree of predictability to an inherently unpredictable line of work.

Led by START, the Canadian whole-of-government community is also developing interdepartmental recommendations, strategies, and policies on a variety of tasks frequently undertaken in fragile and conflict-affected states. Examples include security system reform, stabilization and mediation, standard operating procedures for whole-of-government responses to conflict-related international crises, benchmarking and the implementation and governance of country-specific engagements. The institutionalization of lessons is an ongoing process.

2. Context-Specific Engagement

Each engagement requires an approach tailored to specific regional, national, and local contexts; the needs and the actors vary, as do the tools that must be drawn upon in pursuit of objectives. In addition, the reform processes initiated to rectify a crisis, can, by their nature, be conflict-producing processes, with winners and losers. Not everyone in partner countries will welcome transparency, professionalism, or accountability, but these are concepts we need to reinforce if we want to address the sources of fragility and conflict. All of this requires a good conflict analysis, including solid awareness of the situation on the ground, to help select and apply appropriate capabilities, clarify roles and responsibilities, and support the considerable engagement with local nationals and host governments needed to ensure adherence to domestic priorities.

The importance of such sound situational analysis is clear with respect to one of the more frequent donor responses: capacity building for state security institutions. Capacity building efforts must begin with a recognition and proper analysis of specific national contexts. Donors are learning to be vigilant in avoiding predestined or supply-driven solutions. The strength or effectiveness of security institutions in partner countries is not the only way to measure impact. Assistance can be most productive in tackling security threats when it is aimed at building institutions that are effective, affordable, and accountable, and that can carry out their legitimate functions in a manner consistent with national law and international norms. In so doing, we are not trying to recreate our own security institutions abroad, but rather to support the development of institutions that make sense in the local context.

Donors may determine that a partner possess a certain capability in order to achieve the security effects that our analysis shows are necessary. However, it will not always be the case that partners will want to invest in those capabilities donors see as priorities. Even if donors are willing to provide or to underwrite a capability indefinitely, this is not sound practice for capacity building. Similarly, too great an international presence in a given sector can unintentionally weaken the capacity or legitimacy of the local actors we are trying to help. In our enthusiasm to do good and to do it quickly, there is a danger of duplication or friction among programs from different countries or in different disciplines. Conversely, focused and priority-driven programs can also create geographic or functional pockets of exclusion that do not serve regional stability and security.

Thus, engagement which is based on sound evidence and analysis has a greater likelihood of achieving positive results. In light of the complexity of such engagements, the Government has developed a set of interest-based considerations that looks into international implications, the level of need, and Canada's resources. These can help inform decision-making and planning processes, including the development of customized responses, identifying and employing the most appropriate "tools" from the Government of Canada "toolbox."

3. Civilian Expertise

An integrated approach to engagement in situations where there is active or residual conflict requires early, substantive and sustained engagement by civilian experts, in addition to the essential contribution that soldiers can make. Such civilian expertise is focused on assisting the host country to build its capacity for security, governance, economic development, and the establishment of the rule of law, through mentoring, training, and the transfer of technology. The role Canadian soldiers will play in future peace support operations should reflect the complexity and diversity of the contemporary context, in which military and civilian colleagues work hand-in-hand to build capacity, support peace processes, and protect civilian populations, among many other tasks.

Canada's current mission to Afghanistan, with an important focus in Kandahar, is viewed domestically and internationally as a potential model for whole-of-government civil-military coordination. However, the current configuration of inter-departmental teams took years to put into place and brought to light a crucial deficiency in the ability to deploy well-trained civilians into difficult, even hostile environments. Some of the hard lessons learned from Afghanistan include the need for extensive training, adequate deployment mechanisms, reporting structures, recruitment, de-briefing, security clearances, and reintegration support. These lessons are reinforced by the Canadian experience in the Balkans, Haiti, Sudan, and Lebanon.

Again, it is important to remember that Canadians who deploy into acutely fragile states and conflict-affected situations are there to enhance and support local capacities – not replace them. A key challenge is to identify the appropriate Canadian expertise based on the demonstrated need and a request of the state, and not to respond based on a supply-driven desire to deploy civilian experts. The timing and durations of deployments are also essential and should align with the OECD DAC Principles for Good International Engagement in Fragile States: "Act fast…but stay engaged long enough to give success a chance" (OECD DCD-DAC, 2007).

In 2009, Canada deployed over 300 full-time civilian police and public servants on numerous assessment and stabilization missions, or as part of humanitarian and emergency response teams. START is currently developing a whole-of-government framework with partners that would provide the Government of Canada with a pool of qualified, trained, and ready-to-deploy civilian experts who can work in acutely fragile states and conflict-affected situations. G8 members, through the 2010 Muskoka Declaration, have specifically committed to work with other international partners to help build capacity for civilian deployments from developing countries and emerging donors. Moreover, they committed to support the deployment of additional experts from their own countries.

4. Institutional Structure to Deliver

Integrated responses to fragile states and conflict-affected situations require appropriate departmental authorities and flexible human resource modalities, as well as the integrated planning processes already mentioned. The "new normal" of joined-up responses requires the adaption of policies, training, and activities in peace support operations. It also demands that we ensure the military, police, and civilian personnel we deploy are armed with greater levels of knowledge and sophistication, and that they are provided with appropriate levels of decision-making powers and resources to take effective action on the ground, within the context of whole-of-government agreed objectives and strategies. The design and delivery of effective interventions requires increased institutional thresholds for risk, including higher tolerance for potential failures in programs.

In response to these challenges, DFAIT and partners across Government are working to improve the Government's strategic framework, governance, and operational capabilities to respond effectively. This includes the work of the START Advisory Board, composed of Directors General from nine government departments and agencies. The board meets on a regular basis to assess progress and foster information exchange among implicated departments, all of which informs advice to senior departmental and agency management, as well as to Parliament and the Government. This integrated, horizontal governance structure allows for an ongoing incorporation of lessons learned and the ability to act on recommendations, while granting the flexibility to adapt to new situations.

5. Communications

Canada's engagements in fragile states and international crisis generally attract intense political and media scrutiny, both at home and abroad. There is an inherent challenge in attempting to communicate results of an international engagement that is perceived to be intense and dangerous, and where the ultimate outcomes are generally outside of Canada's control.

Effective public communications, therefore, should be an integral part of any country-specific engagement strategy. The experience in Afghanistan has shown that small public affairs initiatives can make a difference often disproportionally larger than their cost. For maximum effect, and to avoid mixed messaging, communications initiatives should be closely coordinated with both civilian and military components, drawing from cross-departmental information and expertise.

A coherent message to the public is not achievable without the Government's full understanding of Canada's engagement. Both Cabinet and Parliament need to be regularly briefed on major international engagements in order to increase their awareness of the mission and to ensure that they are able to deliver clear and consistent messages. In 2008, for example, the *Independent Panel on Canada's Future Role in Afghanistan* (Manley Panel) recommended a more coordinated management of Canada's engagement in Afghanistan and more regular reporting to the public. Following the panel's report, the Cabinet Committee on Afghanistan (CCOA) was created in order to monitor diplomatic, defence, development, and security issues related to Canada's mission in the country. The CCOA reports to the Prime Minister and the Priorities and Planning Cabinet Committee, as well as to Parliament and the public through the quarterly reports.

Way Forward

Canada's recent experiences in Afghanistan and Haiti, for example, have highlighted that coordination and cooperation between civilian and military actors has become the norm in addressing crises, state fragility, and situations of armed conflict. The coordination and cooperation process has improved dramatically, and in a very short period of time, but constant nurturing and vigilance are required to maintain these gains and move forward.

There is still work to be done to more effectively coordinate the diverse elements of the Government's engagement through all phases of an intervention. This should include enabling capacity for rapid, sustained, and multifaceted civilian deployments (such as an expert deployment unit); developing mechanisms to ensure overall strategic clarity while preserving operational flexibility (e.g., SOPs, joint analysis, etc.); defining ways to ensure coherence of efforts that involve multiple departments while respecting Ministerial accountability; reflecting frankly on past experience; and making sure we are all taking away, and applying, the same lessons. Moreover, cooperation among the various elements of Canada's engagement should take place as early as possible, and not simply when a crisis arises. An early response should include joint training and inter-agency personnel exchanges. Coordination on the ground will never be as effective as it should be unless Canadians are working in an integrated fashion before we deploy, developing an understanding of and acknowledging the cultural differences and respective strengths and expertise of various civilian and military institutions.

After a decade of integrated operations, government departments and agencies continue to improve the ways in which we work together, and new players are becoming involved in Canada's international engagements. Although there is no single individual ownership of Canada's engagement abroad, START remains a valuable resource and whole-of-government platform (i) by reaching out to other government departments; (ii) by working with multilateral agencies and others who are active on issues of fragility and conflict; and (iii) by its experience and lessons gained by working in fragile states across the geographic reach of DFAIT. Enhancing whole-of-government coordination, integrated planning, and action is an ongoing process, and it is imperative that we not lose the momentum most recently and forcefully created by our experience in Afghanistan. This will not be the last time the Government of Canada is called upon to help respond to a complex situation requiring a whole-of-government response.

Chapter 9

CIVIL-MILITARY COORDINATION: CANADA'S EXPERIENCE IN KANDAHAR, 2005-2009

GAVIN BUCHAN

When civil-military relations are discussed in the context of Canada's engagement in Afghanistan the tendency is, quite naturally, to focus on decision making at the strategic level. Debate about military influence over policy, and in particular what impact then Chief of Defence Staff General Rick Hillier had on Canada's decision to commit troops to Kandahar province, has given civil control of the military a higher profile than at any time since the 1960s. However, it is at the operational level that civil-military relations are currently undergoing a test that is, for Canada, unprecedented.

In southern and eastern Afghanistan, Canada and NATO Allies are engaged in a full-fledged counter-insurgency, and as military professionals who have studied the subject will be the first to volunteer, a counter insurgency is never won through force of arms. As the Canadian Army manual on counter-insurgency operations states:

> insurgencies are rooted in political and social issues and thus the military has an overall supporting role to those other agencies and institutions that will create the enduring, indigenous-based conditions for peace. In essence, the military, particularly the land force, provides the manoeuvre space for those other agencies and elements of power working to a shared campaign end state. (Department of National Defence, 2008a, 1)

Security Operations in the 21st Century: Canadian Perspectives on the Comprehensive Approach, ed. M. Rostek and P. Gizewski. Montreal and Kingston: Queen's Policy Studies Series, McGill-Queen's University Press.
© 2011 Queen's Centre for International Relations, Queen's University at Kingston. All rights reserved.

Coordination of effort towards this "shared campaign end state" is difficult to achieve. The heart of the challenge is that while the military are dominant in numbers on the ground and possess the great majority of the organizational capacity, the keys to actually resolving a counterinsurgency are largely held by civilians. This places a unique premium on civil-military coordination.

In recent years, efforts to foster civil-military coodination have taken place under a number of different banners. The North Atlantic Treaty Organization refers to the Comprehensive Approach, an all-embracing concept that includes all actors within the international community, be they governments, international institutions or non-governmental organizations (North Atlantic Council, 2008, para. 11). This in turn had its origins in a Danish initiative that put questions of civil-military coherence on the NATO agenda in 2004, under the more prosaic heading Concerted Planning and Action (Peterson and Binnendijk, 2007, 1). Some practitioners describe close civil-military collaboration as 3-D, after the three main pillars (defence, diplomacy, and development) that have to work together; the term is, notably, in widespread use in the Netherlands (Gabriëlse, 2007, 67). In the UK, the Blair government popularized the phrase "joined up government" to describe an integrated approach to addressing complex problems that implicated multiple departments or levels of government. (United Kingdom Cabinet Office, 1999, 5) In Canada, most now refer to the whole-of-government approach, although it is Australia that has presented what is arguably the clearest definition for that concept:

> whole-of-government denotes public service agencies working across portfolio boundaries to achieve a shared goal and an integrated government response to particular issues. (Australian Public Service Commission, 2004)

Each of these labels conveys a slightly different meaning, but ultimately they all represent efforts to develop systems in which government departments, military and civilian, work together to achieve a common goal.

Since Canada's joint civil-military effort began in earnest in 2005, with the deployment of the Provincial Reconstruction Team to Kandahar, the approach taken to synchronizing civil and military activities has undergone a significant evolution. This chapter traces the changes that have occurred and identify some of the primary themes and conclusions. In so doing the focus will be on the operational and tactical levels, rather than on the Ottawa dynamic. This is not to discount the importance of changes that have taken place at the national level – including the creation in early 2008 of a special Cabinet Committee on Afghanistan and an Afghanistan Task Force within the Privy Council Office – but they lie outside the scope of this document.

Before examining the nature of coordination arrangements, it is important to have a basic grasp of the command practices of the principal players, and the relative degrees of independence enjoyed by the personnel deployed to Afghanistan. In the interests of consistency of analysis I have used the three types of command described by Thomas Czerwinski as the basic template for comparison: command by direction, command by plan, and command by influence (mission command) (Czerwinski, 1996, 122). Application of these concepts to civilian departments is not, of course, a perfect fit, but it does serve to highlight the different styles.

The most rigorously studied practices are those of the Canadian Forces (the CF). The CF subscribes to the philosophy of mission command, which allows subordinates "maximum freedom of action consistent with commander intent" (Canadian Forces Leadership Institute, 2005, 12-13). A good case can be made that over the past two decades or so this philosophy has been eroded, partly because of improvements in information technology and partly because of factors related to the more complex operations being conducted, and the pressures of media and parliamentary scrutiny (Gosselin, 2006, 20-1). In Afghanistan, however, despite intense scrutiny from Ottawa, the robust staffing of the operational headquarters deployed and the sheer volume of daily decision making required do appear to have restored significant substance to the concept of mission command. This was demonstrated by the substantial shift in approach adopted after Brigadier-General Vance assumed command of Joint Task Force Afghanistan (JTF-A) in 2009 (Government of Canada, 2009a, 3). The Campaign Plan, issued by the Canadian Expeditionary Forces Command (CEFCOM) and subject to regular updates, has also been a significant influence. Under this JTF-A's own plans have been nested, with most headquarters rotations putting in place a single overarching operational plan within which sub-plans can be created.

The Department of Foreign Affairs has some elements of the mission command tradition, most notably as embodied in the traditional letter of mandate for Ambassadors departing on post. The Terms of Reference that are given to officers deployed in non-traditional roles, such as Political Advisors, can also be seen in this light. Documents like these provide a sense of higher goals, and as such could be considered analogous to commander's intent. There is, however, a parallel history of headquarters providing explicit instructions to Canada's delegations at the UN, NATO and other multilateral institutions before they commit Canada to a formal position on an issue. This command by direction is less widespread in bilateral relationships, but raises its head whenever a stance on an issue commits Canada to assuming a national position. There is very little tradition of command by plan, and even the Country Strategies that were introduced for all countries shortly before Canada's deployment to Kandahar did not provide anywhere near the level of detail required to shape ongoing operations.

The Canadian International Development Agency is (and with the exception of a brief flirtation with decentralization at the end of the 1980s has long been) a heavily centralized department. It is focussed on delivering programming that is ultimately approved in Ottawa, albeit after significant dialogue between headquarters and personnel deployed in the field. Other than for small-scale local initiatives the approval authorities for individual projects rest in Ottawa. The green light for financing and the choice of implementing partner have to be given by headquarters, although once these are approved field personnel have significant latitude in advancing projects locally. The philosophy is therefore closest to command by direction, as decision making authority is not delegated to the field. Since 2008, however, an exception to this practice has been made for Afghanistan, with significantly enhanced authorities being delegated to Canadian International Development Agency (CIDA) personnel in theater. This created what is, for CIDA, a highly atypical element of mission command. It can, however, be argued that because project decisions still take place under programs approved at headquarters, CIDA's operations also have an element of "command by plan."

The Royal Canadian Mounted Police (RCMP), the fourth major player in Kandahar, attached sufficient importance to the judgement of the personnel on the ground that they could be said to respect the principle of mission command.[28] However, there were two significant constraints on this. One was that if the field significantly overstepped what Ottawa expected, control would be reasserted (as seen when the head of the Civilian Police detachment in Kandahar was removed from command in the spring of 2008). The second was that because nearly all the funding for their operations in Kandahar came from Foreign Affairs, their programming had to be negotiated with Department of Foreign Affairs and International Trade (DFAIT).

Even from a superficial assessment such as this, it is clear that the departments engaged in Kandahar have different traditions and expectations when it comes to command and control. These represented a significant complicating factor when the time came to synchronize actions on the ground in Kandahar.

The reporting chain for personnel deployed to Kandahar also varied between departments. All CF elements reported through JTF-A to CEFCOM; DFAIT was in principle under the Ambassador in Kabul but in practice was more likely to be tasked directly from Ottawa; CIDA had an ambiguous relationship with the Head of Aid in Kabul and received the majority of its direction from headquarters in Ottawa; and the RCMP consistently reported directly to Ottawa. The key point to be drawn from this is that when Canada began its deployment, the varying degrees of delegated authority and the incompatible reporting chains meant that most coordination was either worked out informally on the ground, or referred to Ottawa. There was no option of in-theater coordination above the working level because the civilian departments had not deployed any in-theater headquarters capability.

A further layer of complexity came from the multinational nature of operations in Kandahar. Military operations fell, after the summer of 2006, under the International Security Assistance Force's Regional Command South (ISAF RC(S)). If ordered to pursue a particular course of action, the CF in principle was required to act, although in practice the command arrangements contained a degree of scope for negotiation when NATO orders were not fully consistent with national objectives. The civilian components of Canada's mission, however, did not have a multinational command chain. The same was true for other NATO partners, leading to sharp complaints by some observers that as far as governance and development were concerned Afghanistan was divided into provincial silos based on whatever country led the relevant PRT, and that this impeded coordination (Atlantic Council of the United States, 2008, 12). The US was the one country that did have development and governance interests in most provinces, and in this regard de-confliction between Canada and the US in Kandahar was largely a matter to be worked out informally between the personnel on the ground. The significance of provincial level co-ordination with the US has grown considerably since 2007 with the rapid expansion of the US presence in Kandahar. Coordination with the United Nations Assistance Mission in Afghanistan, assorted UN Agencies and other partners active in Kandahar also required considerable ongoing effort, with the majority of this work falling to CIDA and DFAIT.

This thumbnail sketch does not attempt to capture the full complexity of multinational interaction in Afghanistan. Most of the coordination required occurs between militaries, but there are times when issues spill over to affect civil-military coordination. For example, the US-led Combined Security Transition Command-Afghanistan (CSTC-A) is responsible for US assistance to the Afghan National Police and deployed Police Mentoring Teams to Kandahar in 2007, where they operate alongside Canada's Civilian Police contingent and Military Police. Their activities need to be coordinated across both the civil-military divide and national chains of command (a challenge met in 2007 by the practical expedient of basing the command element for the US Police Mentoring Teams in Kandahar at Canada's PRT).

Coordination with the Government of Afghanistan is, of course, at least as important as how we work with NATO allies or the UN. It lies, however, beyond the scope of this chapter, except to note that effective interaction with the host government becomes significantly harder if Canada's internal coordination is deficient.

There were, then, a series of structural obstacles to effective civil-military coordination of Canada's efforts in Kandahar. The two most significant were that the departments deployed had different command philosophies, and civilian departments lacked an in-theater headquarters capability to interact with JTF-A. The net result was a reliance on ad hoc working level coordination. Conflicts or major coordination issues could certainly be referred back to Ottawa, but that meant dealing with them through interdepartmental machinery that was by its very nature ill-equipped for providing rapid responses to operational questions, and inclined to take issues of departmental mandate very seriously.

It is against this background that the evolution of Canada's civil-military coordination efforts in Kandahar has to be considered. In tracing developments, I have used five major markers:

- deployment of Canada's Provincial Reconstruction Team (PRT) in August 2005;
- the first significant increases in civilian personnel strength, from summer 2007 until February 2008;
- deployment of the first Representative of Canada in Kandahar (RoCK) in February 2008;
- the major influx of civilian personnel in summer and autumn 2008;
- the first iteration of the Kandahar Action Plan in 2008.

In the first period, from August 2005 to summer 2007, the number of civilians on the ground was so low that coordination was achievable through an ad hoc approach. When the PRT was deployed in 2005 there were only five civilians present (two DFAIT officers, one CIDA and two CivPol). After the DFAIT Political Director was killed by a suicide bomber in January 2006, there was a period where only the two CivPol remained at the PRT. Although that drawdown was temporary, by spring of 2007 the tally had still only increased slightly, with 11 personnel at the PRT (three CIDA officers, one DFAIT, five CivPol and two Correctional Services Canada). In terms of raw numbers three further positions could theoretically be added: the Political Advisor (POLAD) and Development Advisor (DEVAD) working for Comd JTF-A, and the DEVAD working for Comd RC(S). These three positions, however, were advisory rather than autonomously operational, and as such did not create civil-military coordination challenges; indeed, by creating informal channels for civil-military communication and providing a civilian perspective in planning sessions they in fact assisted coordination efforts.[29]

During this period the PRT evolved two main coordination mechanisms – the Targeting Board, which was used to collectively review project proposals, and the Board of Directors model. The latter was the more important of the two, as it placed the senior representatives from each department around a single table, where they were able to make decisions on issues that cut across departmental lines. Although the Commanding Officer of the PRT gave up none of his exclusive authority over CF assets, use of this model gave all departments a degree of influence over PRT operations and resources. With limited numbers of civilian personnel deployed this model provided effective working level coordination, but it remained very much subject to the personalities involved.

Civilian representatives from the PRT would on occasion travel to JTF-A to participate in discussions on planning or operations. This was not, however, something that occurred consistently, and as such did not ensure effective input from civilian operators into JTF-A planning. Inevitably, this had negative implications for civil-military coordination. Travelling to JTF-A also reduced the time PRT civilian personnel had available for their operational responsibilities.

The bottom line during this period was that a mere handful of civilians (a maximum of 11, not counting the advisors) were operating alongside some 2500 CF personnel. Under these circumstances ad hoc coordination between peers, largely at the level of the PRT, was sufficient for synchronization of day to day operations. However the civilian contribution to the JTF-A led planning process was inconsistent and lacked depth, which led to less than fully integrated civil-military operations.

The second period (summer 2007 to February 2008) saw few substantive changes to structure or process, but a significant increase in civilian numbers. DFAIT and CIDA now each had five personnel at the PRT, CivPol eight and CSC three. The increased size of the civilian contingents put more strain on the ad hoc coordination arrangements and led individual departments to focus more on their own internal coordination, increasing the risk of developing departmental silos.[30] The rise in numbers also increased the need for coordination between civilian departments. This could be characterized as the phase where ad hoc coordination began to meet its limits.

The response to the need for enhanced coordination was the deployment, in February 2008, of the first Representative of Canada in Kandahar (RoCK). This position was mandated to be the senior civilian representative of the Government in the province (on an equal footing with Comd JTF-A), to provide leadership to civilian personnel and to coordinate Canada's civilian efforts. Assigned objectives included unifying civilian engagement in Kandahar, advancing integrated civil-military planning (with Comd JTF-A) and developing a unified concept of operations for the PRT (Government of Canada, 2008d).

The deployment of the RoCK was intended to address two structural weaknesses in the previous system. The first was the lack of an effective mechanism for coordinating civilian departments – as was clear from the analysis of departmental approaches to command and control, the diversity of traditions did not lend itself to effective coordination. Unity of civilian effort also formed an essential precondition for the second objective, enhanced civil-military coordination. In this regard, creation of the RoCK established a civilian equivalent for Comd JTF-A, one that could act as a single point of contact and a partner for planning.

Deploying a trusted senior civilian with robust Terms of Reference also created a significantly greater degree of "mission command" for civilian operations. The difficulty of managing multiple departments meant that this was unlikely to ever fully match the authority available to Comd JTF-A, but the situation was nonetheless in much greater balance than previous. At the same time, the RoCK was placed under the authority of the Ambassador in Kabul, which perpetuated one difference between the civil and military structures. The RoCK's reporting chain had the advantage of ensuring greater coherence between Canada's provincial-level approach in Kandahar and the approach taken at the national level, but did not provide a true parallel to the JTF-A – CEFCOM relationship.

There were several challenges facing the first RoCK in her initial efforts to enhance civil-military coordination. One was that it took some time to establish the exact nature of the relationship between the position and the senior civilians from departments other than her own (the position was staffed by DFAIT). The Terms of Reference spoke of providing "leadership," which was a term sufficiently vague as to be acceptable, but the question of whether departments would accept direction, and to what extent, was more challenging. Issues like respect for the RCMP chain of command and CIDA's financial accountabilities meant that other departments argued for preserving departmental reporting chains.[31] A second factor was that at first the RoCK had too small a team (in spring of 2008 only two staff) to provide the strong civilian role in the planning process that was desired, although the situation was still a clear improvement over what had gone before. A third issue was the extent of delegated financial, policy and programming authorities to be assigned to the RoCK. Part of the intent behind the deployment was to enable a meaningful degree of "mission command" for the civilian side, but the levers for giving this practical effect were not initially in place.

In the second half of 2008, measures were taken to address these challenges. In the absence of an agreement establishing a definitive command relationship, time, dialogue, and precedent were key elements in defining the practical extent of the RoCK's coordinating authority over departments other than DFAIT. There were also some creative solutions – for example the question of CIDA's departmental financial accountabilities was resolved by giving CIDA staff in Afghanistan enhanced financial authorities, so that they could sign alongside the RoCK in a "dual-key" system. A significant increase in civilian staff was approved, to take the civilian footprint in Kandahar from 24 to 71. While many of these were to be operationally focussed and based at the PRT, allowance was made for placing some 16 staff at Kandahar Airfield to enable better integration of the civilian and military components of the mission. This meant that the civilian departments were finally able to engage on a significant scale in in-theater planning. On a slightly slower timeline a civilian Director was deployed to lead the PRT, with the aim of further strengthening coordination of departments at the working level. Significant delegated authorities were also approved for the RoCK, not least $2 million in signing authority for project approval and contract selection.[32] In combination with robust Terms of Reference this meant that the first RoCK was able to say, on returning from Afghanistan:

> [T]here was never a need for us to call upon our superiors. That's the benefit of having mission command, if you will, on the civilian side and on the military side, because our senior managers trust us to make those decisions and to come to an agreement with them. (House of Commons, 2009)

That is not to say that the system established was without stresses. The reluctance of departments other than DFAIT to insert the RoCK into their own chain of command reflected the structural reality of discrete departmental accountabilities. There was also the significant challenge of running operations under the direction of two co-equal senior figures. This may not be the most efficient of systems, but it was seen as the only appropriate structure. As one senior Foreign Affairs officer put it, "In practical terms, the civilians... and the military are on an equal footing. There is no hierarchy. The military and us [sic] must come together. We must work together, as we are partners" (House of Commons, 2009). In practice this came to mean dual signoff on planning documents and on key reports to Ottawa. Such a system, however, is inevitably dependent to a certain extent on good will and the quality of the relationship between the two leaders, civilian and military.

Adoption in fall 2008 of the Kandahar Action Plan (KAP) played an important role in reinforcing arrangements for civil-military coordination, making it less dependent on relations between the leaders. This over-arching operational plan was produced in theater as an integrated civil-military effort, an accomplishment that was made possible by the civilian staff increases in the preceding months and the increased scope for mission command on the civilian side. As the RoCK at the time said, "we have had strategic plans, and this is all that we required from Ottawa. We, the people working in the field, are the ones responsible for executing the strategic plan and adapting it to Kandahar" (House of Commons, 2009). The process of generating the KAP gave departments on the ground an opportunity to debate the best approach to take and so develop a shared position, and as such was a tool for generating buy-in for the decisions it embodied. Equally important, by setting out the goals to be pursued it defined parameters within which operators, civilian and military, could set to work in full confidence that their actions were consistent with the "whole of government" intent. It brought an element of "command by plan" to Canadian civil-military engagement in Kandahar, and was a tool to strengthen synchronization of effort (Australian Public Service Commission, 2004).

When the US began to deploy troops to Kandahar in significant numbers, the Kandahar Action Plan proved to be a useful tool for integrating not just civil and military efforts, but American engagement as well. With troops and civilians from more than one nation operating in the province, the KAP offered a way to ensure efforts were mutually supporting regardless of the evolution of multinational command arrangements. In late 2008 the RoCK explicitly described the KAP as more than just a Canadian product: "We have a Kandahar Action Plan, which is a multi-national and multi-agency strategy. This sets a clear direction in terms of where we want to go. It builds on what the Afghans have told us. It builds on what the Canadian and US governments have said they want to do."[33]

Not everything, however, was as tidily resolved as it might initially appear. From a CF perspective, the KAP was a useful document, but it did not have a neatly hierarchical relationship to the CEFCOM Campaign Plan. Under normal circumstances, the CEFCOM plan would have provided the higher level guidance that shaped the KAP. Now, however, the plan generated in-theater was both an integrated civil-military product and a multinational one, and the CEFCOM document (despite best efforts to encourage civilian departments to contribute to its development) was neither of these things. This meant that the CEFCOM Campaign Plan became one element to consider in drafting the KAP, rather than definitive strategic direction. Seen from this perspective it becomes clear that evolution of an effective mechanism for civil-military coordination involved compromises for the CF as well as for civilian departments.

An inherent weakness of Canadian civil military coordination remained that outside of Kandahar departments reverted to their traditional accountabilities; the creation of the Privy Council Office Afghanistan Task Force was one effort to address this. Another initiative that helped to improve coordination at the interface between Ottawa and theater was the creation in 2008 of what were dubbed "Communities of Practice" (CoPs). These were essentially interdepartmental committees with representatives from Kandahar, the Embassy in Kabul and Ottawa. A CoP was formed for each of the Government of Canada's six priorities for Afghanistan, and they were charged with providing regular reporting against established benchmarks. While labour intensive, these committees did have a harmonizing effect, ensuring that key personnel at all levels of the system shared an understanding of where progress stood on each of the priorities, as well as any anticipated problems. Because the information from theater was fed directly into this process, Kabul and Ottawa were aware of issues at an earlier stage than would normally have been the case, and in a better position to provide rapid support where required.

It should be acknowledged that Canada's solution to the challenge of working level civil-military coordination is not the only one. The US, for example, while it recognizes that counter-insurgency "requires a mix of familiar combat tasks and skills more often associated with non-military agencies" (United States Army, 2008) has in Afghanistan chosen an approach in which the representatives of the State Department, the US Agency for International Development and the Department of Agriculture are subordinated to the military at the operational level (Gauster, 2008, 21). This approach can clearly ensure effective coordination but as subordinated elements the civilian contributions to the operation are unlikely to achieve their full potential. The UK, by contrast, has placed significantly more emphasis on plans and on civilian leadership. The British deployed in 2006 under an interdepartmental civil-military plan (the UK Joint Plan for Helmand), which was replaced in April 2008 by the much more detailed "Helmand Road Map," a document that had its origins in theater. Moreover in late 2008, after two years of shifting civil-military command relationships, the UK merged its task force headquarters and the PRT into a combined Civil-Military Mission in Helmand which is led by a senior civilian from the Foreign and Commonwealth Office (Farrell and Gordon, 2009, 669-73, 682). As these examples make clear there are alternatives to the "partnership of equals" that Canada has established with the RoCK and Commander JTF-A. As yet, however, no one model has conclusively proved its superiority.

The goal of effective civil-military coordination was clear from the beginning. However, differing departmental approaches to command were a significant practical obstacle to coordination above the working level, something that became increasingly apparent as Canada's civilian footprint in Kandahar began to expand. A major structural problem was that because none of the civilian departments had a headquarters element in Kandahar there was no real civilian counterpart to Joint Task Force – Afghanistan. Issues above a certain level of importance therefore had to be referred to Ottawa (or on occasion the Embassy in Kabul), and the Canada-based interdepartmental process was inherently poorly suited to providing rapid decisions on complex operational issues.

Of the steps taken to address this challenge, probably the most important was deployment of the Representative of Canada in Kandahar. This provided in one person a coordinator for the disparate civilian elements deployed to Kandahar, a counterpart for Commander JTF-A on civil military coordination issues, and a degree of "mission command" on the civilian side so that a greater proportion of military and civilian coordination could take place in theater. Development of a civilian planning capability in theater, through deployment of additional personnel, also had a significant impact. Lastly, development of the Kandahar Action Plan as an integrated civil-military product provided a useful tool for coordinating not just military and civilian efforts, but those of multinational partners as well.

If Canada in future chooses to mount a truly whole-of-government civil-military intervention, there would seem to be several lessons implicit in the first four years of operations in Kandahar. These should, in principle, be applicable to any intervention whose scale is such that it can no longer be managed by ad hoc working level coordination. The first is that civil-military coordination requires unity of civilian leadership; or put slightly differently, civil coordination is a precondition for effective civil-military coordination. The second is that the military and civilian sides must both enjoy a reasonable degree of mission command; without this, coordination issues will tend to revert to the inter-departmental machinery at headquarters. The third is that coordination by plan brings significant benefits in a situation where the civil and military sides retain separate chains of command; this approach, however, requires that both sides invest resources in joint civil-military planning.

Chapter 10

THE ROLE OF DEVELOPMENT IN A COMPREHENSIVE APPROACH

MICHAEL KOROS AND XIANG HE[34]

Introduction

The standard dictionary definition of "comprehensive" is: *of large scope; covering or involving much; inclusive*. Yet, comprehensive and specialised knowledge are consistent. It appears possible and indeed highly desirable in our current age to acquire comprehensive, specialised knowledge within a domain of human endeavour. At the same time, many prominent thinkers, such as Jared Diamond, Thomas Homer-Dixon, Ronald Wright, Wade Davis and Jane Jacobs admonish policy makers and practitioners for inadequate integration of knowledge and experience from a variety of disciplines in response to complex real-world problems. In fact, several of these authors argue that this fault has led in the past, and could lead in the future, to errors that damage our civilisation in profound and possibly irretrievable ways.

This chapter suggests possible ways to integrate such knowledge and experience by exploring and focusing on the role of development in comprehensive security and stability operations. The aim will be to demonstrate how the challenge of poverty reduction has generated repeated calls for comprehensive approaches to developmental assistance for suppliers and clients alike. Development assistance and violent conflict may be viewed as different ways of accomplishing what are in essence political goals. As such, greater interaction between disciplines in addressing problems of violent conflict, insecurity, and poverty would benefit from greater investment in inter-disciplinary cooperation.

Security Operations in the 21st Century: Canadian Perspectives on the Comprehensive Approach, ed. M. Rostek and P. Gizewski. Montreal and Kingston: Queen's Policy Studies Series, McGill-Queen's University Press.

The International Context and Challenges for Development

Before discussing the role of development in a comprehensive approach, it is necessary to define a common starting point or diagnostic of what the current international context and development challenges look like. This will provide a clearer understanding of a comprehensive approach for those who work in development.

Current global problems demand *comprehensive, integrated, and multidisciplinary responses* because the international context is characterised by more frequent, complex and interdependent global challenges and crises. These are driven by at least three factors. First, it is not clear whether the lingering impacts of the food, energy and economic crises in recent years will dissipate or remain a structural feature of the global economy. A period of profound global structural economic change is underway. The implications of the economic crisis for those already most vulnerable to and affected by crises, disaster, instability and violent conflict are difficult to assess due to imperfect statistics and limited data collection capabilities in many low-income countries.

Second, the effects of climate change and environmental degradation – which may precipitate more frequent, and more intense, severe weather events – are straining the ecosystems that the majority of those living in the poorest countries rely on for their very survival. Coastal and arid zones affected by these events will generate large and sudden population movements. Migration due to low intensity conflict and instability associated with competition over scarce natural resources such as water and arable land will persist.

Third, while the overall number of active violent conflicts have declined in the last two decades, civil conflicts are still persistent. This may be attributed in part to the growth and expansion of global, regional and national criminal networks and gangs. The persistence of internal or civil conflict undermines security and the rule of law, especially in places where capacity in these areas is the weakest in the first instance. States are therefore less able to manage conflict through peaceful means.

Together, with other global trends, these drivers will increase the complexity of humanitarian crises, violent conflict and natural disasters, undermining prospects for achieving the Millennium Development Goals (MDGs) by 2015. Preliminary research by the World Bank indicates that the situation in "fragile and conflict-affected states,"[35] a subset of low- and middle-income countries, is worse still, due to their difficulty in achieving MDGs.

The challenges presented by fragile and conflict-affected states are especially difficult to address. Contributing to such conditions are the following: the extension of violent conflict beyond national boundaries, the proliferation of organized crime and terrorist networks, trafficking of humans and illegal goods, increased refugee flows, the spread of HIV/

AIDS and other infectious diseases, environmental degradation and un-regulated natural resource exploitation, and reductions in foreign direct investment and trade due to regional instability, etc. How to ensure that these states are not further impoverished is emerging as one of the key concerns for the international community between now and 2015 (OECD Development Assistance Committee 2010).

Certain policies are having positive effects. Peacekeeping and peace support operations now involve military, police, and civilians working in a range of capacities. During the 1990s, the United Nations carried out four times as many peacekeeping missions as in the previous 40 years (UN-DESA, 2008). According to one report, 200,000 people are currently in the field, costing $8-$9 billion per annum (Center on International Cooperation, 2010). The nature, extent, and scope of these missions have contributed to the decline in violent armed conflict mentioned above.[36] The recently released G8 Muskoka Accountability Report notes con-siderable financial and technical contributions to training peacekeepers, supporting civilians and police in peace operations, building the African peace and security architecture (including maritime security), addressing the proliferation and misuse of small arms and light weapons, grants for reconstruction, and combating conflict resources (Government of Canada, 2010).

Corresponding to growing demand for humanitarian and develop-ment support in fragile and conflict-affected states, a rapid increase has occurred in the number and range of governments and non-governmental organisations involved in responses to complex humanitarian emergen-cies, including peace and stability operations. Recent participation in the Consolidated Appeal Process, for example, has grown sixteen-fold to include 350 organizations in 2010, up from 22 in 2000.

These response trends are generating policy questions regarding ef-fectiveness, coverage and legitimacy. This includes the extent to which development, as an instrument of any state's foreign policy and power, is or should be part of a comprehensive approach. It is well known that many of those operating in the "humanitarian space" are deeply affected by the tensions between military operations in settings where the humani-tarian principles of humanity, neutrality, impartiality and independence should be paramount.

How can the costs associated with violent conflict and state fragility or failure be reduced, or better yet, effectively prevented? Which states are of "sufficient" concern to Canadian interests and values to require our engagement? When needs exceed fiscal and institutional capacity, how does Canada select and prioritise while avoiding neglect? Should Canada seek in all cases the involvement of the United Nations in future peace sup-port operations, so that mandates have broad international support and legitimacy and robust peace support can be balanced with peace-building, reconciliation and humanitarian and development components? The success of such *comprehensive, integrated, and multidisciplinary* operations requires consistent financial support from the international community and improved cooperation among regional, international and multilateral organizations. This has implications of immediate relevance to Canada's whole-of-government or "3D PLUS" operations.

A Comprehensive Approach to Poverty Reduction

Complex interactions between agents, institutions, and instruments, operating from the global to the local level, can generate situations where peace and socio-economic development are mutually supportive. Compounding such complexity are any number of shades of grey that involve weak state capacity, violent conflict, war, and criminality. Empirical studies of these interactions demonstrate strong correlations between infant mortality (as a surrogate for standard of living) and violent conflict (Goldstone et al., 2005), and between state fragility and gender empowerment (Carment et al., 2006). Context specific factors contributing to these correlations are extensively documented in assessments of fragile and conflict affected states published by think tanks and academics as well as NGOs and multilateral agencies. They are also reflected in conceptual frameworks that have been prepared by, for example, the UK Prime Minister Strategy Unit to address instability risks (The Prime Minister's Strategy Unit 2006), or by the Clingendael Institute (2005) whose *Stability Assessment Framework* is now employed by the Netherlands government.

The origins of these contributions to our understanding of peace, violent conflict and development stem from the tragedy of growing inter- and intra-state violence and conflict that followed the end of the Cold War. Following nightmares such as Rwanda and the Former Yugoslavia of the first half of the 1990s, demand grew for more systematic attention by the development community to these challenges. In 1997, the Organisation for Economic Co-operation and Development (OECD) Development Assistance Committee, at a meeting among Ministers and Heads of Agencies, released a policy statement endorsing a comprehensive approach that demands development to play its role in conflict prevention and peace-building alongside economic, social, legal, environmental, and military instruments available to the international community (OECD Development Assistance Committee, 1997).

Reflection on lessons learned across the globe and by all OECD donor agencies, was broadened to include "policy coherence for development" in 2001. This document, that calls for increasing coherence among trade, finance and investment, foreign affairs and defence, and development polices that impact on conflict prevention (OECD, 2001, 13).

The OECD is not the only multilateral organization that has sought to define a "comprehensive" approach to human security. In 2001, the World Bank published *Voices of the Poor* – a study based on interviews with upwards to 20,000 impoverished people. Generated was a summary noting "sources of insecurity" that included health, livelihood, and institutional factors. In 2004, a UN General Assembly report highlighted the importance of development in a prevention framework. Articulating further the report stated "it is the indispensable foundation for a collective security system that takes prevention seriously" (UN General Assembly, 2004, 12).

In close cooperation with the Department of Foreign Affairs, the Canadian International Development Agency has contributed to the evolution of international norms that should guide all operations in fragile and conflict-affected states, including those of the military. Other relevant documents that represent a growing consensus among OECD countries and many multilateral organizations on what a comprehensive response to violent conflict, political instability, state fragility and poverty entails include the Millennium Development Goals (United Nations General Assembly, 2000), the *Principles and Good Practice of Humanitarian Donorship* (United Nations, 2003), the *Principles for Good International Engagement in Fragile States and Situations* (OECD Development Assistance Committee, 2007), the *Paris Declaration on Aid Effectiveness* (OECD, 2005) and the *Accra Agenda for Action* (OECD, 2008), the 3C Roadmap (Swiss Agency for Development and Cooperation, 2009), and the recent Dili declaration (OECD 2010) on a new vision for peace-building and statebuilding.

Those working at the intersection of development, peace, conflict prevention, peace building and peace support operations have a strong evidence-based perspective on what constitutes a comprehensive approach to this set of inter-related problems. This consensus reflects the views of several inter-related disciplines. Further improving practice, and achieving success over the longer term depends on deepening and widening this consensus and including other related disciplines and capabilities. It also requires sustained fiscal and political support and policy dialogue with national governments and other legitimate representatives within low-income countries struggling with these challenges on a daily basis.

Comprehensive Development in the Context of Violent Armed Conflict and Insurgency

Since 1990, Canadian Operations have continued to evolve toward a comprehensive approach of integrating security, governance and socioeconomic development activities. Grasping how to deal effectively with situations of active conflict and insurgency, while establishing a safe and secure context for recovery and development has become an arduous challenge. Without basic security and safety, efforts to trade, invest, and deliver services will remain stifled, undermining the impact and sustainability of external assistance.

A strategic framework for the role of development in multinational stability operations involves "blending civilian and military tools and enforcing co-operation between government departments" (Director General Joint Doctrine and Concepts 2006, p.11). In general, the formulation of such a strategic framework should assess the following: the legitimacy, authority, and capacity of the current regime; operational uncertainties and risks; financial, human and technical resources available to a donor country and their relevance to the requirements and needs; and other context specific features such as geography, climate, history, and culture. The various components of multidimensional operations need to be aligned with this initial diagnostic so that development programming can be situated within the social, political and economic reality on the ground.

The integration of security, governance and socio-economic development activities to achieve shared goals such as stability and legitimacy does not mean that the military delivers development or humanitarian assistance. In fact, the military does not have the required skills or capabilities to undertake such a task. For example, troops often rotate out of an operational theatre every six months, while development requires consistent presence over longer periods and strong country knowledge and experience. Instead, security forces create a positive space for humanitarian and development assistance by ensuring that local (formal and informal, state and non-state) security actors "stay in their lane." In the best cases, the military actually contributes to security system reform more generally and can ensure that all armed services are subject to civilian political control, the rule of law, financial accountability, and fiscal discipline.

Civil-military cooperation will always be a part of peace support doctrine and campaign planning. However, new types of operational arrangements need to be created so that assistance is offered in accordance with humanitarian principles. Legitimacy will accrue to operations conducted in ways that are visibly and consistently aligned with the humanitarian imperative, which includes the duty to protect civilians from harm, and to ensure that humanitarian action can proceed in a context of safety and neutrality. Concomitant to this imperative is an ongoing requirement to pursue all avenues available to reach an alternative, peaceful political settlement with those who choose armed violent conflict. This means effectively communicating and supporting avenues to sanctuary for those who wish to defect from groups using armed violence rather than non-violent political and social forms of protest and opposition to existing authority. In these settings, the basis for the legitimate conduct of counter-insurgency requires that international conventions and standards associated with the conduct of war, and the treatment of prisoners and detainees, be observed.[37]

The Role of Development in the "Clear – Hold – Build" Military Paradigm

Stability will remain elusive where other means of generating a political settlement are absent. Deploying an advanced military force into defined areas to conduct "clear" operations will end organized violent conflict and deprive insurgents of their base within the population. Operations that aim to "hold" such gains will reduce volatility within the affected geographic area while establishing a secure perimeter and linking these areas with other stable regions. In advancing toward "build," unity of effort increases to a tempo and level that can moderate insecurity and begin working on the structural requirements for recovery. The uncertainty associated with these processes is very high and they can be subject to reversals and setbacks. Progress can proceed at different rates across operational zones.

Effective stability operations must start with coherent, military-civilian collaboration to define and shape the engagement. This requires ongoing local analysis of the conflict, the insurgency, and the state, current social and economic development level and related capacity and governance. Paramount at the strategic level, is a broader knowledge of the insurgency, its protagonists, their capabilities, and the identification of opportunities to support other emerging leaders while building momentum and incentives for recovery.

During the "clear" phase, development operations will generally be limited to humanitarian action and support to local civil society actors and the protection of civilians and non-combatants. A balance must be struck between exclusively needs-based (humanitarian) and mission-based (strategically-targeted) programming. Early results, demonstrating commitment to justice and the rule of law, can be achieved by documenting human rights violations or other grievances that the local community has experienced.

During the "hold" or stabilization phase, development operations continue humanitarian action, and project further commitment to justice and the pro-active mediation of differences. Development activities that are geared specifically to the practical needs of the local community are supported, basic services are re-started, and vital infrastructure is rehabilitated by local civil and community development actors (to the extent possible). Central to the success of this effort is the management of expectations through proactive information outreach activities and open dialogue with local leaders, formal and informal. The goal is to create the necessary confidence and conditions for safety, security, civilian protection and political consensus required for long-term recovery.

In the "build" or early recovery phase, development objectives will most often be fully aligned with local and national development plans, geared to sustainability, and designed to further reinforce the confidence of citizens in a legitimate and accountable civil authority that can maintain public order (i.e., the rule of law and civilian security), and deliver basic economic and social services.

Within these unified operations, the nature of the humanitarian and development response will be context specific and will depend on the level of the security threat. The extent to which a donor government can build on the leadership, participation and capacity of local actors, while working to neutralize opposing forces, protect civilians and pursue stability and peace through negotiation and mediation at national and local levels will depend on the degree of security achieved. This is consistent with the US Army's approach to counter-insurgency (COIN) (US Marine Corps 2006).

To achieve unity of purpose and effort throughout these operations it is necessary to focus on those key elements that are the basis for national ownership and effectiveness. First, national civil and local authorities and NGOs demonstrate capabilities and performance in the provision of basic services that is required to win the consent of the population. Second, legitimate private sector activity increases, providing jobs and incomes that are independent of political or other power structures. Third, political dialogue and negotiation is ongoing at all levels to deal proactively with grievances to ensure that gains in reconciliation and peace-building are maintained. Fourth, the core functions of the state are supported, and the national, provincial and local functions of the executive, legislature, and judiciary are reinforced in the roles defined by the political settlement, the constitution and the national budget. Finally, there is a clear commitment to the protection and rehabilitation of the natural environment, including national and cultural monuments and non-renewable, high value, natural resources.

Different Means and Common Goals

Development assistance and armed violent conflict are very different ways of accomplishing what are in essence political goals. Research by Meisel and Aoudia on the role of "good governance" in the promotion of socio-economic development points out that it is a complex and difficult process as profound breaks and changes are implied for both groups and individuals. This involves "a radical transformation of the systems that lay down social, economic, and political rules on the basis of personal relations and rules that are in most cases not written down, to systems founded on impersonal law and the written word" (Meisel and Aoudia 2008, 24).

The study argues that social regulation systems in developing countries are mostly dominated by insider groups who can destabilise the balance of power in place by associating with violent factions or coalitions of factions, thus blocking the countries' development trajectories. If:

(a) Radical transformations in the "rules of the game" are required for economic growth, and;

(b) Economic growth is the most reliable long term means of reducing poverty and aid dependency, and increasing security, stability and legitimacy; then

(c) Integrated and comprehensive programming approaches need to recognize that development is inherently conflictual, and should include the skills, abilities and attitudes essential to effective negotiation, mediation and conflict resolution.

Development, understood as radical transformation will involve conflict and require efforts to address and build capacities that ensure that conflict remains non-violent and does not lead to state fragility and collapse.

The practical implications are significant. Investment in justice and security system reform is required to protect people from harm and abuse in order to avoid violent conflict. This principle became a new international security and human rights norm in September 2005 when the UN General Assembly formally adopted the doctrine of Responsibility to Protect (R2P): the principle that sovereign states have a responsibility to protect their own citizens from avoidable catastrophe, but that when they are unwilling or unable to do so, that responsibility must be borne by the broader community of states.

In 2007, the OECD DAC endorsed a Ministerial Statement on Security System Reform (SSR). The first requirement of good practice articulates three overarching objectives for donors' engagement in SSR: (i) improving basic security and justice service delivery; (ii) establishing an effective governance, oversight, and accountability system; and (iii) developing local leadership and ownership of a reform process to review the capacity and technical needs of the security system (OECD, 2007, 10).

The primary importance of civilian protection is at the heart of the hard lessons learned in counter-insurgency. Ensuring security in relation to the factors identified by the "Voices of the Poor" study mentioned above, will help win support among the population. They will also increase legitimacy, capacity and authority to block those movements toward radical transformation identified by Meisel and Aoudia. Additional recent academic research corroborates these views.[38] Not surprising security and justice systems in Afghanistan remain significant challenges. Without a safe and secure environment, enabling development and economic growth, the ability for Afghanistan to be removed as a haven for terrorism, is jeopardized.

In situations of active violent conflict and insurgency, the robust kinetic capabilities of armed forces are most likely to be deployed along side development and diplomatic capabilities. In addition to promoting peace through negotiations and making defection from insurgency attractive and viable, diplomats and military leaders must provide adequate and sustained support to ensure that military justice and security systems, are controlled by political processes that are legitimate and based on the rule of law. Development is aimed at improving social and economic conditions and opportunities while ensuring that related governance mechanisms exhibit increasing levels of national ownership and fiscal capacity for poverty reduction. As the economy becomes more diverse, resources for justice and security provided by the international community should be replaced by domestic financial, human, and technical capabilities.

Conclusion: Toward Principles for Comprehensive and Integrated Effectiveness

Given the above, the following principles should inform policy, operations, expectations, assessments of risk, and performance expectations:

Greater levels of integrated military/civilian planning and professional interaction are required. The goal is shared generation of alternative scenarios and plans, including performance measures and course corrections. Coordinating these scenarios and actions with other actors is essential and requires ongoing communication and consistent messages.

To be comprehensive, coordinated and coherent, the 3D PLUS arrangements need to exhibit high levels of whole of government and whole of system commitment from the political level to the operational. Siloed approaches to armed violence, insecurity, poverty and weak governance will not work. Alignment with other donor nations and regional, international and multilateral organizations is required.

Context-driven responses will constantly seek to encourage and reinforce local ownership, build legitimate local institutions, prevent setbacks into violence or the collapse of civil order, and promote accountability, transparency, and the rule of law.

Donor governments and implementing agencies need more bench strength. Donor governments need to invest in a deep pool or cross-trained personnel accustomed to working in diverse organizational cultures and settings. This could include personnel recruited and trained in the affected countries and regions as long as talent is not pulled from the affected state and society on a permanent basis.

Personnel from across the 3D PLUS construct require familiarity with a wide range of bureaucratic and specialized language, as well as a deep appreciation for local languages, customs, cultures, and practices. Without this degree of dexterity and flexibility, donor nations will have difficulty adapting to rapidly changing conditions and will not be able to communicate effectively to sustain political support for their mission.

Human capabilities that involve both security and civilian actors should balance short-term, visible gains while establishing the foundations for the rule of law, livelihoods, and sustained economic growth and employment. In this regard, a full spectrum of mutually-reinforcing development operations will be required within the period of stabilization – to ensure conflict prevention and crisis response and continuous focus on the foundations for long-term institution building that can be owned and advanced by the legitimate national and local authorities. This means that no single donor nation or organization can or should respond to these challenges alone.

While strengthening overall unity of effort, alignment and coherence, comprehensive operations require high degrees of delegated control and authority for implementation decisions. This operational flexibility and agility supports the overall strategic vision and recognizes that stability, security and socio-economic progress is reached at different rates across a country or region. A simultaneous mix of clear, hold and build activities will be required at any one time across the national territory and in bordering regions in order to ensure that insurgents, conflict entrepreneurs or rent seekers are not able to capitalize on power vacuums or grievances in any one locality.

The systematic consideration of risks, results and the potential for unintended consequences is assessed continuously and communicated clearly to the political level in order to sustain support for the mission.

An inclusive approach, that identifies marginalized groups and key constituencies, and reflects the different needs and requirements of women, men, and children, must ensure equitable access, participation and the sharing of benefits. Where possible, those disaffected with the insurgency need support and confidence to find sanctuary or safe haven within their communities, or to move to other communities where they can live in security and dignity.

The goals of the mission need to be defined in ways that are commensurate with available political, financial, and technical capabilities. This will encourage focus on a limited set of realistic, monitorable actions. These should be established where possible in full consultation with local and national authorities, with a critical mass of local and external resources and within a time frame that is adequate for the stated goals and objectives.

These principles are intended to demonstrate that it is possible to integrate knowledge and experience from a variety of disciplines so that truly comprehensive approaches may emerge as viable and effective solutions to the complex real-world problems of violent armed conflict, chronic instability and insecurity, and global poverty.

Chapter 11

MILITARY CONSIDERATIONS IN ASSISTING FRAGILE STATES

RICHARD ROY

For most who served in Western militaries from the late 1970s to the early 1990s, there was a clear and predictable threat, the Warsaw Pact. Those years, as well as those stretching back to the start of the Cold War, were spent training to repel the hordes expected to inundate Western Europe in conventional war. Subsequently, from the fall of the Berlin Wall until 9/11, the prime focus for many militaries was participating in humanitarian interventions or complex peace support operations. Here military forces were employed impartially to assist efforts to stabilize intricate yet largely internal conflicts under United Nations (UN) authorization and in many instances UN leadership. Since 9/11, while neutral UN missions continue, global threats to peace and security have changed. Militaries are now being used as a counter to more amorphous threats such as organized crime, piracy and terrorism, and other threats that erode international security. These emergent, difficult challenges call for new techniques and procedures. The different and evolving security responses that have developed were neither obvious nor entirely predictable beforehand. Likewise, the exact manner in which military forces will be employed in the future security environment is difficult to predict with any degree of certainty; however, there are indicators shedding some light for military planners.

Beyond the current international security situation, there are some obvious indicators of where and how military forces will be employed in the future. The "where" seems apparent; that is, failed or failing states will continue to exist within the global community of states. One method of promoting international security involves addressing the root causes

Security Operations in the 21st Century: Canadian Perspectives on the Comprehensive Approach, ed. M. Rostek and P. Gizewski. Montreal and Kingston: Queen's Policy Studies Series, McGill-Queen's University Press.

of threats, typically in the poorly governed areas of fragile and conflict-affected states. Historically, and often under the UN banner, the Canadian military has frequently been deployed to such areas. While fragile and conflict affected states are expected to remain a fixture within the community of states for the foreseeable future, how military forces will be specifically employed is less clear. But there are some constants. Military forces do what is prescribed in tactics, techniques and procedures (TTPs) and described in doctrine as a type of operation. While military TTPs are continually adapted on operations in response to an adversary's actions, they retain a baseline purpose and functionality. For instance, there remains a need for communications, cordons and checkpoints during all operations. Operations, such as non-combatant evacuation, forcible entry and others, are broad strokes of the application of military power. Between TTPs and the broad parameters of a military's type of operation most contingencies can be addressed. However, there is a recurring theme within conflict situations – a requirement to work collaboratively with a host of others organizations that now populate the battle space. The requirement to interact and collaborate with a multitude of actors in order to effectively contribute to the resolution of complex crises is called the comprehensive approach.

This chapter will discuss the utility of the comprehensive approach during operations in a fragile state. It will commence by examining the construct of the comprehensive approach within a number of models used by Malcolm Gladwell in order to clarify and emphasize the utility of the comprehensive approach in modern operations. This will be followed by a brief sketch of how a complex problem is generally solved. The chapter will then outline how the comprehensive approach was applied in three different cases: Haiti, Sudan and Afghanistan. Finally, the chapter will conclude with a statement on the overall value of a comprehensive approach.

A Glimpse of Gladwell

A coherent unified national strategy for all international engagements has great value. The works of Malcolm Gladwell reinforce this view postulating that the idea of seeking tipping points, the importance of norm entrepreneurs and the 10,000 hour journey to expert status can contribute to resolving conflict situations in an efficient and effective manner.

In *The Tipping Point: How Little Things Can Make a Big Difference* (2002), Gladwell discusses the importance of tipping points, how a seemingly insignificant action can push a system dramatically in a new direction. This concept is based on seeking a fuller understanding of the network or the complex adaptive system. In essence, Gladwell argues that the main challenge is to try and understand the best place to act upon a complex adaptive system in order to affect change and discover what activities might yield exponential shifts. From a strategic perspective, this can be seen as a preference for the relative merits of conflict prevention vice crisis intervention, a re-balance in the attention afforded a troubled system before a tipping point is reached that begets greater violence.

The tipping point is significant when considering fragile states for a number of reasons. First, it demonstrates the non-linearity of a modern complex crisis. Linear planning and purely quantitative solutions – more troops or more aid – are severely constrained and may only contribute to success in a minor way. Second, highlighting the necessity of framing the problem from a qualitative perspective demonstrates that economy of effort is possible in assisting fragile states. A detailed awareness of the networks can show where small, incremental, quality actions can deliver dramatic improvement particularly if wedded to the desires of the host partners. Fewer resources are therefore required in-country if they are narrowly focussed; this allows assistance to be provided to more partners albeit at lower levels but with more value-added. Third, evaluations of progress need to be undertaken cautiously to ensure the right things are measured when tipping points are being leveraged. Monies handed out, infrastructure projects completed, or even social engineering programs do not necessarily sway the local balance of influence and power sufficiently to tip progress in a positive direction. Even if they do sway favourably, measuring the depth and degree of that movement is purely subjective. Those conducting the campaign, somewhat reflecting Gladwell's concept of "coup d'oeil," are best placed to judge progress (Gladwell, 2005, 44). As previously mentioned, the concept applies at the strategic level not only with regard to conflict prevention but in selecting where to best deploy Canadian resources so as to cause a relative benefit domestically which may in turn free up further resources for additional engagements.

A second Gladwellian aspect is that of the requirement for norm entrepreneurs. A norm entrepreneur seizes on new norms and acculturates them, carries them forward until they are well accepted, become the standard. The Government of Canada (GoC) has performed this function with respect to the Anti-Personnel Land Mine Treaty and its continuing advocacy of aspects of the *Responsibility to Protect* project. Militaries themselves filter through this process as new trends and ideas emerge, are examined and, if validated, integrated into doctrine and training; a phenomenon seen in the militaries' evolving use of the revolution in military affairs, the effects based approach to operations and most recently the re-discovery of counter-insurgency. For fragile states there is a key norm that has yet to be discovered and carried forward but enormous energy is being invested in discovering it. This norm is the clear vision of how to meld the disparate actors together to achieve success – a vision of victory in military parlance, though the comprehensive approach is giving some hints at the broad measures needed. Three types of actors are trying to build a useful vision. The first is the current practitioners in the field. Existing practices and operational policies are under continual review in those fragile states where the international community is present. Organizations deployed today are more agile and adaptable in analysing and modifying their plans and approaches. The second is the think tanks and institutions that study and publish in the functional areas that support state building in fragile states. Their work aids in further developing the range of potential tasks and solutions that can aid in work in these nations. The final actor includes historians and other academics that provide details of options for alternative future approaches based case studies of what worked or did not work on past campaigns. While this discussion has weighed heavily on how we can adjust our norms for greater success within a broad comprehensive approach framework, the key individuals to carry norms forward, of course, must be the local population. Greater study and understanding of the norms, and the entrepreneurs who move these norms forward, will provide the foundation from which we are better able to understand what needs to be done, including cross–organizational functionality, in failed and fragile states.

Gladwell postulates that it takes over 10,000 hours to become an expert in any particular discipline. Gladwell's examples included music and hockey but are also applicable to diplomacy, development and defence (Gladwell, 2008, 15-68). Expertise is developed in a number of ways – practice, experience and study – but of course this all demands time. It takes many hours to become a professional, a process much easier when there is a professional body of knowledge available. Responding to the wide variety of needs in a fragile state reflects the need for a wide team of experts to address its myriad problems through a comprehensive approach. It is more than evident that teams from across departments, agencies, nations and international organizations must join together to address the complex and disruptive issues facing a fragile state. Some of this team formation improves with recognizing the roles, tasks and accountabilities of other actors involved in a mission. Despite the experiences shared in an operational theatre some aspects are best left to the individuals with the requisite functional and the professional expertise. For example, while frequent contacts will be required between military leaders and local authorities, detailed political plans and planning are best left to diplomats. While military resources will be committed to short-term construction projects they should be used to shape the longer term programmes based on the advice and planning of development experts. Finally, the details of the security aspects of a counter-insurgency are best left to military professionals.

The Modern Security Environment

All challenges in the modern security environment involve the interaction of complex adaptive systems (CAS), the search for useful knowledge and the need of suitable partners for planning and implementation.[39] Within all situations multiple CAS are interacting. Spawned by conditions that normally develop over a long period of time, a crisis in a host nation will involve an intricate interaction of dynamic local, national and regional social networks either competing or cooperating to achieve their own ends. Intervening elements themselves are CAS that bring increased layers of complexity to a situation as they attempt to coordinate and collaborate with the multiple entities that populate crisis environments. Not surprisingly, the activities and interests of adversarial groups starkly influence what can be accomplished. Organizational complexities aside, it remains difficult to properly frame the nature of the problem without the required detailed research and study of the condition in any particular fragile state. While sufficient information may be available in government once it becomes seized of an issue, frequently, outside sources of knowledge – subject matter experts – that have monitored and studied the country are required for effective strategic framing. It is widely acknowledged that military forces alone cannot provide the complete solution to many of the challenges facing a fragile state. It is also true that no singular organization, agency or actor can deliver viable long-term solutions. Partners are required – security, development and diplomatic and others – in all cases to help fragile state build the capacities necessary for effective governance.

Complexity in the modern security environment has a direct bearing on both planning and the requirement for adaptability. Planning for most militaries, to a great degree, is about risk mitigation and managing the inherent complexity of its own forces and functions. There are three important planning norms that demand careful attention in complex operations. First, military linear planning – a presumption of the ability to link cause and effect – is unhelpful. Notwithstanding the claims of the "apostles" of effects-based planning, such linkages rarely exist. This is especially evident in the presumption that second or even third and fourth order effects can be somehow predicted. Second, the deeply embedded planning culture in militaries often conditions them to believe their methodologies have universal application. While an awareness of other organizations' planning methodologies is valuable, many other organizations have thrived without the benefits of military planning. Third, kinetic operations retain a primacy in most military plans despite the useful contribution military forces can make delivering stability and reconstruction. So, for collective planning to improve, militaries need to be cautious about becoming fixated on linear processes, about imposing the mantle of their planning methodologies on others, and they must explore ways of applying their organizational mass differently within the networked environment. No plan is ever perfect. As a plan is executed it must be closely monitored and assessed so that it can be modified as conditions change and CAS respond to it. Adaptation must be responsive to the level at which a plan is implemented: immediate at the micro/tactical level, rapid at the operational level, and timely at the macro/strategic level. In order to retain the initiative to shape and drive progress during an intervention, all elements must be capable of adaptation as conditions change. This does not apply to military forces alone.

Finally, when dealing with the modern security environment, there is a requirement for the formulation and translation of strategy from the national to the tactical level. The purpose of a strategy for a particular intervention is to determine the scale and scope of national involvement. It must ensure participation, supports national interests and objectives, and must set limits on the dedication of national resources, energy, and attention. Pragmatically, Canadian interests are best served when all national efforts in a specific area are coordinated under an overarching unifying strategy. The formulation of this coherent strategy tends to be problematic. In the host country, particularly in hostile environments, facing shared risk and danger and operating under an intense sense of urgency, whole-of-government (WoG) teams coalesce and can integrate effectively to manage the combined Canadian contributions. Equal focus and seamlessness is not mirrored at the national level as the distractions of bureaucracy, accountabilities, routine and distance impede crisis management. Furthermore, viable national strategies can be obscured by a fixation on reporting a mass of details that while revealing our own activities confirm little of the actual, local progress – measurement substituting for strategy. Therefore, even without including political considerations, the formulation of national strategy remains a significant challenge and they may continue to be only incrementally constructed over time.

Recently, with the completion of the inter-departmental study *Sustaining Canada's Engagement in Acutely Fragile and Conflict-Affected Situations* (Government of Canada, 2009b), there has been some work dedicated towards refining Canada's strategic procedures. This is critical considering the likelihood of our future involvement in these types of situations. The study outlines collective initiatives that could advance the formulation of Canadian strategy including revising funding mechanisms, developing a deployable civilian capacity for Government of Canada (GoC) and integrating intelligence preparation and advice more fully. Streamlining intelligence is seen as particularly important as it serves as the baseline for strategic framing and is crucial to help identify key trigger points and gateways when planning interventions. The study includes suggested criteria to aid in the evaluation of when Canada should intervene though recognizing that such decisions are solely within the purview of Cabinet. The study prompted a review of the tools individual departments commonly use to assist in international interventions that helped expand shared inter-departmental understanding. It points to useful techniques, such as horizontal management, that are tested models to help understand whole of government and comprehensive approach measures. The study is an important first step in addressing a select strategic issue. Further improvements could be accomplished by continuing the definition, clarification, and promotion of shared awareness of departmental roles. Much more is left to be done to improve the ability of the GoC to frame and conceive coherent strategy.

The Use of Military Forces

The purpose for which military forces are used at the strategic level is extremely important. Their commitment to operations represents an immediate and direct demonstration of national intent. Even when folded into coalition or UN operations, they signal national intentions; witness India's contribution to peacekeeping missions as it bid for a UN Security Council seat (Krishnasamy, 2003, 263-80). Fundamentally, military force achieves its ends through three means: coercion, deterrence, persuasion or combinations thereof (Schelling, 1966). To be effective, the means must be underpinned by operational and tactical competence. To be prepared and responsive for deployments, military forces must be constantly scanning the current operational environment to determine where they will likely be committed. An intelligence and analytical heavy process, this allows for the preparation of contingency plans and option analysis. In combination with this predictive stance, doctrine is usually developed for the typical type of operations that the GoC may order, such as a non-combatant evacuation operation (NEO) or peace support operations (PSO). The ability to pre-plan for deployment, use non-prescriptive models (doctrine), and benefit from deeply embedded planning cultures, allows military forces to be well prepared, adaptable, and forward looking on modern operations. This has proven particularly useful in assisting fragile states.

There are a number of other factors that are important when considering the employment of military forces. First, they generally derive their effect by being employed in mass. It is through their mass presence that they can achieve the effects of coercion, deterrence and persuasion. Mass allows for the application of overwhelming, carefully planned and controlled force and violence to deliver those effects. Sufficient mass provides the blanket security that permits other actors to deploy on a smaller, more selective scale. Some of this mass is associated with the military's need to be self-sufficient. Second, militaries by and large formulate doctrine for all types of operations so that the knowledge of how to best respond to particular challenges is well distributed and well understood across the deployed forces. Most other actors have their own doctrine though they may choose not to recognize it as such.[40] Third, the use of military force, certainly in the case of Canada, remains bounded by the Law of Armed Conflict (LOAC) and tightly prescriptive rules of engagement. They do not conduct international operations under human rights law, the underpinning of most national legal systems, an issue leads to confused expectations from some actors (Watkin, 2004, 1-34). Additionally, the expectation that stepping away from our own Western legal norms will confer some advantage, often suggested due to the practices of our irregular adversaries, are unfounded given that LOAC generally treats the conditions and requirements of irregular warfare. Fourth, existing military capabilities have generally proven their utility in conflicts in fragile states. Finally, to a great extent military forces can provide security assistance to a host nation on a relatively value-neutral basis. From a Canadian perspective, Western militaries are not deployed to promote imperialist or post-colonial agendas.

Select Cases

In the following section three atypical examples of how the Canadian military has been used to assist in fragile states will be advanced as general models for potential future involvement. The first is the disaster response in Haiti, the second a combination of capacity building and advice in Sudan, and the final, a full scale counter-insurgency campaign in support of a nascent government in Afghanistan.

Haiti. Reflective of both Canada's policy to aid those touched by disaster and its close ties to the affected nation, mere hours after an earthquake struck Haiti on the 12 January 2010, Canadian government mechanisms were mobilized to guide the urgent assistance required. The Interdepartmental Task Force on Natural Disasters was convened that evening and the Interdepartmental Strategic Support Team (ISST) was despatched to evaluate the situation early the next morning. The ISST, composed of personnel from Canadian International Development Agency (CIDA), the Department of Foreign Affairs and International Trade (DFAIT) and members of the Disaster Assistance Response Team (DART) of the Canadian Forces (CF), arrived in Port-au-Prince within 24 hours of the earthquake. This initial element, flown in on the newly acquired C-17s of the CF, was quickly augmented as the magnitude of the disaster became evident. Besides the availability of strategic airlift, the capability of Canada to respond quickly was based on the well established procedures in the GoC for responding to disasters of this nature: the interdepartmental task force convenes regularly, well established standing operating procedures exist, and an immediate response team, the ISST is well organized and trains regularly. The departments worked closely together ensuring rapid inflow of Canadian aid, personnel, troops and materiel and the outflow of those Canadians who wished to be evacuated. Haiti did reveal the need for an additional higher level decision-making mechanism, for greater cross government awareness of the parameters of strategic movement and for clarification of chains of authority, but in general coordination functioned well at the strategic level.

The close coordination at the national level was evident on the ground in Haiti. The CF elements worked intimately both with its whole-of-government partners and diverse range of other actors, typically in a supporting role. The CF Joint Task Force Commander clarified and maintained this supporting focus from his first meeting with the Head of Mission (HoM), the Canadian ambassador to Haiti. Their subsequent close partnership allowed them to improve the delivery of Canada's assistance. A temporary defence attaché was placed at the embassy to facilitate communications and effective use of liaison officers (LOs) proved crucial. LOs were exchanged between all departments deployed as well as with other key actors such as the UN and the US forces. CF plans within theatre were closely tied to the HoM's objectives and woven into the activities of the UN cluster system,[41] the overarching mechanisms for coordination. The comprehensive approach informed the activities in the various sectors: in Jacmel, for instance, the DART, working through their CIDA and DFAIT LOs, assisted and complimented the work being conducted through the local UN cluster groups; the DART provided security details, reinforced by naval landing parties, delivered clean water, constructed latrines and conducted a medical outreach program. The DART's capability to rapidly integrate into the response was based on joined-up pre-deployment exercises with other government department actors and its core focus and understanding of humanitarian operations. Within the Royal 22 Regiment (R22R) sector, a different approach was employed but was equally successful and primarily rested with a command driven philosophy. Based on his previous experience, the commanding officer knew of the value, role and potential contribution of many of the other actors operating in his sector. He ensured that members from other government departments were fully welcomed and supported as team members and that most activities were orientated towards developing the capabilities of others to deliver assistance in lieu of the CF.

Sudan. Canada's support to the African Union's mission in Darfur was organized along different lines. It started as more of an ad hoc structure. The Ottawa portion thereof was known as the Sudan Task force. The nucleus resided within DFAIT but drew heavily on the advice and assistance of the other departments involved in the mission. The lead components of the team operated out of the Canadian embassy in Addis Ababa, Ethiopia and carried out the daily, detailed liaison and coordination with the African Union (AU) and its Darfur Integrated Task Force (DITF). Request for support received from the AU were filtered through the embassy back to the Sudan Task Force. The Task Force would determine whether the request could be filled, whether simple or complex, through consultation with the other government partners. For example, aviation fuel for the Canadian contracted airframes in Darfur was continually a troublesome issue. Ensuring adequate and sufficient supply involved extensive consultation with both CF aviation fuel quality experts as well as the participation of CIDA fuel contracting experts. Rarely accorded the attention or credit the mission may have been due, a thorough lessons learned study was conducted at its conclusion to aid in preparing for future missions.

The response on the ground – in Addis Ababa, Khartoum, and Darfur – was focused on the singular goal of building African capabilities and capacities to deal with peace support operations. Similar to Canada's supporting role in the Congo in the 1960s (Moir, 1962), the objective was to enable the African Union to carry out the ongoing mission and build core competencies for future missions. Support included advice pertaining to operational planning in general, the relevance and importance of rules of engagement, general aspects of peacekeeping, and the importance of phasing and coordinating strategic air movements. Assistance to DITF, provided by embedded staff, included planning and controlling air operations, contacting and logistic mentoring and training to operate a joint intelligence centre. For the troops in the field, Canada provided a wide range of equipment and supplies. This included everything from the complex (helicopters and fixed winged aircraft and their fuel supplies) to the relatively simple (flak vests, goggles and maps). The most operationally significant items may have been the 105 armoured personnel carriers, 100 Grizzlies and five Huskies, provided in 2005. This fleet required that the operators be provided detailed training beforehand, that they be painted an acceptable colour – white, that ammunition be stockpiled for them, and that suitable maintenance arrangements be organized. All these activities benefited from the close cooperative interaction between government partners to implement programs with a wide variety of actors (comprehensive approach) thereby allowing the African Union to focus on the support and protection of the people of Darfur.

Afghanistan. The structures for the current counter-insurgency campaign in Afghanistan are much more robust than those for the previous two examples. The higher levels of government have been more directly involved with a Cabinet Committee on Afghanistan having been established and the Privy Council Office exercising a more direct oversight role. In this instance, the lead departments have core staff that focus solely on Afghanistan; this includes elements in DFAIT, the CIDA Afghan Task Force and Canadian Expeditionary Force Command. Many other departments and agencies, in their own ways, have contributed enormously; this includes components of Public Safety Canada, Correction Services Canada, Canadian Border Services and others. The governance structures both in Ottawa and in Afghanistan have grown and evolved since the 2006 deployment to Kandahar. This mission has pointed to a serious gap in government capabilities, a limited ability to deploy civilians. The ability to deliver effective administrative services reflects on a government's legitimacy and can be a critical component in resolving a counter-insurgency (Joiner, 1967, 540-58); capacity building in this area demands civilian experts, making this a critical issue. This point, raised in *Sustaining Canada's Engagement,* has led to a set of initiatives to improve this capability thereby signalling the importance and contribution to modern operations.

The Canadian mission in Afghanistan has been continually improved as greater familiarity with the environment was gained and better working accommodations with partners were established. The organization of the provincial reconstruction team (PRT), initially just a mirror of what was being trialed elsewhere, shows this incremental evolution. At first a military centric entity operating within a limited geographic area, it grew into a multi-functional WoG team carefully integrated with the Task Force staff, participating fully in joint planning and operating across the breadth of the province. The conceptualization and conduct of Canadian counter-insurgency has been improved and reformed in response to the actions of the Taliban. Given the massed target that the Taliban mustered in 2006, the conventional-battle orientated OP MEDUSA was the appropriate counter. With a shift in Taliban tactics, the Canadian approach was modified (Forseberg, 2009). In mid-2009, OP KANTALO refocused Canadian priorities onto Kandahar City where over 80 percent of the province's population resides. This new village-focus put population security rightly to the fore of the Canadian mission. This series of operations has reinforced the need for detailed coordination at many levels, for instance, streaming quick impact projects into development and linking together the steps of clear, build, hold – that reflect the benefits from a unified national strategy in theatre.[42] The wealth of contacts within Canadian networks in theatre allowed for the Canadian WoG plan to be linked to the actions of a multitude of partners. Granted, achieving this sophistication has been part of a slow and incremental process for no initial plan survives its launch and sufficient information is not usually available to resolve a complex situation when observing from afar. It took time to learn the intricacies of the Afghani networks that needed to be identified, monitored, moderated and molded. Both Afghanis and Canadians have been well served from this ability to adjust and adapt.

Conclusion

The military has many distinctive roles to play in providing assistance to fragile and conflict affected states. As cited in the examples above, these missions extend from humanitarian assistance, to advice and mentoring, to full-scale and complex war fighting. What is certain is that the modern operational space is populated by an enormous number of actors. From a military perspective therefore, there is value in knowing the roles and functions of the other actors within that space. All these actors combine in an array of complex adaptive systems. As suggested by Gladwell, there is a need to seek out the experts to help us understand these networks and help select effective points of action that may serve as tipping points. At a minimum the CF must prepare itself to work with all and any that can aid in the resolution of a complex challenge.

The GoC will continue to employ its resources to solve problems both on the domestic and international front. There are some general maxims that now inform these engagements: they are never *only* a military problem, though the military may be a key enabler; complexity demands mobilizing all actors possible to contribute to both defining the problem and executing programs designed to ameliorate the problem; strategic resources are scarce and must be well spent; and solutions, procedures, lessons and detailed analysis are often best considered ahead of time and not in the urgency of the moment. Heeding these general maxims will improve Canada's ability to respond to international crisis thereby reinforcing its role as a key contributor on the international stage.

PART IV
COMPREHENSIVE
APPROACH TODAY –
DOMESTIC OPERATIONS

Chapter 12

COMPREHENSIVE APPROACH, DOMESTIC OPERATIONS: INTEGRATED BORDER ENFORCEMENT TEAMS

TODD HATALEY

This chapter discusses the comprehensive approach in the domestic context, more specifically in the context of policing, with a specific example drawn from an operational section within the Royal Canadian Mounted Police (RCMP) called Integrated Border Enforcement Teams (IBET). To be sure, the incorporation of a multi-agency approach for ensuring security within the domestic environment is not a new concept. For decades, police agencies have worked with partner agencies and community groups, which has served to increase effectiveness and the ultimate goal of creating a safer domestic environment. At the same time, however, the relationship between police and partner agencies is not static, and has evolved along, what the present author argues, is a path dependent trajectory. The result is an ever-increasing move towards cooperation and coordination between domestic agencies (at the municipal, provincial and federal levels), as well as at the international level, suggesting an increase in horizontal and vertical integration. Using the RCMP's Integrated Border Enforcement Team program as an example, this chapter argues that domestic law enforcement has moved from a model of joint enforcement to a model of joint jurisdiction. Moreover, this shift towards joint jurisdiction can be tracked along a path dependent continuum marked by points of critical juncture.

Security Operations in the 21st Century: Canadian Perspectives on the Comprehensive Approach, ed. M. Rostek and P. Gizewski. Montreal and Kingston: Queen's Policy Studies Series, McGill-Queen's University Press.
© 2011 Queen's Centre for International Relations, Queen's University at Kingston. All rights reserved.

Introduction

The security goals of most police agencies in Canada today are not remarkably different from the goals of NATO allies currently operating in Afghanistan. According to the NATO website, ISAF's major objective in Afghanistan is "assisting the Afghan authorities in providing security and stability, in order to create the conditions for reconstruction and development" (North Atlantic Treaty Organization 2010). By comparison, the Toronto Police Service states that their mission is to deliver "police services in partnership with our community to keep Toronto the best and safest place to be" (Toronto Police Service 1999). Canada's national police force, the Royal Canadian Mounted Police, similarly echoes this goal of providing safe communities in their mission statement, committed to "preserve the peace, uphold the law and provide quality service in partnership with our communities" (Royal Canadian Mounted Police 2006). Within these three examples are two important similarities: the goal of creating secure environments; and doing so in partnership with local stakeholders, in short, a comprehensive approach to creating the necessary conditions for legitimate governance.

From a policing perspective, the comprehensive approach to creating secure domestic environments has been around for some time, but has not been articulated by a common name or model. The Community Policing Model, which has been used by many police forces in North America and Europe, is one of the most widely used and promoted policing models. The United States Department of Justice defines the Community Policing Model as a strategy that promotes the use of partnerships and problem solving models to proactively address issues of public safety. Community Policing is composed of three components: community partnerships, organizational structures to support those partnerships and a problem-solving model that includes the use of stakeholder partnerships. (United States Department of Justice 2009). In the Province of Ontario the Ontario Chiefs of Police adopted the Community Policing Model in 1996 (Community Policing Advisory Council of Ontario, 1996). Similarly, the Royal Canadian Mounted Police have operationalized a community-policing model using an approach known by the acronym CAPRA (Clients, Acquiring and Analyzing Information, Partnerships, Response, Assessment) (Royal Canadian Mounted Police 2009a). The CAPRA model encourages a problem solving method that incorporates partnership with local and other interested stakeholders.

For police agencies, the development of partnerships for solving law enforcement related problems has become a standard training and operating procedure. From the time of initial training, new recruits are taught that engaging partnerships with community stakeholders is an effective strategy for augmenting limited resources as a means of achieving secure communities. Moreover, by engaging community stakeholders in the problem solving process, the community takes some of the ownership for the problem, the process and the solution.

The engagement between law enforcement and other stakeholders exists on multiple levels. Up to this point the paper has focused almost exclusively on community policing – what might be described as uniformed general duties police work. Examples of partner agencies frequently engaged on this level include social services, schools, health agencies, community groups, and courts, to name a few. With an operational focus on the local or community level, relationships between law enforcement agencies and the partners they engage, tend to reflect common goals within their respective area of operation.

Beyond the community level, specialized law enforcement units, have continued to apply the partnership model on an increasingly larger and complex scale, integrating partnerships within unified organizational structures. Specialized law enforcement units refer to investigational teams with a specific mandate. For example, Proceeds of Crime units have a mandate to investigate and prosecute criminal activity pertaining to offense related property, the property gained through criminal activity and money laundering (Royal Canadian Mounted Police 2009b). Moreover, many of these units are integrated both horizontally and vertically, including amongst them partners from various levels of government and various government agencies. The RCMP's Integrated Proceeds of Crime unit, for example, contains partners, working within the same office, from the following agencies:

- Public Prosecution Service of Canada
- Canada Border Services Agency
- Public Safety Canada
- Seized Property Management Directorate
- Canada Revenue Agency
- Forensic Accounting Management Group
- Various Provincial and Municipal Law Enforcement Agencies (Royal Canadian Mounted Police 2009b)

Examples of specialized and integrated units in the RCMP also include:

- Integrated National Security Enforcement Teams (INSET)
- Integrated Market Enforcement Teams (IMET)
- Marine Security Enforcement Teams (MSET)
- Commercial Crime Investigations
- Drug Investigations
- Immigration and Passport Investigations
- Integrated Border Enforcement Teams.

The Comprehensive Approach as a law enforcement concept shares many similarities with the concept as it is expressed by the military. In law enforcement the comprehensive approach uses a different terminology, but it effectively shares the same goals – that being creating a more secure environment for legitimate governance in partnership with other stakeholders. Increasingly, as noted above, law enforcement agencies have moved towards an integrated policing model for specialized investigational units. The next section of this paper will look specifically at the model used by Integrated Border Enforcement Teams to fulfill their mandate of intelligence gathering and law enforcement along the Canada – United States border.

Integrated Border Enforcement Teams

The first Integrated Border Enforcement Team was developed in 1996 in response to the trans-border drug trade in the lower mainland of British Columbia. The model was developed to bring together partner agencies dealing with the specific problem of cross-border drug criminality (initially defined as trafficking), but was soon expanded to include other cross-border criminal activities such as the illegal movement of people, weapons, money and cigarettes. Following the events of September 11, 2001, IBET was rapidly expanded to cover the entire Canada-United States border with 15 separate teams. The expansion of IBET in the post 9/11 period represents, in my opinion, simply the continuation of policies initiated before 9/11 (this will be expanded on further in the chapter). Paul Pierson would explain this expansion in terms of institutional continuity, accelerated by a focusing event (9/11) (Pierson 2004). In addition to this expansion, the mandate changed from trans-border criminality to national security, defined as identifying, investigating and interdicting persons and organizations that pose a threat to national security.

The IBET structure is one composed of partner agencies operating under a joint management structure that is led by the RCMP. Partner agencies are drawn from across all levels of government and international partnerships as well. Although IBET is a RCMP led program, partnerships include: Canada Border Services Agency, Provincial and Municipal police, tribal police and American agencies such as the Border Patrol, Immigration and Customs Enforcement, Customs and Border Protection and state and local law enforcement. At the most senior level, IBET is managed by an International Joint Management Team, and at the local level by a regional or Local Joint Management Team. Local management meetings take place on a regular basis (generally weekly). Frequent meetings allow for partner agencies to establish the necessary working relationships, determine group priorities, share information and intelligence, set priorities and to plan operations.

Integration with core members of IBET is done through a close working relationship, which in many cases means working in the same office space, formal scheduled meetings, and regular informal contact. In addition, IBET maintains open lines of communication through predetermined links, interoperable communications systems, standardized mapping capability and open lines of intelligence sharing.

The joint management arrangement is critical for the working relationship of partner agencies, as well as for setting objectives and priorities. Joint management provides one of the key mechanisms for joint enforcement. The idea of joint enforcement is important since it sets a baseline for evaluating where we have come from in the last fifteen years and where we are heading. In the simplest terms, joint enforcement means that law enforcement units, from different levels of government and different governments work together sharing information and resources for the purpose of investigating criminal organizations operating on both sides of the border. Although there is a shared enforcement mandate, the jurisdiction of the respective agencies remains relatively intact. In other words, American law enforcement officers are not operating in Canada and vice versa.

In April 2009 the International Joint Management Team produced a strategic plan and future vision for IBET. That plan concluded that by 2015 all IBETs would be: fully integrated and strategically located, have a cross-designated law enforcement capability, and operate within a standard and common model with appropriate legislation on both sides of the border (Oliver 2009). In short, the future of IBET is a move beyond the joint enforcement model to a joint jurisdiction model.

Joint or shared jurisdiction means having designated Canadian and American law enforcement agents empowered to operate on both sides of the border with some enforcement capability. The border becomes a zone in which certain agents are trained and authorized to enforce the laws of either country. This represents a totally integrated and seamless enforcement blanket that is not interrupted by the presence of an international boundary. There are currently two programs in existence that represent this kind of joint jurisdiction arrangement: Shiprider and Border Enforcement Security Task Force (BEST).

The Canada – United States Shiprider program, official known as the Integrated Maritime Security Operations is a cross-border maritime law enforcement operation conducted in shared waters and co-managed by the RCMP and the US Coast Guard. Shiprider involves reciprocal arrangements by which law enforcement personal from Canada and the United States work along side on board each other's vessels in sovereign waters of both countries. The 2007 Canada – US Framework Agreement on Integrated Cross-Border Maritime Law Enforcement Operations is the agreement under which the program operates (Public Safety Canada

2009). Shiprider is governed in Canada under Part 1 Section 7.(1)(d) of the *RCMP Act*.[43] In the United States the Shiprider program is governed under Title 19 USC 1401.[44] Currently Shiprider is restricted by time and geography. Operations can only take place in designated locations for designated periods of time. Shiprider projects have taken place in Cornwall, Detroit/Windsor, during the Olympics and most recently during the G8/20 in Toronto.

Border Enforcement Security Task Force (BEST) is an United States Immigration and Customs Enforcement (ICE) led operation, that like Shiprider, allows law enforcement agents from Canada to operate along side ICE agents in the US to enforce US law. BEST was initiated along the US – Mexico border in 2005, but has since expanded to include locations along the border with Canada at Blaine, Washington, Detroit, Buffalo, and Massena, NY. Canadian partners working with the ICE led BEST program include: Canada Border Services Agency, the RCMP and the Ontario Provincial Police.[45] Like the IBET and Shiprider Programs, BEST allows for an integrated enforcement strategy, and the ability to conduct operations beyond the traditional restrictions imposed by international boundaries.

IBET, Shiprider and BEST represent an evolution in a comprehensive approach to border security. Cooperation between Canadian law enforcement agencies and between Canadian and American law enforcement agencies has always been high. However, these programs have pushed the institutional arrangements, developing frameworks for working together and integrating not only Canadian resources, but also American. The next section of this chapter will develop a theoretical argument detailing an explanation for why changes in border enforcement have occurred in this manner.

Borders, Security, Institutions and Change

Theoretically framing any political investigation presents a number of issues. While the goal of conceptualizing theoretically any political issue is to move beyond the descriptive, to explain the phenomenon in question in a normative context, and in doing so to provide some degree of predictive capacity, all theoretical lenses present some degree of bias. This section illustrates that a constructivist/institutional analysis incorporating a framework based on timing, path dependence and critical events can be useful for explaining the changing dynamic of borders and border security.

The one term that needs to be clarified is "institutions." This paper takes the position that borders are institutions that direct and constrain individuals and groups (used interchangeably) to behave in a certain manner, and therefore, using an institutional analysis to explain strategic and functional change to border security is appropriate. Immergut (1998) identifies three separate branches of institutional scholarship: rational choice, organization theory and historical institutions. Although these approaches appear diverse (Hall and Taylor, 1996) she argues that there is a common theme linking these institutional approaches. All institutional approaches, she maintains, are concerned with analyzing the effect of rules and procedures on the preferences expressed by human actors (Immergut 1998, p.25) Institutions have two roles: they both constrain certain behaviours, as well as induce other behaviours. Institutions act as filters that value particular behaviours over others, either in the goals that political actors seek to achieve or in the means they use to achieve these goals. Institutions do not determine behaviour, but rather "provide a context for action that if we examine them with sensitivity to their purpose, help us to understand why actors make the choices they do" (Hall and Taylor, 1996, 26).

March and Olsen (1998) define institutions as a "relatively stable collection of practices and rules defining appropriate behaviour for specific groups of actors in specific situations." The practices and rules, they maintain, are embedded in "structures of meaning and schemes of interpretation that explain and legitimize particular identities and the practices and rules associated with them." Moreover, they also assert that the practices and rules are embedded in the resources and allocation of resources that make it possible for individuals and collectivities to act in a certain way, and to penalize those that challenge proper or expected behaviour.

Onuf, Kubalkova, and Kowert (1998), in concurrence with March and Olsen (1998), maintain that institutions are a stable, but not fixed, pattern of rules and related practices, which make people into agents, who in turn conduct themselves within the context of the institution, maintaining some degree for human choice. Thus, individuals act as agents[46] constrained and directed, to varying degrees, by a contextual understanding that defines appropriate behaviour. Borders, and the security frameworks in place at borders, therefore, can be understood as a process that is constructed and maintained by not only material items, but also, and possibly more importantly, by social and discursive practices. Therefore, as an institution, borders are dynamic, in not only the material context (resources and size of force used for security), but also in the context of the ideas that organize, motivate and frame the issues (security or trade, for example) that define each respective organization.

Institutions play an important role in defining social reality in the constructivist agenda. Wendt (1992), who defines institutions as a relatively stable set or structure of identities and interests, claims that they are often codified as formal rules and norms, and as Onuf et al. (1998, 61) asserts, give society structure. Despite this, institutions have no motivational force except by virtue of actors' participation in collective knowledge. Wendt (1992, 398) further argues that institutions are primarily cognitive entities that do not exist apart from actors' ideas about how the world works. Thus, institutions are by no means homogenous amongst the general population. In the context of borders this means that some groups may view borders as necessary for the maintenance of sovereignty and security, while other groups may see borders as an unnecessary barrier to trans-border commerce.

Collective identity creates what constructivists term social facts. The acceptance by the collective consciousness of a norm or behaviour creates at the simplest level meaning and at a higher level a constitutive role. The fact that the existence of institutions is linked directly to the will of collective identity does not detract from the power of institutions to affect the behaviour patterns of individuals or social groups. Wendt (1992, 398) explains, as a collective knowledge, institutions have an existence over and above the individuals who happen to embody them at the moment. In this way, institutions have a persuasive character that directs and bounds individual and collective behaviour, and to some degree choice. Institutions are, however, at the same time human constructs, (Grafstein 1988) and as such can be altered by human or agent input. While institutions can be static, characterized by a stable set of behaviours and expectations, they can also be dynamic, producing new sets of expectations and behaviours.

Viewing the provision of border security as a dynamic institution suggests that it has an inherent capacity for the production of their primary function (Wendt 1992, 398), which could be defined as maintaining territorial integrity by combating cross-border criminal activity. Understanding the production and reproduction of border security, as well as its capacity for change, requires an awareness of the social conditions under which borders were initially produced and subsequently reproduced. And while the purpose here is not to trace the point of origin, it is important to understand that institutions emerge out of a given material and social context that will to some degree direct institutional change.

The initial development of the border between Canada and the United States starts with the nation building process in the United States and a very substantial commitment of physical and sociological/ideological resources required to build a new nation. The political climate at the time can be characterized by the American relationship with Britain and the struggle for regional power and spheres of influence in North America. Following the American Revolution, the United States approached the security of the northern border in the context of a possible invasion route for the British. Between 1775 and the signing of the Treaty of Paris in 1783, the British and Americans fought 39 land battles along the northern border (Sweeney 1996). The result of this bordering process was a commitment to a defensive border, including a material and ideological commitment to constructing that border. This was the beginning of the border institution. Over time the material and ideological commitment was reinforced by certain events, further embedding the existence of the security function along the border,[47] creating what Laitinen as defined as a security border.[48]

Given that institutions are also characterized as being resistant to change (Newman 2003), comprehending the initial process through which borders emerge, provides some direction for understanding the production and reproduction of border institutions in space, time and function. Paul Pierson (2004) argues persuasively that institutions have a point of origin, and at that point in time a substantial initial investment of resources was required. In the presence of a given initial or "historic" event a particular outcome is generated that requires an investment in resources and commitment. In addition, at the same time an ideological/sociological meaning is attached to the entity being created (border). The construction of a border can be initiated by any variety of events. The common element, however, is the bounding of territorial identity, known as the "bordering process" (Newman 2003, p.15), motivated by a real or perceived threat to the territorial integrity of the state. In whatever manner borders were created, whether through a power struggle or imposed, each state has experienced the bordering process as a unique event to its population. In this sense, as Paasi (1996, p.72) notes, the bordering process creates boundaries that exist in unique socio-cultural action and discourse.

In addition, as Pierson (2004, p.34-35) notes, the development of institutions further encourages or generates a greater investment in resources and skills, deepening the social commitment to the institution. At the same time, the institutional constraints imposed by the institution on social behaviour are reinforced. In other words, even though the event that set in motion the development of borders and/or border security institutions does not re-occur, a level of initial investment is significant enough to reinforce the function or existence of the organization, the application of resources, as well as the ideological/sociological meanings. Once the genie is out of the bottle it becomes difficult, although not impossible, to put it back in the bottle. Alternatively, the institution develops an existence removed from its initial purpose, which moreover includes changes in both the material and social context within which the institution is understood. For both borders and the organizations that provide security along borders this could mean a shift in tactics, strategy or even its raison d'être.

Pierson (2004, 20) argues that a significant commitment of resources sets the course for some degree of institutional continuity, since reversing course would be too costly, both politically and possibly financially. This condition is known as path dependency. Pierson (2004, p.20) defines path dependency as "social processes that exhibit positive feedback and thus generate branching patterns of historical development." William Sewell (quoted in Pierson, 2004, 20) contends that path dependency means that what has happened at an earlier point in time will affect the outcomes of events at another point in time.

A key concept in any dynamic definition of path dependency, as Pierson notes, is positive feedback or self-reinforcement. Path dependency does not suggest that institutional change is predetermined, but rather that the range of actions that may be available or acceptable to an actor are limited (Campbell 2004, p.65). Moreover, the greater the levels of feedback, coupled with persistence over time, makes the cost of changing the institutional trajectory difficult. In other words, seeking alternatives becomes increasingly more difficult.

Explaining when institutional change occurs is another issue. Pierson (2000) has argued that the timing institutional change is a result of events occurring at critical junctures in the development or evolution of an institution. These are referred to as focusing events. Because institutions are regulated by human choice (within a pre-determined context), individual or group reaction is what motivates or directs institutional change along a specific trajectory. As Koslowski and Kratochwil (1994) have illustrated, the critical level of analysis for understanding change is found at the agent or individual level. Indeed, Peters, Pierre, and King (2005) argue that change occurs because of conflict between political agents.

Cooperation, Joint Enforcement and Joint Jurisdiction

Examination of the post-war history of cross-border cooperation between Canada and the United States illustrates that the two countries have shared a commitment to cross-border cooperation, especially in the context of economic development. The *Autopact Agreement* in 1965 stands out as an example of a cooperative cross-border trade agreement. The *Canada – United States Free Trade Agreement* in 1988, and the follow up 1994 *North American Free Trade Agreement* seemed to re-iterate this cooperative relationship. The 1995 *Canada – United States Accord on Our Shared Border* committed the governments to improving the relationship and brought border security into the mix for the first time. More importantly, the 1995 agreement suggested for the first time taking law enforcement beyond the cooperative level, to a shared enforcement level, with the formalization of the security relationship. The 1995 agreement was followed by the first official arrangement for cross-border law enforcement, with the development of the IBET in the lower mainland of British Columbia in 1996. This first IBET was a response to the problem of cross-border drug trafficking.

An important question at this point is to ask why the cross-border law enforcement relationship emerged with the characteristics it did in the mid-1990s? What we see emerging during this time period is an organizational structure that is cooperative and that sees a particular problem (drug trafficking) as a criminal or law enforcement issue. It may seem strange to question how the problem of drug trafficking was framed, but it is important to note that this issue could have just as easily been framed as a community issue, a health care issue or even an educational issue. At the same time the Canada – United States relationship could have been marked by animosity or unilateral action rather than a cooperative approach. There are three points here that return to the theoretical argument outlined above. First, the border, as an institution, and therefore the resources that exist to construct that border, were developed in the context of security. Thus the issue of drug trafficking was most easily framed in the security context, rather than in a social or educational context. Second, cooperation between Canada and the United States with regards to border issues has always been high, both in a formal and informal level. Therefore that natural evolution was the development of a formalized relationship. The advantage of the formalized relationship, as opposed to having maintained the status quo, was the ability to work within the legislative parameters that define legal or criminal codes of each state. Prosecuting cross-border crime required formal and legal arrangements. Third, the timing of the creation of the first IBET corresponds with the American decision to designate the border along the Washington/British Columbia corridor as a High Intensity Drug Trafficking Area (HIDTA). By giving the region this designation, the American government was putting the border between Washington and British Columbia on par with drug trafficking corridors along the US/Mexico border, a status that threatened the movement of legitimate trade within the region.

What can be observed, following the events of September 11, 2001, is a continuation of changes that had taken place before 9/11, but in an accelerated fashion and for different reasons. Whereas IBET, for example, was being implemented slowly at points along the Canada – United States border, the *Smart Border Accord* committed Canada and the United States to immediate development of fifteen teams in total to cover the entire border for the purpose of ensuring national security (defined largely in the context of terrorism). Along with this expansion came the necessary increase in manpower and material resources, further entrenching the security mandate along the border. More significantly, however, was the commitment to a formal arrangement for joint enforcement along the border. For the first time, dedicated teams of law enforcement officials from both sides of the border shared intelligence, resources and set investigational and enforcement priorities as an integrated and international unit. The comprehensive approach to border security had an official binational mandate for joint enforcement.

The shift towards shared jurisdiction, a shift that is evident in the development of the Shiprider and BEST programs, represents simply the continuation of an institutional arrangement going back to the beginning of the post-War era. Although these current programs are restricted in scope, they do represent a comprehensive approach that goes beyond the traditional restrictions imposed by different levels of government, state boundaries and sovereignty. Consequently, these programs are illustrative of the capacity for institutional arrangements to develop well beyond their initial incarnation in order to address, or respond to, changing political pressures.

Conclusion: The Way Ahead

The comprehensive approach in policing is about developing and working with appropriate partners. This is done for a number of reasons. The overall goal of a comprehensive approach is to create safer communities. Partnerships allow for increased operational effectiveness through the sharing of resources, manpower and intelligence. Partnerships further provide alternative solutions to common problems through the sharing of knowledge and experience. As law enforcement agencies become more comfortable working with partners, not only will those relationships become more integrated, but they will evolve to include more stakeholders: private citizens, businesses and non-governmental agencies. For police agencies working along the border this list could include: property owners, trucking and shipping companies and environmental groups, as examples.

Partnerships however, are not without their challenges. Policing along the border presents one distinct problem – jurisdiction. As noted, as the border institution evolves so too will the problem of jurisdiction. Already the International Joint Management Team responsible for IBET has committed itself to a cross-designated law enforcement capability, to be in place by 2015. This development will effectively remove the issue of jurisdiction for law enforcement officers with the appropriate training and designation. Shiprider and BEST are the beginning of this process. This is not to say that sovereignty issues will not arise. Sovereignty, like the border, is an institution that is equally imbued with ideological and material meaning. However, like other institutions, sovereignty is not a static concept, as the development of the EU has clearly demonstrated.

The final challenge worthy of note is the issue of trust. Institutional arrangements are important for developing a framework within which a working relationship or partnership can be established. The establishment of that partnership aside, institutions remain, by and large, human creations and are therefore subject to human behaviour. From the individual to the group level, being able to trust partners and partner agencies is a critical component to the success of a comprehensive approach. Trust is doubly important in work being carried out in the security sector, where poor working relationships can jeopardize the safety of others. As institutions evolve, the ideological/sociological meaning of that institution has to change in a manner that includes trust as a characteristic component of that institution. Trust, in turn, has to be supported by material resources, which, in the case of border enforcement units may include shared or integrated working space, common communications systems and shared databases.

In its most basic form, the comprehensive approach in law enforcement is expressed in community policing models that stress the development of partnerships with other agencies and community stakeholders.

More complex partnerships are created within institutional frameworks that include horizontal and vertical integration, as well as integration across international boundaries, as is illustrated by the IBET case study. Integrated policing partnerships, like IBET, are products of institutional frameworks that evolve along a path dependent trajectory, accelerated by focusing events. With reference specifically to the IBET model, we have moved from frameworks based on cross-border cooperation, to shared enforcement and are now moving towards a model of shared jurisdiction. In the end, a comprehensive approach will provide more secure communities. At the same time, however, issues such as trust, leadership, mandate and sovereignty will have to be addressed in order to provide the necessary guidelines for integrated units to effectively fulfill their shared objectives.

Chapter 13

CANADA'S NORTHERN STRATEGY: A CASE STUDY IN HORIZONTAL MANAGEMENT

JOHN KOZIJ AND SYLVIA BOGUSIS

Introduction

Military engagements are often precipitated by a sharp triggering event and a Comprehensive Approach is a profound horizontal organizing principle intended to marshal a breadth of resources and talents to task. For the *Northern Strategy*, such circumstances – a triggering event or set of events – are absent. There is no war, no combatants, no current threat to life and democracy in or around the Arctic. There are compelling reasons for a Northern Strategy, and a horizontal approach, but these must fight for political/policy attention in a world where there are other important, pressing issues. The first part of this document will focus on why the federal government has stepped up its efforts in the North as this background is relevant in explaining why the *Northern Strategy* is both a horizontal policy endeavour and a successful one.

Since the federal government has had "Northern Strategies" in the past, there is a need to explain why the North has become the focus of attention once again and why there is another strategy. The 2009 *Northern Strategy* differs from its predecessors in a number of respects but, in particular, because it is so closely linked to the Government's core priorities. *The Northern Strategy* responds to several key trends and developments which, taken together, represent an unavoidable set of inter-related challenges. Many of these issues are common to the Arctic coastal nations. It is also true that there have always been issues and challenges in the North.

Security Operations in the 21st Century: Canadian Perspectives on the Comprehensive Approach, ed. M. Rostek and P. Gizewski. Montreal and Kingston: Queen's Policy Studies Series, McGill-Queen's University Press.

Captain John Franklin would have said so in the 1850s, and the Inuit could have iterated their own list of challenges generations before that.

That being said, some of these issues, many of them exogenous forces impacting the North, have a new, pressing and strategic importance, so they require attention and action. There are also internal factors that are different from before. Chief among them is the current Government which has a different view on the appropriate federal role, where powers are divided, by our constitution, between federal and provincial governments.

Indian and Northern Affairs Canada (INAC) has worked hard and collectively with a number of federal departments, including many colleagues from the Department of National Defence, to bring the *Northern Strategy* together. However, there would not have been as much impetus for such interdepartmental collaboration without the leadership of the Prime Minister and his personal, as well as his professional, interest in the North.

The sections which follow: (i) provide an overview of the exogenous and endogenous factors that underpinned the development of the *Northern Strategy*; (ii) examine success factors and lessons learned in horizontal program and policy development; and, (iii) summarize accomplishments thus far.

The Arctic: Focus of Attention, Time of Transition

Why has the Arctic[49] region become a focal point of international interest? The salient issue is that this region is undergoing profound environmental change, which is evident in its ice, permafrost, and weather systems. This catalytic change has altered our perception of the North from the standpoint of accessibility, marine traffic, resource wealth, and sovereignty.

External Policy Factors – Environmental Change

There is clear evidence of environmental change in the Arctic region: the sea ice is thinning more rapidly than predicted; there has been a tremendous net loss of multi-year ice; the permafrost is thawing and releasing greenhouse gases; coastal erosion is apace; and weather and climate patterns are far more variable. The magnitude of these changes worry many, especially those who live in the Arctic region and are experiencing the impacts first-hand: structural damage to infrastructure as the ground shifts, reduced ice-road seasons because of shorter winters, inability to rely on traditional knowledge of ice conditions, and changes in species' patterns of behaviour.

Many scientists regard the Arctic as an early-warning system of global climate change. The Arctic sea ice extent plummeted to a record low in 2007, equivalent to the size of Ontario and well ahead of climate model predictions. Summers 2008 and 2009 also saw the further diminishing of

FIGURE 5: CIRCUMPOLAR MAP

© 2001. Her Majesty the Queen in Right of Canada, Natural Resources Canada. / Sa Majesté la Reine du chef du Canada, Ressources naturelles Canada.

the thick, multi-year ice cover. Because of the half-century of warming trends in the Arctic region, ice-free summers in the North are more likely. It is important to understand why there is such concern about Arctic sea ice conditions. These play a critical role in the climate, ocean currents and the ecosystem of the Arctic and beyond.

Figure 6 below shows the "calving" of the Ayles Ice Shelf, a development that provides further evidence of a dramatically changing Arctic environment. While few will have heard of this event, it is unarguably more important than another piece of geography in the Arctic called Hans Island. At 1.3 square kilometres, the uninhabited Hans Island, which straddles Nares Strait between Greenland and Ellesmere Island, is about 50 times smaller and has much less to tell us; the territorial dispute over Hans Island between Canada and Denmark is much less complex and meaningful than the inter-related set of factors that led to the calving of the Ayles Ice Shelf.

FIGURE 6: AYLES ICE SHELF[50]

Source: NASA's Earth Observatory.

External Policy Factors – Economies in Air and Marine Traffic

Another driver for the strong international interest in the Arctic region is its potential as a cost-reducing and time-saving transportation corridor (see Figure 7). Over the past several years, the number of air and sea transits has been steadily increasing as commercial operators seek shorter and more economical routes – over the pole flights and new marine passages. It is true that marine traffic in the Canadian North has been growing at a very gradual level. However, the Northeast Passage witnessed a first in September 2009: two German cargo ships successfully navigated across Russia's northern shore from South Korea to Siberia – without ice-breakers to clear their path. This northern route trimmed 4,000 nautical miles off the usual 11,000 mile journey via the Suez Canal and generated significant time and fuel savings for the operating company.

FIGURE 7: ARCTIC MARINE AREA

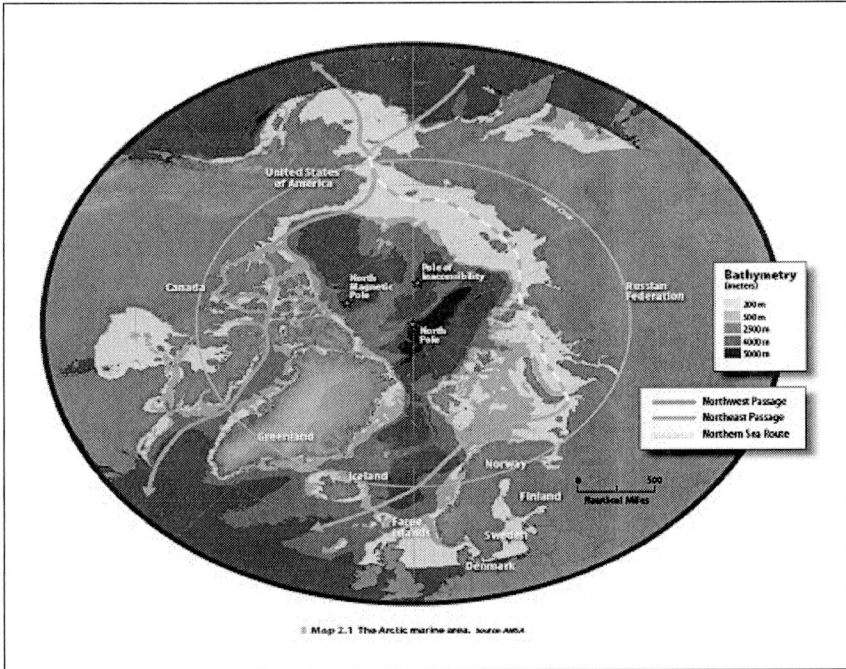

Map 2.1 The Arctic marine area. Source: AMSA

Arctic Council AMSA Report 2009.

External Policy Factors – Economic Potential

The entire Arctic region is richly endowed with minerals, oil and gas. For example, once the Diavik, Ekati and Snap Lake diamond mines in the Northwest Territories went into production, Canada catapulted into the diamond producing global elite in just over a decade. It became the world's third largest diamond industry by value and the fourth by weight. Our world-class mines are at a mature stage now so Canada may not continue to hold its diamond-producing status. But there is more to the North than diamonds.

The Arctic region, including the off-shore, is high in oil and gas potential. The Arctic is estimated to hold a large percentage of the world's undiscovered oil and gas (United States Geological Survey, 2009). Development projects have been slow to come on stream because of the harsh operating conditions, environmental concerns, market conditions and various regulatory issues. However, price and technology have allowed Norway to conquer the issues of off-shore development in the Barents Sea. Exploratory offshore oil drilling will begin in Greenland's west zone in summer 2010.

External Policy Factors – Geopolitical Developments

Sometimes an event can capture the world's attention and draw strong reactions from the media, politicians, analysts, and the public. On August 2, 2007, the Russians accomplished an amazing technical achievement at the North Pole, in international waters. Had the Mir-1's crew just placed a bottle of vodka on the sea floor at the North Pole and not a titanium Russian flag, the media probably would not have been as quick to react with such headlines as "who owns the North Pole"? Also, the reaction of Canadians might have been quite different. In polling that was conducted after the North Pole dive, 85 percent of Canadians responded by saying that the Government should protect Canadian sovereignty. Subsequent to this event, media and various analysts began to focus their attention and speculation on which country was doing what in the Arctic and with what ultimate intention.

Colleagues at Foreign Affairs and International Trade Canada have helped to educate NAO/INAC on boundary and territorial matters in the Arctic. There are international rules in place, which all the Arctic coastal states are respecting. Contrary to media descriptions of "conflict," "a race" and "competition" in the Arctic, the actual behaviour of the Arctic coastal nations is characterized by cooperation and collaboration. Joint scientific research, including in seabed mapping, is under way to determine the extent of continental shelves of the Arctic states. Decisions on countries' extended continental shelves will not be based on a race to resources, or gunboat diplomacy, but on rules, scientific facts, cooperation and negotiation.

The Ilulissat Declaration of 27-29 May, 2008 also underlined this point (see Appendix A). Ministers and high-level representatives of the five Arctic coastal states (Canada, Denmark, Norway (Greenland), the Russian Federation and the United States of America) met in central west Greenland and re-affirmed their commitment to the existing legal frameworks of international cooperation (particularly the United Nations Convention on the Law of the Sea, or UNCLOS) and to the orderly settlement of any possible overlapping claims, as well as their intentions to continue to contribute actively to the work of the Arctic Council and other relevant international fora.

More recently, the foreign affairs ministers of the five Arctic coastal states communicated the same message about working closely together. At a meeting hosted by Minister Lawrence Cannon on 29 March 2010, the Ministers re-affirmed their countries' commitment to the orderly resolution of any possible overlapping claims on continental shelves and indicated that they will continue to cooperate closely in scientific and technical work.

External Policy Factors – Arctic Policies and Strategies

Around 2007, Canada and the member states of the Arctic Council,[51] as well as other international players, started to undertake strategic assessments of their interests and roles in the Arctic. Much was happening in parallel. As Canada and its Arctic coastal neighbours were reviewing developments in the Arctic and updating their policies and approaches, other non-Arctic countries and international organizations were doing the same, albeit from different lenses. For example, because of the environmental changes in the Arctic, some (e.g., Greenpeace and European Union) have called for a new governance structure – a treaty or some other international instrument – to protect this remote and pristine area.[52]

External Policy Factors – Continental Shelf Submissions

At the same time as various countries and international organizations were reviewing their Arctic strategies or policies, work by UNCLOS signatories to collect scientific data for their continental shelf submissions was also well under way. Up to 50 countries, including Canada, may have extended continental shelves and are conducting scientific surveys to establish evidence of these.

Some of the seabed data collection under UNCLOS is being carried out in the Arctic Ocean. The photo below shows Canadian and US icebreakers working in tandem using seismic and sonar technologies to map the Beaufort seabed. While the US has not yet ratified UNCLOS, it is collaborating with Canada in mapping the seabed and sharing data. Canada and Denmark also have a similar work and data sharing arrangement. This underscores the point that, while the media has often portrayed this seabed mapping effort as a race, it is not. Rather, it is a systematic scientific effort being undertaken by a number of countries under the terms and conditions set by UNCLOS. Canada is working hard to meet its deadline of 2013 for data submission to the UN Commission on the Limits of the Continental Shelf (CLCS).

Internal Policy Factors – A Government Priority

On January 26, 2006, the Conservative Party of Canada formed the new Government of Canada. What many do not realize is that the North figured in the Conservative campaign platform and was an area identified for early policy attention. In August 2006, Prime Minister Stephen Harper made the first of his annual summer trips to the North. During the early stages of his government, the Prime Minister's Northern visits focused on the issues of exercising sovereignty and the need to strengthen Canada's military presence and capacity in the North.

FIGURE 8: CANADA'S ICEBREAKER, LOUIS S. ST-LAURENT, WORKS WITH US COAST GUARD CUTTER HEALY

Photo: Jon Biggar, Canadian Hydrographic Service.

While exercising sovereignty continues to remain an element of the government's Northern agenda, the Prime Minister's latter visits to the North demonstrated the government's broadening approach to Northern issues. For example, Prime Minister Harper announced the expansion of Nahanni National Park in 2007, measures to extend the reach of the *Arctic Waters Pollution Prevention Act* in 2008, and the creation of the Canadian Northern Economic Development Agency (CanNor) in 2009.

A number of other developments point to the priority that the government has given to Northern issues. The North figured prominently in the October 2007 Speech from the Throne (SFT) and subsequent Budgets and SFTs. The Prime Minister held the first-ever Cabinet meetings in the North, in Inuvik (August 2008) and Iqaluit (August 2009). The Prime Minister's leadership on Northern issues led to subsequent high-level public service attention to the North.

The summer of 2007 was a watershed period in focusing the world's and Canada's attention on the Arctic region. The Russia flag planting, the lowest sea ice extent ever recorded, and Prime Minister Harper's announcement that Canada would build two military facilities in the far North[53] all happened within the space of several weeks.

Marshalling the Northern Strategy Team

The Northern Affairs Organization (NAO) of INAC has worked hard and collectively with a number of federal departments to bring the *Northern Strategy* together. The *Northern Strategy* is a shared agenda and NAO has acted as a convenor, bringing key federal stakeholders together at the policy table. In addition to the Assistant Deputy Minister (ADM) Coordinating Committee on the Arctic, the Clerk established, in the fall of 2007, the Ad Hoc Committee of Deputy Ministers on the Arctic, chaired by the Deputy Minister of INAC with the Associate Deputy Minister of the Department of National Defence as the vice-chair. Various committees have also been struck to respond to key issues and to keep work planning for the *Northern Strategy* ever green (Figure 9).

FIGURE 9: GOVERNANCE STRUCTURE FOR THE *NORTHERN STRATEGY*

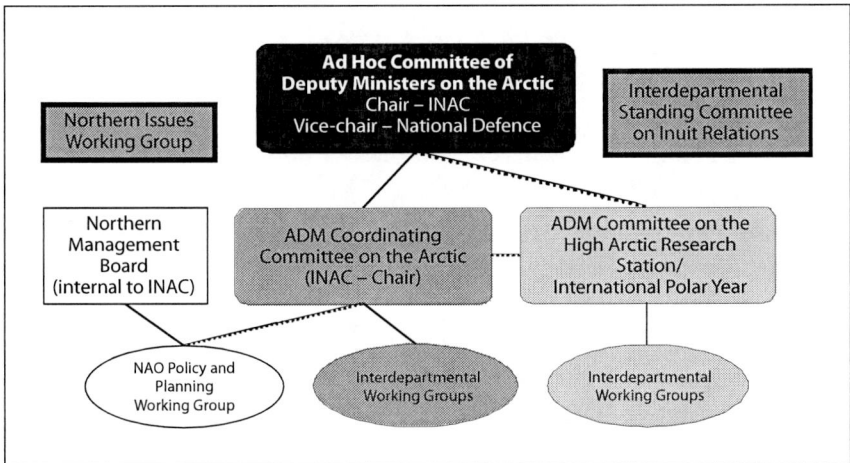

Overview of the Northern Strategy

The purpose of this chapter has been to explain how the *Northern Strategy* came to be and how it is being managed, not to provide an exposition of the *Northern Strategy* itself. Yet it is worthwhile to address this topic briefly. Figure 10 below provides an encapsulation of its content. First announced in the October 2007 Speech from the Throne, the Government issued its public version of the *Strategy* in July 2009.

A number of initiatives under each of the pillars of the *Strategy* have been launched, highlights of which are found in Appendix B. The federal government continues to keep its eyes North, assessing and responding to systemic and emerging challenges in the North.

FIGURE 10: CANADA'S NORTHERN STRATEGY

Key Success Factors of *Northern Strategy* Horizontal Work

In reviewing events and developments since 2006, NAO has identified key elements that led to success in moving the *Northern Strategy* forward. These elements may offer some guidance and insight for other horizontal initiatives or even comprehensive ones.

Clear Accountability. In his response to the 2007 Speech from the Throne (SFT), the Prime Minister stated that many of his Cabinet colleagues would be working on the *Northern Strategy* and that this work would be led by the Honourable Chuck Strahl, the Minister of Indian Affairs and Northern Development. That statement affirmed the importance of the ongoing efforts of a number of departments to advance the *Northern Strategy* and solidified the Minister's and INAC's leadership and accountability for this horizontal policy file.

Leadership and Staying Power. Since August 2007, INAC's leadership on the *Northern Strategy* has benefited greatly from stability – same Minister, Deputy Minister, Assistant Deputy Minister, Director General, Director and even some senior analysts. Consequently, the INAC team has built a solid, in-depth knowledge of Northern issues, as well as strong relationships with federal partners and other stakeholders. Since managing the transition of new players never arose for INAC, policy continuity and focus have been steadily maintained.

Nimble and Opportunistic. Working on a number of policy fronts simultaneously with a number of federal partners has resulted in policy and program readiness for SFTs and Budgets. Strong communication efforts, coupled with effective interdepartmental working relationships, have meant that INAC is able to keep abreast of the multiple moving parts of the Northern agenda and help other federal departments situate their priorities within the overall vision and work plan for the *Northern Strategy* over successive periods.

Acting Corporately. This is perhaps a rare distinguishing feature of how the *Northern Strategy* is being managed horizontally. INAC's senior management team for the *Northern Strategy* – from Deputy Minister to Director – have all worked in the Privy Council Office previously. In considering Northern priorities and potential government responses, NAO takes a broad, whole-of-government perspective, not just a departmental one.

To illustrate: in the summer/fall of 2007, INAC, as the lead department for the *Northern Strategy* proposed three "big ideas" – signature initiatives – to the government. These initiatives were developed in response to the significant transition going on in Canada's North, the state of our largest ice-breaker, and major gaps in our awareness of our own Arctic domain. All three "big ideas" were adopted as priorities by the government. Two were funded in Budget 2008: a new icebreaker and a major geo-mapping initiative in the North. The 2007 SFT announced the third big idea, a High Arctic Research Station, and Budgets 2009 and 2010 provided initial funding. At the time, none of these initiatives were considered to be INAC programmatic areas. After the 2007 SFT, however, NAO was advised that INAC would lead the development work for the High Arctic Research Station. This came as a surprise to NAO/INAC, not being a major science-based department. However the task was undertaken with strong support from the departments and agencies which are the science leaders.

Sensitizing the System to the High Cost of Doing Work in the North. INAC has been able to help other federal partners with their policy proposals by underscoring the North's reality to the central agencies: it is complex and costly to operate in the North. Reasons include: extreme winter cold and highly-variable weather; a very short season for some activities, especially construction; the remoteness of and distance between Northern communities; high transportation costs for food and other essential products, such as lumber, fuel and steel, that must be shipped; long lead-times for infrastructure projects; and, some capacity gaps across the territories. This reality translates to projects and programs that will cost much more in the North, compared to southern Canada.

Doing the Basics Right. NAO puts much effort into ensuring interdepartmental meetings are planned well in advance and run smoothly. As examples: NAO produces a six-month forward agenda for both its Deputy Minister and Assistant Deputy Minister committees; it tracks progress on initiatives through regular reporting; it distributes briefing materials a week in advance of meetings; it prepares detailed minutes of meetings; and, it keeps its membership and distribution lists up-to-date. In 2009/09, the Treasury Board Secretariat assessed NAOs performance in managing a horizontal policy file and accorded it the highest rating – strong.

Conclusion and Lessons Learned

Timing matters. External events can have a galvanizing effect on policy profile, development and coordination. Since 2006, the Government's attention to the North has not wavered through successive SFTs and Budgets. The Prime Minister's sustained focus is of significant note and has stimulated a strong public service response to the issues of the North. As an example; in July 2009, sixteen deputy ministers participated in a full-day retreat at which they considered and discussed potential long-term trends in the Arctic and their implications for federal response. Building a federal community of interest has taken time and hard effort, but it has brought considerable rewards, including a high degree of engagement, openness to new policy approaches and strong partnerships.

APPENDIX A
Ilulissat Declaration

THE ILULISSAT DECLARATION

ARCTIC OCEAN CONFERENCE

ILULISSAT, GREENLAND, 27 – 29 MAY 2008

At the invitation of the Danish Minister for Foreign Affairs and the Premier of Greenland, representatives of the five coastal States bordering on the Arctic Ocean – Canada, Denmark, Norway, the Russian Federation and the United States of America – met at the political level on 28 May 2008 in Ilulissat, Greenland, to hold discussions. They adopted the following declaration:

The Arctic Ocean stands at the threshold of significant changes. Climate change and the melting of ice have a potential impact on vulnerable ecosystems, the livelihoods of local inhabitants and indigenous communities, and the potential exploitation of natural resources.

By virtue of their sovereignty, sovereign rights and jurisdiction in large areas of the Arctic Ocean the five coastal states are in a unique position to address these possibilities and challenges. In this regard, an extensive international legal framework applies to the Arctic Ocean as discussed between our representatives at the meeting in Oslo on 15 and 16 October 2007 at the level of senior officials. Notably, the law of the sea provides for important rights and obligations concerning the delineation of the outer limits of the continental shelf, the protection of the marine environment, including ice-covered areas, freedom of navigation, marine scientific research, and other uses of the sea. NAO remains committed to this legal framework and to the orderly settlement of any possible overlapping claims.

This framework provides a solid foundation for responsible management by the five coastal States and other users of this Ocean through national implementation and application of relevant provisions. Therefore a need does not exist to develop a new comprehensive international legal regime to govern the Arctic Ocean. Developments in the Arctic Ocean will be monitored and implementation of appropriate measures will continue.

The Arctic Ocean is a unique ecosystem, which the five coastal states have a stewardship role in protecting. Experience has shown how shipping disasters and subsequent pollution of the marine environment may cause irreversible disturbance of the ecological balance and major harm to the livelihoods of local inhabitants and indigenous communities. INAC will take steps in accordance with international law both nationally and in cooperation among the five states and other interested parties to ensure the protection and preservation of the fragile marine environment of the Arctic Ocean. In this regard INAC intends to work together including through the International Maritime Organization to strengthen existing measures and develop new measures to improve the safety of maritime navigation and prevent or reduce the risk of ship-based pollution in the Arctic Ocean.

The increased use of Arctic waters for tourism, shipping, research and resource development also increases the risk of accidents and therefore the need to further strengthen search and rescue capabilities and capacity around the Arctic Ocean to ensure an appropriate response from states to any accident. Cooperation, including on the sharing of information, is a prerequisite for addressing these challenges. NAO/INAC will work to promote safety of life at sea in the Arctic Ocean, including through bilateral and multilateral arrangements between or among relevant states.

The five coastal states currently cooperate closely in the Arctic Ocean with each other and with other interested parties. This cooperation includes the collection of scientific data concerning the continental shelf, the protection of the marine environment and other scientific research. Efforts will be made to strengthen this cooperation, which is based on mutual trust and transparency, inter alia, through timely exchange of data and analyses.

The Arctic Council and other international fora, including the Barents Euro-Arctic Council, have already taken important steps on specific issues, for example with regard to safety of navigation, search and rescue, environmental monitoring and disaster response and scientific cooperation, which are relevant also to the Arctic Ocean. The five coastal states of the Arctic Ocean will continue to contribute actively to the work of the Arctic Council and other relevant international fora.

APPENDIX B
Achievements under the *Northern Strategy*

Some of what we've accomplished under the Northern Strategy

Sovereignty	Environmental Protection
✓ Polar Icebreaker – CCGS Diefenbaker ✓ Arctic/Offshore Patrol Ships ✓ Docking and refueling facility in Nanisivik ✓ Expansion of the Canadian Rangers ✓ Military training centre in Resolute ✓ Launch of RADARSAT II ✓ NORDREG – mandatory ship reporting ✓ Strategic meteorological and navigational services (MET and NAVAREAS)* ✓ Scientific work to support continental shelf delineation	✓ Commitment to establish an Arctic Research Station – including $2M for a feasibility study and $18M for pre-construction design phase* ✓ Arctic Research Infrastructure Fund ($85M) ✓ Leading International Polar Year research ✓ Expansion of the Nahanni National Park ✓ Feasibility study for creation of marine conservation area in Lancaster Sound ✓ Extended the *Arctic Waters Pollution Prevention Act* ✓ Accelerating reclamation and remediation of federal contaminated sites ✓ Community-based environmental monitoring*
Economic and Social Development	**Governance**
✓ $100M for geo-mapping in the North ✓ Northern housing development, including social housing ✓ Significant investments in Northern infrastructure ✓ $50M to establish CanNor ✓ $90M to renew the Strategic Investments in Northern Economic Development program ✓ Northern regulatory improvements and reducing red tape* ✓ Extending the Mineral Exploration Tax Credit* ✓ $1.8B in oil and gas exploration licenses in Beaufort Sea ✓ Commercial fisheries harbour in Pangnirtung ✓ Renewed Food Mail Program* ✓ Extending Territorial Health System Sustainability Initiative* ✓ Labour Market Agreements with territories ✓ Enhanced broadband access in Nunavut and NWT	✓ Negotiating and implementing land claims and self-government agreements ✓ Advancing transfer of federal responsibilities in Nunavut ✓ Strengthening Nunavut's Financial Management capacity ✓ Extended Yukon self-government financial agreements ✓ $2.5 billion through Territorial Formula Financing 2009-2010 ✓ Ilulissat Declaration by Arctic States ✓ Meeting of Arctic Ocean Foreign Ministers *Denotes new investment from Budget 2010*

Chapter 14

FAMILY RELATIONS: A PRELIMINARY ANALYSIS OF THE USE OF THE COMPREHENSIVE APPROACH AT THE VANCOUVER 2010 WINTER OLYMPICS

BERNARD BRISTER

Domestic Canadian application of the Comprehensive Approach (CA) is not a new phenomenon and can be traced back at least as far as the multi-agency security effort in support of the 1976 Olympic Games in Montreal as a reaction to the massacre of Israeli athletes at the 1972 Munich Games (Kozij, 2010). More recently, it has been employed to good effect in the national responses to the Red River floods in 1996, the Ice Storm in Ontario and Quebec in 1998, and the forest fires in British Columbia in 2004 (Roy, 2010). Contemporary and ongoing examples of the use of the CA in security applications include the RCMP-led Integrated Border Enforcement Teams (IBET), and Ship Rider and Border Enforcement Security Task Force (BEST) (Hataley, 2010).

Nonetheless, the planning and execution of the security strategy for the Games is seen by many as unique in both scope, size, and by virtue of its deliberate nature. The Games involved the participation of over 300 government agencies in three levels of government, two countries, the Olympic organizations (Vancouver Olympic Committee – VANOC, and the International Olympic Committee – IOC) and a multitude of sports federations charged with the oversight of the conduct of each of the events

Security Operations in the 21st Century: Canadian Perspectives on the Comprehensive Approach, ed. M. Rostek and P. Gizewski. Montreal and Kingston: Queen's Policy Studies Series, McGill-Queen's University Press.

(interview with Mercer, 2010). Within this structure, the execution of the security plan involving more than 140 government agencies and 13,000 security personnel in rural and urban areas ranging from high alpine remote to high density inner city in weather that varied from sub-zero blowing snow to balmy sunshine has been touted as the largest, most comprehensive domestic security operation in Canadian history. With this many agencies and people involved, the security environment was said to contain at least as many sensitivities (insecurities) as there were security and interagency partners (Barr, 2010).

Given the reality of the magnitude of the Olympic security effort, the application of the CA to a comprehensive analysis of this event is beyond the limited scope of this work. Instead, this chapter will focus upon a single dynamic involved with the CA, that of the interaction between individuals, groups and agencies in the achievement of the common goal of a secure and peaceful Olympic Games. The thesis of the chapter is that the benefits to be derived from the application of the CA in any given security situation will be limited by issues of hubris and tribalism.

The analysis leading to this conclusion, as well as the conclusion itself, must be seen as preliminary in nature as the final research and evidence is not yet available. While extensive before and after research interviews have been conducted and some of the departmental reports on the Games have recently been issued (at the time of writing) the end-state implementation/revision of these reports has yet to be completed and as such, absolute conclusions at this stage of the process are premature. The examination of the security operations associated with the Games starts with an overview of how the Canadian security infrastructure that was established for the event evolved.

Strategic oversight and control of the security functions for the Games was coordinated by Ward G. Elcock. Mr. Elcock was designated the "Coordinator for the 2010 Olympic Games and G8 Security" and reported directly to the then National Security Advisor (NSA), Marie-Lucie Morin in the Privy Council Office (PCO) (interview with Senior Games Operations Officer, 2008). The Royal Canadian Mounted Police (RCMP), as the lead security agency charged with the planning and execution of the Games security strategy, reported through their chain of command to the Coordinator in the PCO (interview with Mercer, 2010).

The primary vehicle used by the RCMP for the planning and execution of the Games security effort was the Integrated Security Unit (ISU). The RCMP ISU was responsible for establishing the overall security plan for the Olympics, and coordinating the input of the international, federal, provincial and municipal government departments that contributed resources, personnel, and capabilities to the security of the Games. The Department of National Defence, via the Canadian Forces (CF), was one such department and the CF was tasked to provide key assets, personnel, and capabilities in support of the RCMP ISU (interview with Senior Official, Department of National Defence, 2008).

The rationale for the establishment of a separate infrastructure for the Games is worthy of some consideration. The establishment of a security infrastructure for the Games that was largely independent of the existing infrastructure may well have been a reaction to an assessment that the existing infrastructure was in some way dysfunctional or otherwise unsuitable for the actual operational planning and execution of a security operation as opposed to the provision of policy support for a security strategy.

While the RCMP had been assigned the responsibility for overall management and control of Games security, the Public Safety (PS) Canada had been assigned the "umbrella" role of inter-departmental security coordination. Notwithstanding the assignment of this responsibility, however, attempts by the Chief of Defence Staff (Hillier) and the Deputy Minister of DND (Mr. Elcock at the time) to get PS to define the role and resource requirements of the CF for the Games were unsuccessful. It also became apparent that the RCMP did not possess the requisite strategic planning or coordination skills that would allow them to effectively manage and control the security effort for the Games. Discussions between the Deputy Ministers and the NSA indicated a lack of progress and direction that established the need for a more effective direction and coordination mechanism for the overall security effort (interview with Elcock, 2009). Another problem that had to be addressed was that in the early stages of planning for the Games it was sometimes difficult to determine who was in charge as no agency was apparently willing to cede authority on any issue of substantive importance. The situation clearly required a greater degree of executive direction and oversight by a senior entity with the established authority to impose a decision on issues when and as dictated by the security situation. The government accordingly took immediate action.[54]

The fundamental reaction was the establishment of a security infrastructure for the Games outside of the existing bureaucracies and agencies. Given the drawbacks and weaknesses of situating the position of Coordinator in one of the rank and file government departments, it was decided that the Coordinator would be located within the Privy Council Office (PCO) and specifically in a relationship that reported directly to the NSA.

The operationally-focused structure established specifically for the Games effectively circumvented the established bureaucracy including its dominant focus on policy making and what might be considered an almost dysfunctional reluctance to adapt current lines of authority and influence to meet evolving security priorities. Research and observation over the course of the Games themselves indicates that this new and separate operational security infrastructure, created outside of, yet attached to, the existing permanent one, worked very well – at least at the tactical level. Inter-agency working relationships established through the interactions of agency staffs at the ISU, problematic at the outset, gradually improved. The flow of information and active participation in the cooperative resolution of security issues associated with the Games steadily increased and improved in terms of both speed and efficiency (interview with Senior Games Security Liaison and Coordinator, 2008).

However, the nature of these changes in terms of their permanence within the Canadian structure can only be determined with time. It may well be that the increased level of trust and cooperation will be a temporary phenomenon that disappears after the impetus of the Games has been removed and the participants have returned to their original organizations and positions. Whether or not a number of improvements to the national security infrastructure are adopted to address operational concerns identified over the course of the Games will be the true test of both the success and the viability of the employment of the CA to national-level security operations.

The analysis and discussion of the use of the CA in the planning and execution of the Games security strategy will address issues at the tactical, operational and strategic levels. At the tactical level, consideration will be given to the issues of information sharing and the degree to which the various corporate cultures were seen to either clash or adapt to some level of harmonization.

The timely and effective sharing of classified information to those with a need to know vs. those with a clearance to know was at times problematic because classification standards between agencies often differed. In other cases, the agencies were not cleared or equipped to deal with classified information that in the context of a whole-of-government operation such as the Games, would have been necessary to effectively address issues of disaster response and/or consequence management. As the Chief Operating Officer of the ISU, Assistant Commissioner Bud Mercer concluded that there exists a need to establish a common system for the classification of information at the national level and to establish capabilities within the government agencies at each level to access and share this information (interview with Mercer, 2010).

Because there was no government-wide system of collation, classification, and distribution of intelligence, information-sharing issues were addressed on an ad hoc basis throughout the Games (interview with Integrated Security Unit Planner, 2010). The CF struggled with the sharing of classified information with police and civil organizations that either had a different classification system and/or a different culture of information management. This issue was particularly sensitive and acute in the cases where the intelligence came from allied sources and was subject to restrictions imposed by those allies that had to be adhered to if the intelligence conduit was to remain open (interview with Integrated Security Unit Emergency Measures Coordinator, 2010).

The RCMP in turn struggled with the constitutional and Charter restrictions on the sharing of information on suspects with Other Government Departments (OGDs). They also had to contend with the fallout of the Maher Arar affair that put significant restrictions on the extent to which they could share such information with American liaison staff within the ISU (interview with Integrated Security Unit Emergency Measures Coordinator, 2010).

Caught in the middle of all of this uncertainty, the civil emergency agencies struggled to understand the intelligence control cultures of the CF and RCMP within the context of their own experience – a disaster response scenario where time was of the essence and any restriction of the flow of information likely had very real and negative consequences (interview with Integrated Security Unit Emergency Measures Coordinator, 2010).

The influence of the information security cultures that were pressed upon the civil emergency agencies had a rather bizarre consequence for their operational effectiveness and the extent to which they were able to interact with their peer organizations across the border in Washington State.

Prior to the advent of the Games, it had often been the case that communication in general and the passage of information in particular had frequently been smoother and more effective between provincial and state officials than between provincial and federal ones. This may have been due to a greater degree of commonality with state officials regarding the nature of the difficulties being faced as well as the priority / degree of immediacy assigned to them. The relationship between the state and federal authorities on the American side apparently was similar to the Canadian experience (interview with Senior Provincial Manager, 2010).

In an interesting twist, the flow of information across the border between the consequence management organizations actually slowed down during the Games as the influence of federal security organizations imposed their sharing restrictions on the provincial-state information flow. The classified nature of some of the information shared with Emergency Measures British Columbia (EMBC) slowed the passage of all information southward as it had to be vetted to ensure that some classified material was not inappropriately disclosed to American authorities (interview with Senior Provincial Manager, 2010).

The information-sharing example outlined above was just one instance of difficulties arising from the confluence of cultures that occurred when the security agencies came together to address Olympic security. Whether the confluence was correctly termed a "clash," a "harmonization" or a "merging" of agency cultures varied with the organizations involved and the circumstances of the interaction. Some organizations were resistant to the embrace of the CA approach. A case in point is that of the EMBC and the RCMP. Many in both organizations did not consider EMBC to be a legitimate part of the security strategy for the region either before or after the Games. Overall, the RCMP did not appear to embrace change in either the nature or types of their relationships and operations. Their preference appeared to be the status quo, bringing others in at the last minute when the situation is becoming desperate (interview with Senior Provincial Manager, 2010). They tended to erect barriers within the ISU umbrella organization that frequently isolated them from other agencies. The reclusive nature of the RCMP, combined with a perception of a pervasive "us vs. them" philosophy, tended to distance them somewhat from their peers/allies in the operation (interview with Integrated Security Unit Planner, 2010). The RCMP can generally be characterized as a very tribal organization on the basis of their performance over the course of the Games and while they emphasized the open and inclusive security culture whenever possible, under stress and/or when pressed by individuals or events, they reverted to type and "circled the wagons" (interview with Integrated Security Unit Planner, 2010). In contrast to this was the Vancouver Police Department who tended to be very open and inclusive and who were particularly good at info-sharing and support of the team-building process (interview with Integrated Security Unit Planner, 2010).

Another example of the different organizational cultures "bumping-up" against one another concerns the military. While the CF clearly understood its support role in the security strategy they nonetheless would tend to push information at the other agencies (including the RCMP) and press for analysis of contingencies, outcomes and consequences (interview with Senior Provincial Manager and Integrated Security Unit Planner, 2010). One consequence of this was that the RCMP may have felt threatened on several occasions and this evidenced itself in a number of restrictive measures intended to reinforce their dominance in the operation and the subordinate or supporting role of the CF (interview with Senior Provincial Manager and Integrated Security Unit Planner, 2010).

The quality and effectiveness of the relationships within the ISU fluctuated over the course of the operation and with the stress level being experienced with particular events and personalities (interview with Senior Provincial Manager and Integrated Security Unit Planner, 2010). Generally, the various cultures did not fit well together, and formed a series of pegs being pressed into dissimilar holes. The system's success over the course of the training and in addressing the limited number of minor issues and events involved with the execution of the Games can be attributed both to the limited nature of those events and the ad hoc inter-agency cooperation procedures that developed at the tactical and personal level. In the fortunate absence of an event requiring a sustained combined joint response to a large-scale event, the ultimate effect that this low-key clash of cultures would have had on the collective response to a major security event is not known (interview with ISU Emergency Measures Coordinator, 2010).

One indicator of the possible outcome that this clash of cultures could have had in responding to an actual large-scale event was the result of a training event involving a 9/11-style crash of an airliner within the Games area of operations. The CF classification of the information associated with this event was such that the first indicator that an event was unfolding to the civil emergency/consequence management agencies might well have been the rain of wreckage and debris on the ground following the break-up of the aircraft. The consequences of this turn of events would have been politically unacceptable (perception of a bureaucratically de-layed response in responding to public need) and morally questionable (interview with ISU Emergency Measures Coordinator, 2010). Although this particular scenario was rehearsed several times, the clash of infor-mation management cultures continued to make the response process an awkward beast and raised the uncomfortable question of how other large-scale events that were not exercised as rigorously would have been handled.

Notwithstanding these difficulties, however, there were successes and improvements to inter-agency cooperation and coordination experienced throughout the planning and execution process, particularly at the tac-tical or grassroots level (interview with ISU Planner and ISU Emergency Measures Coordinator, 2010). Proof of this occurred not only within the Games themselves but also in a real life multi-agency event that took place proximate to theGames. The event was the tracking, reception, and processing of the people on board the illegal migrant ship Sun Sea. The smooth and effective coordination of effort among a variety of agencies including EMBC in the handling of the activities related to the Sun Sea incident demonstrated that at least within the immediate timeframe of the Games, and at the tactical level, the Games security experience has borne fruit (interview with Senior Provincial Manager, 2010).

Unfortunately, the news is not so positive at the operational or regional level of the Games security strategy. It would appear that hubris and tribalism have significantly interfered with the use of experiences and issues encountered during the planning and execution of the secur-ity strategy for the Games. Further, this interference might have actually resulted in the degradation of the ability of security organizations do-mestically and bi-nationally to address national security interests both now and in the future (interview with Senior Games Security Liaison and Coordinator, 2010).

During the planning and execution of the Games security strategy, there was ongoing friction between the tactical, operational, and strategic levels as the security realities "on the ground" rubbed against the polit-ical realities within and between security organizations and government bureaucracies at every level. In several cases, this friction was created by the fact that the thin veneer was peeled off years of claims that plans were in place when in reality there were no real plans, only concepts and policies.

These policies and procedural directions flowing from the strategic level met increasing resistance as they made their way from the strategic or national level to the operational or regional one, where they had to be operationalized or translated into a useful plan that met the Games security objectives. The reason for the resistance was that the policy and procedure had often been developed in isolation without input or collaboration from those on the ground. It was also common to see greater and greater resistance to requests or recommendations for changes or amendments to policy and procedure as it moved up from the tactical level to the strategic level for the same reasons (interview with Senior Games Security Liaison and Coordinator, 2010).

Over the course of the planning and execution phase of the Games, security professionals from all agencies involved worked together to make sense of higher-level policies within the context of the security realities present for the Games and also to determine which were genuine policies and which were just the preferences of one or more levels of bureaucracy (interview with Senior Games Security Liaison and Coordinator, 2010).

In order to achieve success in their respective mandates, there arose a series of changes/amendments/alterations to the tactics, techniques, and procedures used by these agencies in the everyday execution of their responsibilities. Initially at both the tactical and operational levels these changes were made informally and became increasingly effective as professional relationships between individuals were established that resulted in increasing levels of trust and cooperation. At the conclusion of the Games, leaders and analysts at the tactical level undertook a formal and detailed review process intended to capture these experiences and lessons with the objective of institutionalizing these changes in order to improve the efficiency and effectiveness of the overall national security infrastructure.

The review and reporting process for the RCMP, the Integrated Public Safety Organization (IPSO) and the CF were examined and in each case, the detailed reports and recommendations coming from the tactical level were subjected to a series of vetting procedures that effectively removed any mention of activities or recommendations for change that did not conform to what was perceived as the best interests of the agency or leadership involved (interview with ISU Planner, Senior Games Security Liaison and Coordinator, and Senior Provincial Manager, 2010).

One such example was the IPS review. It initially contained a proposal for a major revision to the operating structure, but by the time it was cleared at the senior levels, much of the proposal that influenced existing areas of authority had been watered down or amended such that it now contains few substantive changes or improvements. Comments or recommendations that implied criticism of existing organizational philosophies, accepted wisdom, or leadership were removed. One estimate indicates that only 15 percent of the observations and recommendations made at the tactical level eventually made it into the after action review or analysis issued by the agencies involved (interview with Senior Games Security Liaison and Coordinator and Senior Provincial Manager, 2010).

Will some of the most fundamental and important lessons of the Games security experience be ignored and lost? Possibly. They will likely exist for a short time and be resident in the organizations that participated in the Games to the extent that the tactical level participants remain in their positions and maintain the contacts established during the Games. Thereafter they will be carried in the professional memories of the participants as they move upward through their respective organizations and thus, after a fashion, they will become an informal part of the national security infrastructure. To the extent that acknowledgment of organizational or procedural shortcomings within a given agency will impede the upward movement of these individuals through their hierarchies, the lessons and knowledge resulting from the Games will be cast aside or used only in an indirect fashion to shape future security efforts. There is unlikely to be any formal institutionalization into the corporate memory of a number of these lessons for the future.

The logic employed to rationalize this outcome, professionally and personally, may well have been that since the Games were a success and there were no security incidents of any significance that the status quo in terms of policy and leadership was obviously sufficient to bring about success. There is therefore no requirement for a process of embarrassing self-analysis or tweaking of the system to maintain or improve its efficiency in carrying out its mandate. The logic employed with this line of reasoning is otherwise known as hubris. The follow-on conclusion to this line of logic is that significant change and improvement to an organization's capabilities will only take place at a very slow pace, or very quickly when a cataclysmic security failure exposes weaknesses and shortcomings previously concealed by organizational defences – otherwise known as tribalism.

This has already evidenced itself in the conduct of the G8/G20 security programme where many of the lessons learned appear to have been ignored or otherwise shelved by the same organizations that participated in the execution of the Games strategy or were key observers of the Games security process. The government's objective that the Games serve as a test bed and learning device for the G8/G20 security effort and future large-scale security endeavours does not appear to have been met and the organization that stood to gain the most from observing, learning and capturing the hard learned lessons from the Games (not to mention that it is their federal mandate) – Public Safety Canada – did not (interview with ISU Planner, 2010).

At the national level, the key issue is the future of the strategic co-ordination function served by the Coordinator resident in the PCO. The question naturally arises that if the position of Coordinator is necessary to facilitate the security effort for planned events such as the Olympics and the G8, would not such a position be equally necessary, or even more so, on an ongoing basis to coordinate the national response to a no-notice attack, disaster, or some other crisis involving the wholesale inclusion of the every aspect of government as well as the security infrastructure? If such coordination is necessary for a planned event, would it not be even more necessary and valuable to address an unplanned one?

Mr. Elcock states that the reality is that they are different situations. In an emergency, everyone would focus on the event under the coordina-tion of the PCO as the immediate priority. The decision to establish the position within the PCO was taken for a couple of reasons. First, the PCO has the ability to organize and operationalize policy – that is to say, to turn a policy into action – a capability that is not shared with a number of government departments that include PS and Transport Canada. Second, PCO alone within the government infrastructure has the clout, the power to mobilize the other departments, to direct them to take action in support of the established policy and would do so if a security crisis or emergency arose requiring a national response. Thus the position of Coordinator is and will likely remain a temporary one (interview with Elcock, 2009).

While this logic and explanation is absolutely true – the PCO has directed, and will continue to direct, government activity in times of crisis – the question remains: would the national security infrastructure not be better positioned to react to a crisis with an established national level operational capability, rather than an "ad hoc" one cobbled together in the heat of the moment? Some of the senior leadership associated with the operational level command and control of the Games certainly think so (Barr, 2010).

The major problem that would be encountered in the establishment of an ongoing mechanism would be the same as for the temporary one established for the Games. This problem would be one of obtaining bureaucratic buy-in by the various departmental mandarins for a long-term subordination of their power and authority, and the selection of a department that actually has the ability to operationalize a plan rather than simply establish policy for an issue.

The mandarins allowed the temporary relinquishing of their power and authority in the case of the Games for two reasons: the agency they relinquished it to was not a peer organization, but one that had clear seniority/authority/power and they understood that it was a temporary situation resulting from a transient set of circumstances. As such there was no surrender of authority to a peer organization and they were as-sured that the pre-Games power status quo would be re-established at their conclusion. Under the conditions that presently exist in terms of inter-agency power issues, the only other circumstance in which the surrender or sharing of power would be contemplated would be in a no-notice crisis where all were convinced that issues of national security superseded those of the acquisition and retention of power by individual agencies within the government security infrastructure – exactly the set of circumstances described by Mr. Elcock in his explanation of why his position as Coordinator would not be a permanent one.

Thus the security legacy of the Games is somewhat mixed and in the eyes of a number of practitioners somewhat disappointing at this early stage of post-operations assessment and review. Whether or not the tactical level or grassroots recommendations aimed at improving the interoperability of the national security effort throughout every level of government will make it into the report and be assigned a priority that allows for their funding and establishment depends in large part on the politics and preferences of the senior level managers and the political masters they serve (interview with ISU Planner, 2010). Initial reports on this process are not encouraging.

EMBC has the lead for the IPS report and as mentioned earlier, preliminary indications are that the grassroots lessons learned are being watered down and thinned out by organizational politics between agencies and also within EMBC. Observations and inputs for change or improvements to the EMBC way of doing things, specifically with respect to the value and utility of inter-agency coordination and cooperation and proposals for integration of consequence management operations under an ongoing IPS are being increasingly opposed as the ideas move up through successive levels of review (interview with Senior Provincial Manager and ISU Planner, 2010).

Similarly, indications of the Games' legacy at the federal level are also disappointing. Execution of the security plan for the G8/G20 indicate that few if any of the lessons learned at the Games were incorporated in spite of a number of specific references by senior managers of the Games forming a template for future large-scale national level security operations (interview with ISU Planner, 2010). The RCMP may conduct a good internal review and revise some of their processes and procedures, but these actions will likely never see the light of day outside of the tribe. Other federal institutions including the CF are likely to follow the same strategy (interview with ISU Planner, 2010).

In the absence of a catastrophic event forcing an open, comprehensive, and detailed enquiry into events, it is unlikely that any substantive change will result from the conduct of the Games in terms of how the security community conducts itself. Equally unlikely is any substantive change in the operating cultures of the individual agencies involved (interview with ISU Planner, 2010).

It would appear that in many cases, the lessons learned from the Games will benefit the national security infrastructure in the short term so long as positively motivated individuals retain their positions and Games-related contacts. But as they move around their organizations these contacts will inevitably weaken and the benefits to the operating capabilities of organizations and the security community resulting from the Games will gradually disappear (interview with ISU Planner, 2010).

Research to date on the use of the CA for the planning and execution of the security strategy for the 2010 Winter Olympics in Vancouver thus does not provide a positive picture in terms of the degree and extent to which the lessons learned will be used to improve the Canadian security infrastructure and ensure that it is as effective and efficient as possible. Those lessons that point to a change, shift, or sharing of power/influence within the infrastructure are unlikely to see the light of day at the strategic level and are even less likely to be implemented should they reach that lofty plane. The best that can be hoped for is that the tactical- and operational-level leaders responsible for the success of the strategy continue to employ the lessons they learned throughout the remainder of their careers as they move up through their respective organizations. Otherwise the very success of the efforts of the thousands of security personnel is probably the greatest obstacle to overcome in affecting meaningful improvement to the national security infrastructure. In the absence of failure or disaster, a combination of hubris and tribalism will likely prevent the true value of the Games experience – improvements to enhance national security – from ever being realized.

The extent to which these statements are true can be assessed in the future based upon the degree and extent to which the two fundamental recommendations coming out of the Games – the creation of a central coordination mechanism for the oversight and control of national-level security operations (Barr, 2010) and the establishment of a government-wide protocol and system for the sharing of classified information (interview with Mercer, 2010) – are implemented.[55]

The application and operational effectiveness of the CA is therefore limited by issues of hubris and tribalism resulting from a concern over the dissipation of power that could result from structural changes to the national security infrastructure. The improvements to the national security infrastructure resulting from the planning and execution of the largest and most comprehensive security operation in Canadian history will probably be limited to those that are successful in passing through several levels of filtering within each of the agencies involved and within the government infrastructure as a whole. In the absence of a significant security event highlighting a failure in the existing system, this combination of hubris and tribalism will limit the benefits that can be realized from the successful efforts to secure the 2010 Winter Olympics in Vancouver.

PART V
MAKING THE
COMPREHENSIVE
APPROACH WORK

Chapter 15

RELIGIOUS LEADER ENGAGEMENT AND THE COMPREHENSIVE APPROACH: AN ENHANCED CAPABILITY FOR OPERATIONAL CHAPLAINS AS WHOLE OF GOVERNMENT PARTNERS

Steve Moore

Introduction

There is an emerging recognition within the international community that a more Comprehensive Approach (CA) is needed to effectively intervene in violent conflict situations that confront us globally – a trend now replicated in response to natural disasters domestically and abroad. In addition, there is an increasing acknowledgement that in many parts of the world the religious dimension of life – in both its irenic and conflictual manifestations – must be taken into account if efforts to resolve conflict are to be effective and lasting. Already, military chaplains in a number of countries have established a track record in working constructively with local religious leaders in conflict zones, initiatives known as Religious Leader Engagement (RLE),[56] a sub-set of Key Leader Engagement (KLE).

Today, military leaders acknowledge the strategic merit of building rapport and establishing cooperation with the religious segment of society as critical to the accomplishment of mission mandates. It is under Commanders authority and in accordance with their intent that chaplains contribute to meeting these operational objectives through engaging

Security Operations in the 21st Century: Canadian Perspectives on the Comprehensive Approach, ed. M. Rostek and P. Gizewski. Montreal and Kingston: Queen's Policy Studies Series, McGill-Queen's University Press.

religious leaders and their faith group communities. Networking, partnering and, in some instances, peacebuilding endeavours among local clerics have proven to be effective means to garnering the much-needed trust of these influential community leaders – something that other initiatives may build on. In addition to Canada, chaplains from the United States (Iraq and Afghanistan), France (Kosovo), and South Africa (Burundi) have worked closely with Command to bring religious leaders together, in some instances, at the highest levels, leading to greater understanding of the *other* and increased cooperation across ethnic lines. To date, the majority of instances of RLE have taken place within the military context and under Command, seminal ministry under development within the U.S. Army and Navy Chaplaincies. Direct linkages to Command will remain the central focus of RLE, as out of necessity all operational initiatives must integrate into mission planning.

Bearing the above in mind, the trajectory of this chapter will include an exploration of the principles and dynamics of RLE, albeit within a different venue – the Whole of Government (WoG). The complexities of contemporary conflict will continue to drive the requirement for innovative ways to navigate such labyrinths. CA, with its WoG emphasis, is one such response. The interagency environment (WoG) continues to expand as greater collaboration with other government departments (OGD) and agencies (OGA) increases in the bid to enhance nation-building capacities. This discussion will consider the potential role of RLE within the WoG domain. Religious peacebuilding within conflicted nations is an emergent phenomenon globally. In the years ahead, the strategic significance of chaplains' engaging religious leaders and their communities, engulfed in the larger conflicts of their respective identity groups, may have a role to play along side their interagency partners.

The Changing Face of Warfare

Since the early 1990s seismic shifts have occurred in the nature and complexity of conflict. The movement from the more traditional *interstate* warfare of earlier times to what is now described as *new wars – intrastate* conflict – has brought us to the abyss of asymmetric warfare. Today, we witness insurgents using more low-intensity and asymmetric methods as a means of throwing larger and more professional troops off balance. Unable to match the military prowess and sophisticated weaponry of Western armies in open conflict, today's insurgents place their focus more on undermining an adversary's will to fight, employing "hit and run" tactics that chip away at the edges, deftly using car bombs, suicide bombers, improvised explosive devices (IEDs), and the like. Clearly, the aim is "to circumvent or undermine an opponent's strengths while exploiting his weaknesses, using methods that differ significantly from the opponent's usual mode of operations" (Fulton, 2003, 63).

Elaborating further, Leslie, Gizewski, and Rostek describe today's operational environment thusly,

> That environment is ever more dynamic, uncertain, and challenging. Often, it involves irregular and asymmetric conflict conducted by a range of foes, including highly adaptive "media-savvy" terrorist organizations, intent less upon defeating armed forces than in eroding their will to fight, warlords seeking to retain power and influence over local populations at any price, and trans-national criminal organizations ready, willing, and able to buy, sell, and trade everything from drugs to armaments for personal gain. Frequently, it involves failed and failing states whose tenuous existence and inability to meet popular demands offer ready breeding ground for rebellion and civil war, as well as a secure base from which adversaries can function. And, it involves complex human and physical terrain – with large, densely populated cities and highly diverse populations (i.e., ethnically, religiously, economically, and culturally) often serving as the backdrop for military operations (Leslie, Gizewski, and Rostek, 2008, 12).

Hostile environments such as these have stirred governments to reassess former approaches to arresting the violent conflict of imploding nations. A more Comprehensive Approach to addressing such complexity has emerged.

The Comprehensive Approach

Multinational coalitions, be they UN or NATO, are now employing what in military circles is known as a Comprehensive Approach, frequently described as collaborative interaction between international and local organizations during times of chaos or disaster (Director General Joint Doctrine and Concepts, 2006). One of the better definitions of CA originates with *The Comprehensive Approach: Road Map*; a document soon to be published by the Chief of Force Development of the Canadian Forces (CF). Draft Version 4 offers the following explanation and description,

The term "comprehensive approach" is widely used and sometimes loosely applied to a range of different circumstances. The whole-of-government approach, much like the United States' interagency concept, describes the collective efforts of a level of government. The Comprehensive Approach concept builds on and expands beyond this to include all actors who could potentially contribute to the resolution of a complex issue. These additional actors could include important allied governments, subject matter experts, functional specialists, non-government actors and others as the situation dictates. It includes those who need to be closely consulted at all levels to ensure activities are coordinated and coherently delivered (Canadian Forces Development, 2010, 4).

In recent years, Canada's experience of CA has primarily focused on nation building in failing or failed states, an approach where Whole of Government (WoG) thinking is nested within the CA (Leslie, Gizewski, and Rostek, 2008), the former being language more familiar to other government departments (OGD) and agencies (OGA). In Afghanistan, Canada employs an overall "comprehensive" strategy with a particular interagency (WoG) emphasis. A number of government departments and agencies are presently working in collaboration, an effort to which the Canadian Forces (CF) provides support and security: the Department of Foreign Affairs and International Trade (DFAIT), the Canadian International Development Agency (CIDA), The Royal Canadian Mounted Police (RCMP), Corrections Services Canada (CSC), the Department of Justice, Canadian Border Services Agency (CBSA), Canadian Security Intelligence Service (CSIS), Elections Canada, and finally the Department of Finance (Mantle, 2008). Added to this list are the various Non-Governmental Organizations, both international and indigenous, that are functioning in the same operational environment. The ideal to which all strive is to see such cooperation develop multinationally among the numbers of nations operating in the theatre of operations.

As noted above, the vagaries of contemporary conflict have summoned actors from a broad range of domains. Operational space still exists for others who may contribute to resolving the enmity among peoples that drives conflict. Unmistakable in the midst of these continuing complexities has been the resurgence of more militant and extreme forms of religion. The recruitment of impressionable youth by these organizations is of alarming concern among more moderate religious leaders everywhere. Of note, has been the increase in calls for empowering those among the tolerant voice of religion whose emphasis is one of peace and inclusivity of the *other*. Engaging religious leaders determined to rise above the violence of their more radical counterparts may be an approach worthy of consideration.

Religion as a Factor of Contemporary Conflict

Harvard's Hebert C. Kelman, known for his work with the Oslo Accord, maintains that the deep-seated "negation of the *other*" is a main driver of conflict, which in turn shapes collective identity (Kelman, 2008) as boundaries are drawn to secure one's safety and identity from the alien *other*. In such situations, this is done "largely by exclusion, placing beyond that boundary those who are 'not us,' who are 'them'…these are the ones made *other*" (Schreiter, 1992, 52). Stirring such animosity, or stoking its embers, becomes an effective means of polarizing ethno-religious communities for political gain, inciting violence by misleading local populations, colluding with the criminal element if need be (Varshney, 2002). Volatility and violence can be expected outcomes if people are outraged by their "victimization" at the hands of the *other* – real or perceived – rendering their deep emotional currents and prejudices easily exploited (Appleby, 2000).

Sadly, religion is often employed as a catalyst for such conflict escalation due to its uniqueness as an instrument of global appeal. Today, "religious identity and affiliation are more transnational and therefore more mobile than identity based on nationality or language" (Appleby and Cizik, 2010, 38). The complexities of conflict may be compounded further when religious leaders who, with their incendiary language, contribute to the congealing of adversarial identity markers, exacerbating the polarization of communities even more (Otis, 2004). "Religious identity *per se* is not exclusive. The problem comes when it turns into the only motivation for political action under the influence of opportunistic leaders with exclusive political programs" (Apostolov, 2001, 13). Co-optation of religion as a means of consolidating power bases – manipulative politicians collaborating with religious leaders either desirous of power or flattered by such undue attention – must be recognized for what it is and resisted.

Recognition of the Role of Religion in Resolving Contemporary Conflict

Among the numerous groups engaged in religious peace-building around the globe, three American based organizations devoted to conflict resolution, research and reconstruction and stabilization efforts bear mentioning. Each in its unique way, challenges the US Government to review its traditional policy of keeping religion at arms length in its efforts to resolve conflict abroad. Insights will be drawn from each as a means of stimulating like discussion in the Canadian context. A nascent domain, these represent but a sampling of the growing body of literature emerging from the research and debate around religious and strategic peace-building. Of significance is the recognition that more than a few of these organizations/think tanks are secular in orientation. The following will serve as a backdrop to the discussion to follow regarding the role of Padres engaging local religious communities.

In their most recent publication, *Engaging Religious Communities Abroad: a New Imperative for US Foreign Policy* (Appleby and Cizik, 2010), emphasizes that for many in today's world, religion is woven into all aspects of life: language, culture, economics, society, art, and politics. Religious affairs experts are needed, necessitating additional training for Foreign Service and military officers. Strategies for respectfully engaging religious actors at the community level would ensue, while supporting credible religious organizations administering health care and education for local populations.

Those familiar with Operations will recognize USAID as a significant player in reconstruction and stabilization. *Religion, Conflict and*

Peacebuilding: An Introductory Programming Guide (USAID, 2010), was designed as a "toolkit" to lower discomfort levels among personnel to making connections between conflict, religion and peace-building. In more unstable situations, the writers state, "inattention to religious identities or to the views and aspirations of religious leaders may result in mischaracterizations about what the conflict is actually about or how likely it is to become violent" (USAID, 2010). Not to underestimate the "challenges" that engaging religious communities may bring – hence, the need for transparency in dialogue – the document underscores the undeniable influence religious leaders have within their communities as well as the integrity and authenticity of religious themes and organizations in the midst of conflict.

The Washington-based Center for Strategic and International Studies (CSIS) is a secular think tank of longstanding. In their view, successfully resolving today's complex conflict will necessitate "government analyses, policy, training, and programming...fully incorporat[ing] an understanding of the varied roles for religion in conflict-prone settings" (Danan and Hunt, 2007, 1). The Report, *Mixed Blessings: US Government Engagement with Religion in Conflict-Prone Settings*, recommends additional government expertise in all departments with respect to religion, expanding outside partnerships with academics in related fields, and linking this community of experts to those in the field as a force multiplier. In addition, the framers of this document encourage broader engagement inclusive of "not only 'religious moderates' but also 'religious conservatives' as opinion leaders and possible drivers of change" (Danan and Hunt, 2007, 52).

More relevant still to the deliberation to follow is the Report's citing of the role of chaplains as a strategic resource in the operational environment (Danan and Hunt, 2007, 26). More than any other contingent member, the chaplain embodies a natural bond with their local counterparts in theatres of operation. As such, they offer inroads to local communities where the intermeshing of religion and culture blur any lines of distinction.

Religious Leader Engagement: An Emerging Role for Operational Chaplains

The Human Dimension (HD) is of increasing importance to the individual within the military environment as well as to the organization itself. To this end, "creativity, innovation, ingenuity and adaptability" (Directorate of Land Concepts and Designs, forthcoming) are viewed as essential components of HD. Accordingly, much emphasis is placed on HD within the military as a functioning body with many members, of which cohesiveness and trust are critical elements. Concomitant with greater capacity to function within the human dimension as an organization – comprise of individuals – comes an enhanced capability to interface with indigenous populations within theaters of operations.

[L]earned *trust* within the organization will ultimately translate into greater opportunities for authentic engagement among the leaders and people of local communities. An increased capacity in this regard will serve to "disarm" potential spoilers as the establishment of a *fragile trust* among the people facilitates a gradual, yet perceptible, shift in allegiances. In this sense, an aspect of Army culture will not only be the ability to adapt to organizational change at the micro and macro levels but also to examine ways and means to integrate with local cultures within Areas of Operation (DLCD, forthcoming).

It is out of this thinking that Religious Leader Engagement emerges.

Identifying the tolerant voice among religious leaders is key to initiating dialogue. These are faith group leaders – community leaders – often desirous of moving beyond conflict, thus transcending the present hostilities and intransigence that are pitting their respective identity groups against one another. Known as "middle-range actors," (Lederach, 1997)[57] they enjoy the confidence of the grassroots while moving freely at the higher levels of leadership within their own communities.

Considering the above from a strictly doctrinal perspective, the Department of National Defence publication, *Land Operations* (2008b), stipulates "…a wide range of capabilities and activities are required in order to influence and affect systems and actors, including the indigenous population, in order to realize operational objectives" (5-24). Of import here are "actors" within "indigenous populations" as centres of gravity, a term defined as "…strengths that create effects; therefore, they are better defined in terms of people – individuals or groups – that can create effects" (510.1, 6-9). Land Force's newly released *Counter-Insurgency Operations* manual (2008a) states: "In all cases, the indigenous population is the *primary* centre of gravity because no insurgency can survive amidst the hostile terrain of an unreceptive public" (511.7, 5-16).[58] "Public opinion," "public will," and "strength of national purpose" are all factors of the abstract and moral perspectives of centres of gravity (Canadian Forces Operations, 2000). More poignant still, Wilson et al. write, "people and ideas are the essence of why wars are fought and for how long" (Wilson, Sullivan, and Kempfer, 2003, 53). Drawing attention to the sway of religious influence, Allan English illumines, "the real centre of gravity is a shared religious/ideological goal where common purpose and zealotry replace military equipment and command structures" (English, 2005, 53). Charismatic religious leaders are identified as having the capacity to shape moral opinion in the public domain – significant centres of gravity within local populations (Land Force, 2008, 508.6 b, (1), 5-11).

As a harbinger of things to come, engaging the tolerant voice among local religious leaders as centres of gravity segues naturally into the operational domain of Key Leader Engagement (KLE). Yet to be documented within Canadian military doctrine, KLE is an influence activity used at commanders discretion. It may be defined as "the conduct of a deliberate and focused meeting with a person of significant importance in order to achieve a desired effect" (Land Force, 2009, 1). Religious communities within indigenous populations – and the inherent influence of their leaders among the people – are worthy of consideration. A modification of KLE, the chaplain engaging local religious leaders may be referred to as Religious Leader Engagement (RLE), a label that originates in American military doctrine.

Again, in *Engaging Religious Communities Abroad: A New Imperative for US Foreign Policy* (Appleby and Cizik, 2010), the authors underscore the core objective of religious engagement to be the building of partnerships and networking that would increase in value over the long run. Here understanding and respect are deepened where actors may otherwise remain wary of each other, thus engendering the trust and confidence that enables the advancement of shared interests and objectives. The Task Force cites as well that such cooperation among local religious leaders and their communities over the long-term may function as "shock absorbers," preventing the manipulation or abuse of religion to escalate conflict or tensions (Appleby and Cizik, 2010).

A leading authority in intractable conflict is social psychologist Terrell A. Northrup. In such situations, she contends that over the long term, a shift in the perception of the *other* touches on identity. If evident, even in one of the parties, "the chances for long-term change are greatly increased, particularly if the change involves core aspects of identity that are directly related to the conflict." Although not a panacea for change, she illumines that where such intractable conflict between groups persists, "the progress for change is somewhat better when changes in the dynamics of the relationship occur" (Northrup, 1989, 70). Embryonic in today's operational environment, tomorrow's chaplains will collaborate with their interagency partners to impact the dynamics of relation among religious communities within indigenous populations. The following diagram and accompanying text is but a brief introduction to this emerging domain.

JIMP

Figure 11 depicts how Religious Leader Engagement may move estranged groups from Encounter among religious leaders to Joint Activities at the community level. This concept finds its origins in the **JIMP** principle (Leslie, Gizewski, and Rostek, 2008),[59] an Army construct designed to more effectively convey the fullness of meaning of the Comprehensive Approach. See Figure 12 below. The following is a brief overview: (i) **"J"** represents Joint or the combined nature of operations where the marshaling of different military elements are used in a complementary fashion to accomplish the mission; (ii) **"I"** stands for Interagency, which is the Whole of Government domain – government departments and agencies collaborating in nation building efforts; (iii) **"M"** or Multinational

FIGURE 11: RELIGIOUS LEADER ENGAGEMENT

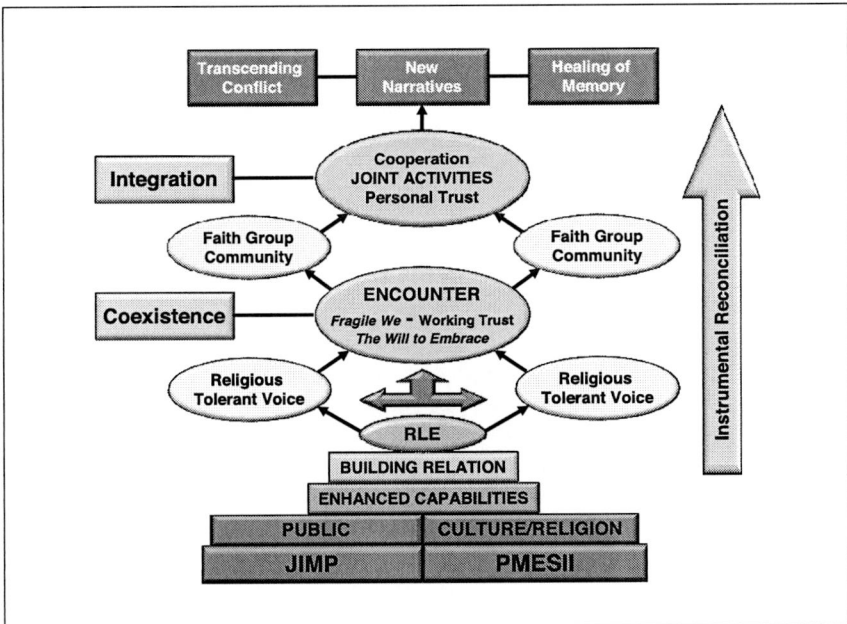

©Major S.K. Moore, PhD

speaks to international will – numbers of nations coming together under the auspices of the UN, NATO or other coalitions, bringing to bear all of their combined resources to create stability and effect change where needed, and; (iv) **"P"** or **Public** domain, which is host to a number of organizations and activities in Operations, but, as has already been underscored, the indigenous population therein is without question the most consequential. As Figure 11 indicates, RLE falls within the **Public** domain of Operations. Local religious leaders are undoubtedly centers of gravity within indigenous populations – middle range actors who, in non-western societies, where the lines of separation between faith and the public space are markedly less defined, carry much influence at community and regional levels. Such influence owes its origins to the almost seamless nature existing between religious communities and local culture and, at times, politics. Chaplains move quite freely within these circles and, most certainly, bring something to the table in terms of their ability to be a positive influence for good.

PMESII

Concomitant to **JIMP** is another aspect of doctrine referred to as **PMESII**. This acronym delineates the breadth of interests in a given campaign:

Political, Military, Economic, Social, Infrastructure and Information. The Social sphere of PMESII runs in tandem to the Public Space of JIMP, for indigenous populations are host to both culture and religion, salient aspects of the Social sphere. Religious communities factor significantly within culture – again, a domain familiar to operational chaplains.

FIGURE 12: SCHEMATIC OF JOINT INTERAGENCY MULTINATIONAL PUBLIC CONCEPT

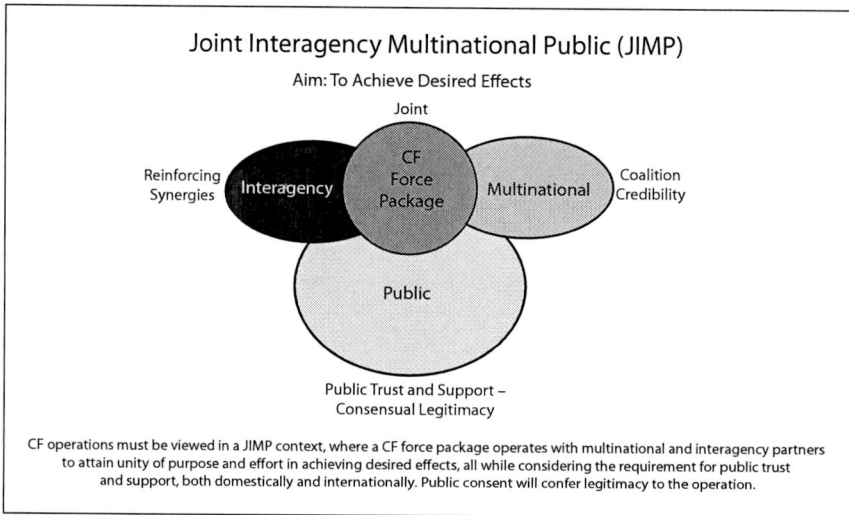

Joint Interagency Multinational Public (JIMP)

Aim: To Achieve Desired Effects

Joint

Reinforcing Synergies — Interagency — CF Force Package — Multinational — Coalition Credibility

Public

Public Trust and Support – Consensual Legitimacy

CF operations must be viewed in a JIMP context, where a CF force package operates with multinational and interagency partners to attain unity of purpose and effort in achieving desired effects, all while considering the requirement for public trust and support, both domestically and internationally. Public consent will confer legitimacy to the operation.

Source: Government of Canada Department of National Defence (2004, 16).

Encounter

Where religious communities are estranged due to their being engulfed in the larger conflict of their respective identity groups, the goal becomes to gradually bring religious community leaders together in *encounter*, a delicate process of dialogue leading to the establishing of what practitioners refer to as the *"fragile we*, a situation…where *us* versus *them* gives way to *we* at least in certain contexts" (Baron, 2008, 284). As progress in relations improve, *working trust* emerges bringing conflicting communities closer to *coexistence* where, initially, the desire may be to live separately in a conflict-free environment. It is the repeated acts of co-operation in achieving common instrumental goals that see such trust emerge, an indispensable element of reconciliation. Social psychologists refer to such collaboration as *instrumental reconciliation* (Nadler and Shnabel, 2008). The emphasis here is not so much the addressing of past wrongs as it is beginning the writing of new narratives together through increased association as a way of moving forward. As Baron notes, his "emphasis is more on creating islands of working trust and cooperation than worrying about who has to forgive whom" (Baron, 2008, 296). Chaplains' pray that apology and forgiveness will come but recognize that in more intractable situations, where each group believes they are the victim, it may be premature to suggest. The hope is that in time such sustained trust and cooperation may move communities closer to *integration* where *personal trust* creates an atmosphere of friendship. It is in such an atmosphere that conflict is transcended, new narratives are written and the healing of memory begins.

Joint Activities: Towards Personal Trust and Integration

A chaplains' ability to network among local religious communities may prove advantageous in situations of intractable conflict where *trust* has been earned and established. With the support of Command and the confidence of OGD actors, the chaplain may aid in identifying and facilitating *Joint Activities* between religious communities that coincide with OGD goals. Local religious leaders, given to *inter*communal cooperation for the greater good, are in a position of influence among their people and with other well-placed community leaders. Continued consultation with other OGD partners would be critical, particularly those functioning in diplomatic and development roles. Any budding joint activity to determine if the identified needs coming from within the faith communities would fall within the parameters of acceptable OGD programming. Here networking becomes partnering. Once a given initiative is identified, the role for the chaplain would remain one of *trusted friend* to the religious leaders but would segue to becoming *facilitator* as WoG members are introduced to the leadership. Out of necessity, the chaplain would remain connected to any such endeavour. US Chaplain (Col) Mike Hoyt (2009) states,

> Religious actors deal in the areas of intentionality, authenticity, credibility, and integrity...When the chaplain (or Commander) fails to follow through on a task, breaks appointments, does not keep promises, or appears prejudicial the observant religious leader sees a break down on two levels: individual character and the value of the spiritual message.

As someone once said, "Perception is very real in its consequences." When dealing with religious communities in non-pluralistic societies, the chaplain's visibility with such processes is essential to their success.

In circumstances where security and opportunity have been favourable, Commanders have authorized chaplains' more intentional peacebuilding activities among religious communities. Padres have brought religious leaders together who, due to existing tensions, have been incommunicado for a number of years. Dialogue and, in some cases, joint activities have resulted, affording occasions to seed reconciliation. Such cooperation among local religious leaders and their communities over the long-term may function as "shock absorbers," preventing the manipulation or abuse of religion to escalate conflict or tensions (Appleby and Cizik 2010).

Of particular importance to joint activities is the notion of super-ordinate goals. These are jointly agreed-upon goals that are of benefit to both groups but cannot be attained through individual effort. As such, greater integration comes to the fore. Through cooperation of this nature, an identity more inclusive of the *other* begins to develop.

Religious Communities: Promoting Local Ownership and Building Local Capacity

A recurring concern among many strategists continues to be the lack of a clear "exit strategy" once personnel and resources have been committed. The cultivation of local ownership from an early stage in the mission is an underutilized approach in building local capacity. The consensus at the Comprehensive Approach Conference in Helsinki was the overemphasis on waiting to engage relevant international actors in nation building efforts to the neglect of integrating local actors at an early stage (Rintakoski and Autti, 2008).

In fragile states, where infrastructure and services have been interrupted and the corruption of political figures is far too common, top down structures frequently have difficulty gaining traction in local communities. Consideration must be given to the employment of religious organizations as credible local actors readily available to aid in the rebuilding of much-needed infrastructure and services. The Chicago Task Force findings stated, "Religious institutions, because of their structure and experience, can and often will fill the vacuum created by the absence, erosion, or collapse of state authority over some or all of its territory" (Appleby and Cizik, 2010, 35). In societies suffering from the strain of conflict, its citizens will search for alternative means of service delivery: one such means is the religious sector. An added advantage that religious institutions bring is that they function well at the grassroots level optimizing networking among the people. Religious centers function as the hub of many cultures and, as such, are most often viewed by local communities as trusted organizations – an available means for building local capacity.

Engaging Religious Communities Abroad: A New Imperative for US Foreign Policy emphatically states, that authentic engagement "entails engaging religious communities on their own terms, listening carefully to their concerns and fears, and entering into substantive dialogue about how to realize their legitimate aspirations" (Appleby and Cizik, 2010, 23). Cementing such gains made must be viewed over the long-term and calls for "collaborative processes that enhance the likelihood of favorable and enduring outcomes within a particular environment" (Department of National Defence, *Land Operations*, 2008b, 514). More than any other contingent member, the chaplain is in a position to engage local religious leaders. The common ground of the spiritual plane is a natural precursor to authentic engagement. What must be kept before us is that activities of this nature – the results of which may be more challenging to measure in the short term – in the aggregate they can have a powerful influence over people's lives (Department of National Defence, *Land Operations*, 2008b). The key here is for the chaplain to be embedded within the interagency environment, to train with as well as work along side other agency partners. When engaging local religious communities in dialogue, needs may be identified, opening the way for other WoG partners to effect change within entire communities that otherwise might remain at a distance to such overtures.

In addition to OGD programming, chaplains are naturally inclined toward *inter*faith dialogue, leading to public celebrations inclusive of leadership from the faith traditions of the identity groups implicated in the greater conflict. Such public displays of unity offer to the people a vision of themes of peace, justice and mutuality that are faithful to the tenor of scripture known to all faith traditions. A number of chaplains attest to conversing with local religious leaders over their concerns for the well-being of their young people and what future lay ahead for them. Where conflict has created chasms between ethnic groups, programming designed to bring their respective youth together has proven to be an effective means of fostering opportunities at building trust and cooperation, as well as dispelling socialized learning about the *other*.[60] Peacebuilders in other contexts speak of cooperative initiatives having revolved around the renaming of a building, street or a park in commemoration of the suffering on both sides of a conflict. A project of this nature implicates people from the communities touched by the conflict, providing a means to move from entrenched positions to begin the work of writing new narratives for the future. Incremental steps, these may be. DFAIT, itself, "promotes dialogue and reconciliation with communities, vulnerable groups and conflicting parties" (Department of Foreign Affairs and International Trade Canada, 2010) as an aspect of the Global Peace and Security Program. A chaplain with enhanced skills could possibly contribute where religious communities are implicated. Given time and resources, much could be done in designing context-specific programming for implementation among religious communities where appropriate.

Peacebuilder and scholar, Rabbi Marc Gopin contends that initiatives of this kind should be judged "one increment at a time and *then* move resolutely with each increment toward lasting change that indeed addresses the deep roots of conflict through paradigm shifts in attitudes, behaviors, and world views" (Gopin, 2009, 64). He advises those implicated in reconciliation efforts to keep in mind the complexities of the task that lay before them, and not to confuse "long-term ends with short-term tasks" (Gopin, 2009, 64). This is sage counsel for a difference exists between first order goals and those of higher order. In a conflict or post-conflict environment, the former – civil dialogue, cooperation, working trust, i.e., peaceful coexistence – is "evaluated on its own merit without any regard as to how events unfold in the long-term," a situation which may sustain a degree of unpredictability. High order goals look to what may be accomplished over the long-term: "justice, the satisfaction of basic human needs, and the creation of a peaceful society that is egalitarian" (Gopin, 2009, 64). Realizing such profound objectives often take decades if not a generation or more.

As noted earlier, CA builds and expands beyond the interagency environment to include all actors potentially capable of contributing to the resolution of the complexities presented by protracted conflict. In many parts of the world, religious communities will undoubtedly remain centres of gravity within indigenous populations well into the future. Given their profile among the people, local religious leaders – middle range actors – desirous of constructive change, could serve as an additional resource in resolving such conflict. Where hostilities have resulted in alienation among communities, building relation through continued dialogue and joint activities with such prominent community leaders may in time aid in ameliorating relations among estranged peoples. Religious leaders in their own right, chaplains are ideal candidates for Religious Leader Engagement (RLE). As CA continues to evolve as a collective strategy, endeavouring to address conflict's convoluted environment, chaplains may prove to be a strategic asset for Commanders whereby one individual may potentially influence larger groups, i.e., religious communities.

Chapter 16

A TRAINER'S PERSPECTIVE ON THE COMPREHENSIVE APPROACH

S*TEVE* F*RITZ*-M*ILLETT*

Introduction

The Government of Canada (GoC) recognises that in the current and future security environment, addressing conflict in the world's hotspots requires more than the application of pure military force (Government of Canada, 2008a, 9). For an enduring peace, states may have to be stabilised or in some cases, extensively reconstructed.[61] The very scope and scale of stabilisation and reconstruction tasks inherent in addressing the challenges of failed and fragile states drives the requirement for a greater integration of military and civilian (people, organisations, groups and movements) capabilities. This was recognised recently by NATO and its constituent states (e.g., UK, US) who are exploring the adoption of the CA (NATO Public Policy Division, 2006, 3) and the development of CA doctrine.

While the Canadian Forces (CF) has yet to develop CA doctrine, the Canadian Army has responded to the need for an improved understanding of the CA with the development of new concepts and studies. *Toward Land Operations 2021 – Studies in Support of the Army of Tomorrow Force Employment Concept* (Director Land Concepts and Designs, 2009) and *Land Operations 2021: Adaptive Dispersed Operations* (Directorate of Land Concepts and Designs, 2007) are illustrative of the pioneering work that is ongoing to establish an intellectual framework for enhancing the Army's capacity to work effectively as a partner within a WoG and CA context. A key concept articulated in these publications is Joint Interagency Multi-National Public or "JIMP," which recognises that

Security Operations in the 21st Century: Canadian Perspectives on the Comprehensive Approach, ed. M. Rostek and P. Gizewski. Montreal and Kingston: Queen's Policy Studies Series, McGill-Queen's University Press.

"an ability to bring to bear all the instruments of national power and coalition power and influence (i.e., diplomatic, economic, military and informational) on a problem in a coordinated, collaborative fashion will be essential to achieving effective results. So too will an ability to address and if possible, effectively engage the views and reactions of the public – both domestic and international – as well as the media – as operations unfold" (Directorate of Land Concepts and Designs, 2007, 23-24). Under this concept, Army organisations able to function in a JIMP environment are described as "JIMP capable" or "JIMP enabled."

Historically, the "Joint" and "Multinational" elements of the JIMP concept are well engrained within the CF and Canadian Army operational culture. Six decades of involvement in NATO, UN and other operations has positioned the Canadian Army well to deal with these aspects of JIMP. The interagency and public components pose greater challenges for the military – most notably in terms of interfacing with civilian entities and organisations that have well established cultures of their own which the military often does not adequately understand (Leslie, Gizewski, and Rostek, 2008, 15). To be truly JIMP enabled, military forces must extend their understanding beyond a small cadre of Civil Military Co-operation (CIMIC) experts at the tactical level. JIMP is a concept that needs to be fully understood and applied throughout the CF. Additionally, this understanding must be operationalized within military campaign plans, directives and practises.

This paper looks at the need for a theoretical foundation for the Army approach to Joint-Interagency-Military-Public (JIMP) in the context of the Comprehensive Approach (CA). A theoretical foundation (McKinsey 7-S) (Waterman, Peters, and Phillips, 1980, and Peters and Waterman, 1982) is applied to examine what is required to ensure further development of these concepts.

Apply-Identify-Adopt (AIA): A Three-Step Process for Enhancing JIMP Capability

Architects of the JIMP concept have argued that there is a requirement for "more conscious, sustained efforts to develop practical tools and metrics capable of ensuring that the implementation and performance of a comprehensive approach is optimised" (Leslie, Gizewski, and Rostek, 2008, 15). This notion is supported by the results of Army Experiment 10 which concludes:

> [v]arious diagram, modelling and discourse capture toolsets need to be incorporated into the ... planning approach to complex problem solving. Such toolsets would need to be capable of adaptation ... (Director Land Concepts and Designs, 2010, 7).

The CF and Canadian Army have a long history of developing processes to aid with complex problem solving. Some familiar examples would be the OPP (Operational Planning Process) for planning, JIPB (Joint Intelligence Preparation of the Battlefield) for intelligence, PMESII – PT (Political, Military, Economic, Social, Information and Infrastructure – Physical Terrain and Time) for operating environment analysis, and FLOCARK (Features, Lanes, Objectives, Canalizing Terrain, Avenues of Approach, Rating of Approaches, Key Terrain/Vital Ground) for ground assessment to name but a few.

This article argues for the CF to adopt a three-step process to enhance its ability to work with civilian entities within the context of the CA. The tool is a three-step process: (i) Apply a Model; (ii) Identify Interests; and, (iii) Adopt a Strategy (AIA). First it examines an organisation using the McKinsey 7-S Model. It then applies interest-based negotiation theory to identify common interests and finally, identifies the optimum CF engagement strategy for a given civilian entity. The end state would be that the CF would have a methodical and holistic approach to understanding civilian entities, their interests in the mission and the optimal engagement strategy the CF should pursue. The result would be an enhanced level of understanding of areas of potential co-operation and just as importantly, areas of potential friction.

Step 1 – Apply

While 7-S was developed for internal analysis of business organisations,[62] its holistic framework makes it a useful tool for the examination of civilian entities, or in JIMP parlance, the "interagency" and "public" players.[63] Understanding the culture of such groups is critical. As an Army Lessons Learned Centre report (2010, 1) observes:

> As part of a whole-of-government approach, the Army should develop a better understanding of the organizational cultures of members from the other government agencies. Presentations and briefings are not enough. Multidisciplinary teams should conduct pre-deployment inter-agency training days where current scenarios and case studies are analysed and solutions are developed. This would facilitate a better understanding of the various interagencies, their capabilities and culture.

Using the results from an application of the 7-S, detailed insights and understanding of an organisation can be derived. The "Ss" of Strategy, Shared Values and Skills should be of particular interest to the CF as it is often along these lines where the greatest potential for collaboration exists. The 7-S is based upon the premise that an organization is not just "structure," but consists of seven interrelated elements (see Figure 13).

7-S recognizes that a change in one "S" can have an effect on one, some or all other "Ss." The seven elements are distinguished as "hard Ss" and "soft Ss." The "hard Ss" (light coloured circles) are tangible and easy to identify. They can be found in strategy statements, corporate plans, organizational charts and other documentation.

FIGURE 13: MCKINSEY 7-s

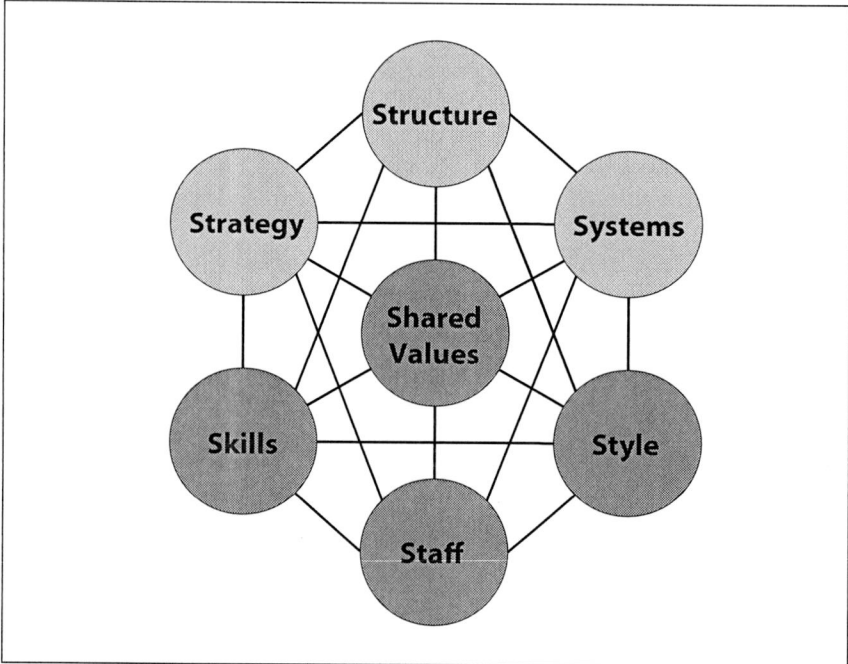

The four "soft Ss" (dark coloured circles) however, are not so easily known. They are difficult to describe since capabilities, values and elements of corporate culture continuously develop and change, or may exist "below the horizon" and only be evident within that organisation. They are also derived substantially from the people who work in the organization. Therefore, it is much more difficult to identify the characteristics of the soft elements. Often, the only way to gain knowledge of these "Ss" is through regular personal and/or professional contact with people who are currently working with these organisations or have worked with them in the past. Although the "soft Ss" are not as visible as the "hard Ss," they have a great impact on the "hard Ss" (i.e., Structures, Strategies and Systems) of the organization.

TABLE 1: MCKINSEY 7-S "HARD" AND "SOFT Ss"

"Hard Ss"	*"Soft Ss"*
Strategy. Actions a company plans in response to or anticipation of changes in its external environment.	**Shared Values.** The dominant values, beliefs, and norms, which develop over time and become relatively enduring features of organizational life.
Structure. Basis for specialization and co-ordination influenced primarily by strategy and by organization size and diversity.	**Style.** This reflects what managers do rather than what they say; How they spend their time and what are they focus attention on. Symbolism – the creation and maintenance (or sometimes deconstruction) of meaning is a fundamental responsibility of managers.
Systems. Formal and informal procedures that support the strategy and structure. (Systems are more powerful than they are given credit for).	**Staff.** The people/human resource management – processes used to select and develop managers, socialization processes, ways of shaping basic values of management cadre, ways of introducing young recruits to the company, ways of helping to manage the careers of employees.
	Skills. The distinctive competences – what the company does best, ways of expanding or shifting competences.

A simple illustration of the application of the first step in the AIA model, which uses the 7-S approach, is offered below. It only examines one "Hard" and one "Soft S" in the context of the International Committee for the Red Cross (ICRC) and is not an in-depth analysis.

Strategy. (ICRC, 2007) The protection work for the ICRC is aimed at helping two categories of people: those being persons deprived of their freedom, particularly those detained in connection with an armed conflict or other situations of violence; and, civilians and others who are not, or who are no longer, taking part in a conflict or other situations of violence, notably persons or groups exposed to specific risks, such as children, women, the elderly, the disabled and the displaced. In situations of conflict, the ICRC coordinates the response by national Red Cross and Red Crescent societies and their International Federation.

The ICRC will participate in coordination and cooperation initiatives with other such organizations by focusing on concrete actions in line with the real needs in the situations in which they operate.

Shared Values. (ICRC, 2010) The ICRC has a permanent mandate under international law to take impartial action for prisoners, the wounded and sick, and civilians affected by conflict. Its mandate is limited to international humanitarian law as both its guardian and promoter. The ICRC is guided by its official principles of "Humanity, Impartiality, Neutrality, Independence, Voluntary Service, Unity, Universality." While not one of the six formal principles, another value that the ICRC subscribes to is that of confidentiality. Because of this, the ICRC will not engage in "name and shame" tactics to fulfill its mandate.

Again, this was a very basic examination of only two of the 7-S elements. Once a detailed understanding of the organisation is achieved using the McKinsey 7-S model as a framework, the second step can be undertaken.

Step 2 – Identify Interest(s)

This step draws extensively on interest-based negotiation theory (The Office of the Executive Director Conflict Management, 2001, 6). If common interests can be identified between parties in a particular situation, the common interests could form the basis of an agreement between the parties. Key to this step is the correct identification of the interests.

Figure 14 illustrates the theory of common interests. The large triangles represent the entirety of a given organisation's interests, Organization #1 in black, Organisation #2 in white. The portions of their respective triangles that overlap, represents the common interest (grey), in other words, that interest that they both share and upon which an agreement might be formed. It is worth noting that in some circumstances, if an agreement can be reached around a common interest, it may also expand to other areas. In such cases, the achievement of the "common interest" can be the "carrot" for additional co-operation in areas that aren't common.

An example from Afghanistan illustrates how two bitter opponents in a struggle can occasionally find areas of common interest. As *Wall Street Journal* reporter Yaroslav Trofimov (2010) notes:

> The antipolio campaign brings together the Taliban, President Hamid Karzai's central government, UNICEF and the World Health Organization in an uneasy but functioning partnership – one that recognizes the reality of the insurgents' stranglehold over large chunks of the country.

While it may strike some as odd that the Taliban would actually co-operate with the Karzai Government (and vice versa), it does indeed happen regularly in the conduct of the anti-polio campaign. This arrangement is possible because both the Government and the Taliban (and several international organizations) have a common interest. Both the Afghan Government and the Taliban have an interest in the anti-polio campaign. First, both have an interest in sparing Afghan children from the debilitating effects of the disease. Second, each has a public relations interest in establishing its legitimacy as *the* health care provider in Afghanistan.

**FIGURE 14: SCHEMATIC REPRESENTATION OF COMMON INTEREST
BETWEEN TWO ORGANIZATIONS**

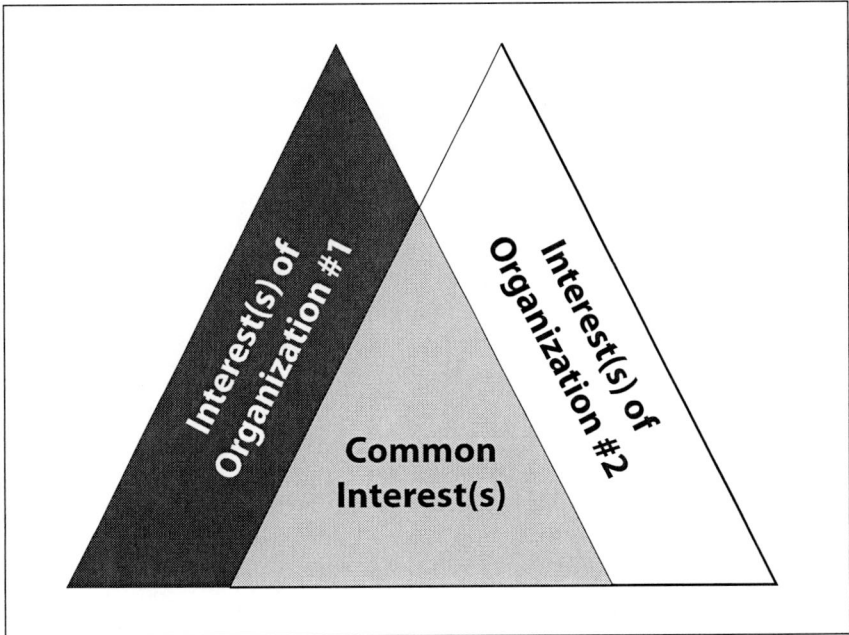

This provides a foundation for the Afghanistan Government – Taliban cooperation, notwithstanding their competition to become the legitimate authority in Afghanistan.

If two groups engaged in a life-and-death civil war can agree on some issues, it stands to reason that various civilian entities and the CF, that find themselves working towards a common goal in the context of the CA for a given mission, should be able to find some common interests upon which they can build their interaction for mutual benefit. Having identified the areas of interest of the civilian entities and having furthermore identified those that the CF has in common with the civilian entities, one can proceed to third and final step in this process.

Step 3 – Adopt the Preferred Engagement Strategy

In the CF context, words are important. Indeed, they are so important that the CF has developed a list of verbs with standardised definitions that are the only ones to be used in giving missions to subordinates. "Mission task verbs" as they are called, provide clarity, ease of shared understanding and simplicity to the process of superiors giving missions to subordinates. For example, the mission task verb "Clear" is defined as follows: *To*

Clear- A tactical task to remove all enemy forces from a specific location, area, or zone. Unfortunately, no comparable system exists for the CF in its interactions with civilian entities. The challenge this poses is that words mean different things to different people and different groups. In the context of recent discussions on the CA, words like "coordinate," "cooperate," "collaborate" etc. are being used rather liberally and often without any clear explanation of what they actually mean, or what is intended. The danger here is that various parties that are looking at working together on something may not have a shared understanding of what these words mean, and this in turn can lead to confusion, miscommunication and ultimately, disagreement. It is not being suggested that the CF would tell civilian entities what the nature of their mutual engagement would be; rather, it would be used and understood internally by the CF.

To address this issue, it is proposed that the CF adopt a standard list of verbs that describe different levels of interaction that might be applied in engaging with a particular civilian organization. This is demonstrated in a linear format in Figure 15, showing increasingly positive interaction as one moves from left to right. In this case, from a CF perspective in the context of Afghanistan, the approach to the Taliban might be "Competing," that with UNAMA "Cooperating" and with CIDA (and other Canadian partners), "Collaborating." Definitions are not provided here but would also need to be developed and standardized.

FIGURE 15: TYPE OF INTERACTION

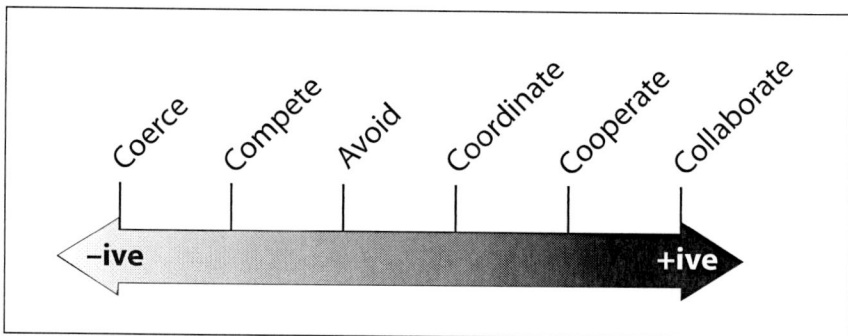

Another possible approach in this step is the use of a two-dimensional model such as that in Figure 16 which identifies strategies based on "Assertiveness" and "Cooperativeness" (Potgieter, 2007). Essentially, each organisation is assessed in terms of these two parameters to arrive at an engagement strategy. To illustrate this in the context of NATO in Afghanistan, the Taliban are both uncooperative and assertive leading you to a "competing" strategy. CIDA could be classified as highly cooperative and assertive suggesting a "collaborating" strategy. The Government of Afghanistan could be classified as cooperative (to a degree) and unassertive (especially in light of the reality of a lack of sub-national governance outside of Kabul) suggesting an accommodating strategy, and so on for each organisation.

FIGURE 16: PRIMARY NEGOTIATION STRATEGIES

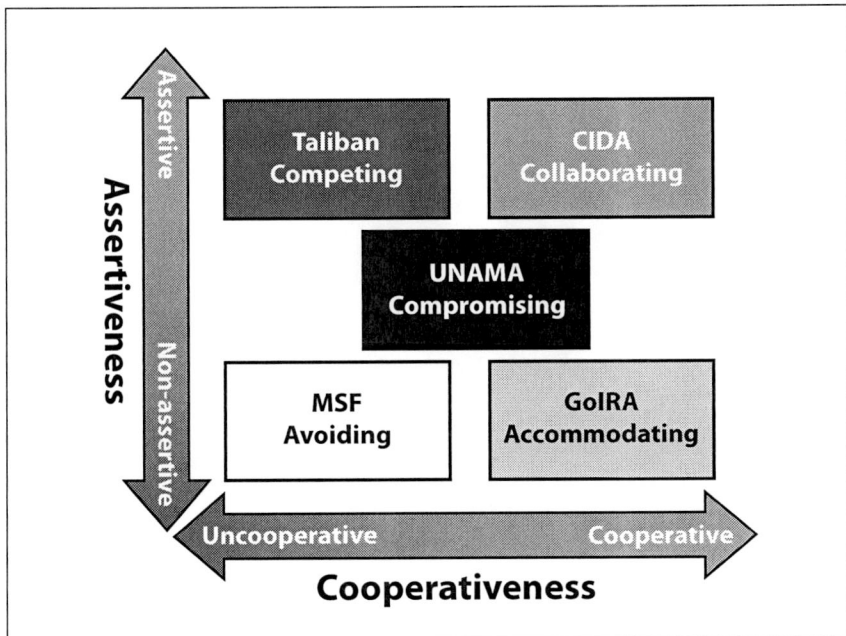

This model has been adapted from the original Thomas-Kilmann Conflict Mode Instrument (TKI), http://courseware.finntrack.eu/learners/cbe_syllabus.htm (viewed 12 February 2010).

Conclusion

Considerable headway has been made in the past few years in developing both our understanding and application of the CA. However, a number of doctrinal, procedural and terminology issues, continue to hamper the CF's application of the approach. This paper has argued for the CF to adopt a three-step process, Apply a Model – Identify Interests – Adopt a Strategy (AIA) to optimize its engagements with civilian entities in the context of the CA. This process could potentially aid the CF in developing a detailed understanding of civilian entities and their organizational cultures, their interest(s) in a conflict, and the optimum engagement strategies that should be adopted to interact with those civilian entities.

Chapter 17

INTERAGENCY TRAINING FOR THE CANADIAN COMPREHENSIVE MISSION IN AFGHANISTAN

MEGAN THOMPSON, ANGELA FEBBRARO, AND ANNE-RENÉE BLAIS

Like many countries responding to the complexity of contemporary international and domestic crises, the Government of Canada is increasingly embracing an integrated or comprehensive approach (CA) to operations (deConing, 2008; Patrick and Brown, 2007; Olson and Gregorian, 2007). The impetus for the comprehensive approach is the understanding that most operations reflect a complexity that is beyond the ability of one governmental department to address. Moreover the CA is rooted in the conviction that an integrated approach of this nature will provide the most effective and efficient responses, facilitate the leveraging based on the strengths of each contributor, and also allow for important synergies to emerge. Accordingly, CA teams are comprised of diverse partners who contribute distinct yet complementary expertise, skills, and resources in order to achieve wider effects and objectives. In practice, a CA can involve various government departments such as defence, foreign affairs and international development, police, border and correctional services; non-governmental and international organizations, as well as the local population. Indeed it is the the explicit emphasis on the coordinated efforts of various government agencies within a single mission space and mandate and working with members of local populations which chiefly defines the new elements of the CA (Leslie, Gizewski, and Rostek, 2008; Olson and Gregorian, 2007; Patrick and Brown, 2007).

Security Operations in the 21st Century: Canadian Perspectives on the Comprehensive Approach, ed. M. Rostek and P. Gizewski. Montreal and Kingston: Queen's Policy Studies Series, McGill-Queen's University Press.

Despite the consensus concerning the benefits of a comprehensive approach, recent reviews of actual CA missions have revealed that they can face significant challenges (Patrick and Brown, 2007; Rietjens, 2008; Olson and Gregorian, 2007). Conflicting political agendas, or at least incompatible objectives, organizational structure disparities (hierarchical and centralized vs. flat and decentralized), incompatible financial, knowledge management and communication systems, different approaches to planning and time frames associated with activities, little or no corporate memory, few formal lessons learned mechanisms, poor funding and personnel shortfalls, and "competition for resources and agency profile" have all been cited as formidable obstacles to effective CA (Olson andGregorian, 2007, 13; see also de Coning, 2008; Morcos, 2005; Patrick and Brown, 2007; Spence, 2002; Stephenson and Schnitzer, 2006; Winslow, 2002). A further source of tension is the "… perceived crossover between civ[il]-mil[itary] functions and lines of operations" (Joint Task Force Afghanistan, 2009, 6). Civilian-based organizations often hold significant concerns about the underlying motives when militaries undertake activities that traditionally fall within development and/or governance activities, fearing that the military will subordinate all other mandates and activities to achieve exclusively security-related ends (Mockaitis, 2004; see also Simms, 2008). Inadvertent knowledge gaps and misunderstandings can also undermine effectiveness, for instance if an organization develops plans based upon inaccurate assumptions concerning another agency's or other agencies' mandates, programs, capabilities, and procedures (Schaefer, Shadrick, Beaubien, and Crabb, 2008).

Interagency training has been suggested as one important way to mitigate at least some of the challenges that can hinder the success of Whole-of-Government (WoG) missions (e.g., Canadian Forces Leadership Institute, 2008). Such training is assumed to provide valuable opportunities for personnel from various agencies to interact in order to provide all participants with a venue for knowledge sharing in order to develop a broader understanding of the overall mission and of each other's capabilities (Schaefer et al., 2008; Stewart, Macklin, Proud, Verrall, and Widdowson, 2004). Jenny (2001) concluded that "[t]raining should be thought of as one of the most important factors for the success of future [interagency] actions. … Indeed, training is arguably the best way to foster understanding … As such it significantly helps in bridging the culture gap and in fostering mutual respect. This in turn facilitates a clear division of labour and helps create channels of communication which will prove of great help should any possible misunderstanding arise during the mission" (31). Similar calls for WoG training have been made by members of the military community (Gizewski and Rostek, 2007; Leslie, Gizewski, and Rostek, 2008; Director General, Joint Doctrine and Concepts, 2006; US Marine Corps Combat Development Command, 2009).

Responding to the need and benefits of this requirement and having the largest capacity for large-scale training, the Canadian Forces have routinely invited Canadian Other Government Departments (OGD) members to their education and training courses that have interagency elements (CFLI, 2008; Thomson, Hall, and Adams, 2010). The largest of these is EXERCISE MAPLE GUARDIAN (EX MG). Conducted over 3 weeks, EX MG was originally developed to provide as realistic a mission-specific training experience as possible for military personnel about to deploy to the Afghanistan mission. While remaining the final confirmation training for CF Battle Groups that are about to deploy to Afghanistan under OP ATHENA, the CF has made continuing efforts to invite Canadian OGD members to contribute to scenario development and to attend EX MG allowing all participants opportunities to practice skills that they will be called upon to use in their upcoming deployment as part of the Canadian WoG team (Land Forces Western Area, 2009).

While assumed to be highly beneficial, it is also the case that large-scale interagency training of the nature of that within EX MG does involve a variety of significant outlays. For instance, travel costs can be quite high, especially for smaller OGD partners, depending on the location and proximity of the training site to the home base of most interagency partners. Certainly this is the case for EX MG, which is traditionally conducted thousands of miles away from Ottawa, at CFB Wainwright, outside of Edmonton, Canada. Further, such intensive training involves significant amounts of additional planning, training, and logistical support. Moreover, such training is quite time intensive and takes OGD members away from their primary jobs. As there are far fewer OGD than military members, OGDs can easily be overwhelmed by multiple interagency training offers/requests from the CF (Thompson and Gill, 2010). Finally, as a result of the global economic downturn of 2008-2009, governments are under increased pressure to be fiscally prudent with respect to resources. For all of these reasons then, it is extremely important to systematically document and justify the benefits of any such resource intensive activities.

Although After Action Reviews (AARs) are routinely conducted after major scenarios in EX MG, and are valuable in many respects, to date there has been relatively little quantitative assessment of EX MG training. The current research was designed to begin to address this knowledge gap via the use of quantitative as well as qualitative assessments of OGD participants' perceptions of the training experience provided by EX MG in terms of two key elements of the comprehensive approach to operations: interactions with the military, and interactions with the local Afghan population. These quantitative assessments allowed us to begin to answer a variety of important questions within this research. For instance, we are able to determine the average amount of prior knowledge and contact OGD members has with members of the CF and the Afghan people, and their general knowledge concerning the amount they knew about the Afghan mission prior to attending EX MG. Moreover, we are able to begin to address if particular aspects of training are significantly associated with valued training outcomes, and whether the training benefits are equal across the OGD groups in attendance.

Method

Participants. 39 of 59 members of Canadian OGDs (11 DFAIT, 14 CIDA, and 14 members of police agencies[64]) who attended EX MG volunteered to complete a short survey assessing their perceptions of the training experience. The length of employment in these agencies and organizations ranged from less than 2 weeks to 36 years, with a mean length of 8 years. Respondents were deploying to Afghanistan in a variety of roles, including as governmental advisors and in various development, governance, political, policing and mentoring roles. On average, respondents reported having "some" prior knowledge of the Afghan mission (i.e., 3.38/ out of a possible score of 4), and indicated they had only "slight" or "little" prior knowledge of and contact with members of the CF (i.e., (2.69 & 2.49/4, respectively). The reported average level of prior contact with members of the Afghan public was quite limited (i.e., the average rating was 1.82/4, close to but still less than a rating of "a little") and, on average, the OGD members indicated having between "a little" and "some" amount of prior knowledge of the Afghan people (i.e., 2.69/4).

Procedure. A DRDC Centre for Operational Research and Analysis (CORA) team member and their representative,[65] who were attending EX MG, provided an overview of the intent of the research and the questionnaire package. Given the hectic training schedule, participants were allowed to complete the questionnaires at their own pace and as their time allowed. Once completed, the OGD participant returned the questionnaire to the DRDC representative and all questionnaires were delivered to the principal investigators once EX MG was completed. We opted to use an anonymous version of the questionnaire although participants could provide us with their contact details if they chose.

Measures. Due to the heavy training schedule we elected to keep the questionnaire as short as possible. Thus we included a few demographic questions including agency worked for, length of time employed by the agency, and deployment work role. We then asked the OGD participants to indicate their prior knowledge and experience related to the Afghan mission, the CF and the Afghan population. Degree of contact with the CF and with the Afghan role players within the EX MG scenarios and via informal contact outside of the scenarios was also measured. Perceptions of training effectiveness was assessed by asking participants to rate a) the amount learned, b) the tools and skills provided by the training, c) the degree of usefulness of the training, and d) the impact of the training on ability to work effectively. Each of these questions was posed separately with respect to perceptions of the CF and perceptions of working with the Afghan population. Response options to all quantitative questions were 1=none/not at all, 2=a little, 3=some/somewhat, 4=a great deal. The questionnaire also provided space for short-answer comments concerning various aspects of the training experience, and suggestions for further improvements to the training from their perspective.

Results

1. Amount of Interaction during EX MG

a. With CF Personnel

Our OGD participants reported that they had "a great deal" of contact ($M = 3.84$, $SD = .36$) with the CF during the exercise scenarios proper. Although the degree of informal contact with the CF was slightly less than was the case during the exercise itself, the average for this variable still indicated that a fair amount of contact occurred informally as well ($M = 3.16$, $SD = .99$). Comments from the survey provided additional detail concerning the perceived value of the interaction with the CF, and in particular suggest the benefits of this training as a way to facilitate a WoG approach to missions.

"[It] helps me [a] great deal to understand [r]oles and responsibilities of both components, [c]ivilian and military within our One Team One Mission umbrella."

"learned a great deal about CF operations, which has prepared [them] to work as part of an integrated team."

"I learned to outreach with CF, to understand their roles and responsibilities. I got the chance to spend time with my team members almost 24 [hours] a day. I am more aware of how to deal with them in [a] difficult situation."

"learned the CF's "way of thinking," the "importance of approaching issues at the correct rank level," and military language.

[Developed a] *"deeper understanding and respect for the CF and its planning and operational modalities"* as a result of the training.

In particular, nearly one-half of respondents (17) provided comments in this area and reported that the training had helped them to establish useful relationships with the CF (and other) personnel with whom they would be working in theatre.

"Face time with [the] military allows for the formation of relationships which will assist in the work environment over in [Afghanistan]."

"The exercise offers the opportunity to meet and build relationships with people in CF/OGD[s] that we expect to work with on the mission – this is invaluable."

b) With Afghan Role Players

On the other hand, the OGD respondents reported that only slightly more than "a little" contact occurred with the Afghan role players during the exercise scenarios. Informal contact occurred even less frequently, and indicated that virtually no contact occurred outside the exercise scenarios. Indeed, mean ratings for the degree of prior contact with the Afghan role players were statistically significantly lower both during the scenarios (M's = 2.35 SD = .66) and with respect to informal contact with the role players outside of the scenario proper ($M = 1.35$, $SD = .57$) than was the case for contact with the CF (t's = 13.54 & 10.37, both p's < .001, d's = 2.75 & 2.21, respectively).

2. Perceptions of EX MG Training Effectiveness

a) Working with CF Personnel

The OGD participants were quite positive about the learning opportunity afforded by EX MG training in terms of working with the CF. Specifically they indicated that the had learned "a great deal" (i.e., M = 3.64, SD = 0.58) about the CF and rated the usefulness of the MG training experience as preparation for working with the CF while in Afghanistan as quite high (M = 3.77, SD = 0.54). They also indicated that the training had provided them with some effective tools and skills to work with the CF (M = 3.34, SD = 0.87) and indicated that the training had affected their ability to work with members of the CF "a great deal" (M = 3.56, SD = 68).

b) Working with Members of the Afghan Population

In contrast to these results with respect to the CF, OGD respondents perceived that the EX MG training has little impact as preparation for working with members of the Afghan population On average, OGD respondents felt they had learned only between "a little" and "some" about the Afghan population as a result of the training (M =2.47, SD = 0.97). The training was also rated as having "some" usefulness in assisting OGD members with working with the Afghan population (M = 2.63, SD 1.06). Finally, on average, the training was perceived to have provided only a few effective tools/skills (M = 2.11, SD =.91), and was rated as only having "a little" impact on the OGD respondents' ability to work with members of the Afghan population (M = 2.11, SD = 0.91). Indeed, in each case OGD participants rated the training effectiveness of EX MG significantly greater in terms of working with members of the CF while deployed, versus working with members of the Afghan public (amount learned: $t = 7.58$, $p < .001$, $d = 1.43$; provided effective tools/skills: $t = 7.78$,

$p < .001$, $d = 1.39$; usefulness of training experience: $t = 5.87$, $p < .001$, $d = 1.36$; impact on ability to work effectively: $t = 7.23$, $p < .001$, $d = 1.41$).

As might be expected comments associated with this question were more mixed. That is, 12 individuals indicated that they had learned about the Afghan culture and people as a result of EX MG, specifically in terms of shuras, maliks, and mullahs; about Afghan customs and attitudes towards women; about local decision-making processes and hierarchy; and about engaging with key leaders. However, 14 respondents (a little over one-third of the sample) indicated that they had learned relatively little about the Afghan culture and people as a result of the exercise:

"I would [have] liked more contacts with Afghan people; it is a must."

"[t]oo few Afghan role players to work with inside and outside [the] exercise. No time for quality 'outside the box' interaction."

"While I attended a number of shuras, I learned very little about Afghan tradition and culture from the exercise."

This theme was particularly apparent from members of the Police group, with fully half of the comments of this nature being written by members of this group.

3. Training Effectiveness as a Function of OGD Affiliation

Results of these analyses[66] showed that the exercise was perceived as equally valuable on all training effectiveness measures related to the CF for the members of the CIDA, DFAIT and Police groups. Results differed, however, for perceptions of training effectiveness with respect to working with members of the Afghan public while deployed, with statistically significantly group differences emerging with respect to perceptions of the degree to which EX MG provided the OGD members with effective tools to work with the Afghan public while deployed and the OGD members' perceived ability to work effectively with members of the Afghan population when deployed.[67] Specifically, members of CIDA rated the EX MG training as more effective in terms of their ability to work with members of the Afghan population than did members of DFAIT, while members of the Police group did not differ significantly from either the CIDA or DFAIT groups. Finally, both the CIDA and the Police groups had significantly higher ratings of the effectiveness of the tools/skills to work with the Afghan public that were provided by the EX MG training than did the DFAIT group.[68]

4. Training Recommendations

Thirty-three of the OGD members provided recommendations on ways to enhance MG as a training exercise. One major theme was the need to have additional information prior to embarking on the training offered at EX MG.

"…it would be useful to receive briefings on how a military operation functions and the roles/responsibilities of the various units. This would provide us with more time to focus on the exercise."

"The CF train for months prior to MG and have detailed briefings on what MG will entail, whereas civilians mostly go in blind. As a result, we are not able to fully contribute and engage with Afghan [and] CF colleagues. More briefings and pre-MG transparency would make it more useful."

"More pre-exercise prep for military [and] civilians about each other's roles, mandate, objectives and protocol."

The importance of incorporating more information about OGDs (in addition to information about the CF) into EX MG was another theme evident in some of the comments.

"CF Personnel should be better informed on the actual roles of the civilian elements being deployed to Afghanistan; [this] will enhance the integration process. We need mechanisms to bridge the military way towards greater understanding [and] integration of civilian ways which are not that bad."

"[m]ost [CF members] are completely unfamiliar with [the] duties, tasks and responsibilities of civilian Whole of Government partners, i.e., CIDA, DFAIT, CSC and CIVPOL."

[There is a need for the] *"PRT [to] visit Ottawa in [the] early part of [the] road to high readiness to learn about CIDA and DFAIT."*

Furthermore, 3 respondents suggested the need to better integrate OGDs into the planning process for EX MG (e.g., for J5 and J35), or to include them at an earlier stage of the planning process, in order to:

"ensure respect/accuracy of their doctrine, function(s) [and] practice in Ex Scenarios."

One final theme (reflected in the recommendation of 4 respondents) concerned the technical aspects of EX MG.

"[e]quipment (comms) …[need to be] … prepared and available at the beginning of exercise."

"[w]orkstations [and] USB drives should be set up/ready at the very beginning of the Ex so that we can do a better job."

Discussion

Although considered to be the most effective means to address the complexity of contemporary missions, many important questions related to achieving optimal effectiveness of the CA remain. One of these questions is the best means to prepare WoG teams for CA missions. Although there have been calls for integrated training, currently few of these opportunities exist. One such opportunity within Canada is EX MG. Although remaining the final confirmation exercise for Canadian Battlegroups deploying to Afghanistan, EX MG is also available to members of Canadian OGDs as an interagency training opportunity. Although After Action Reviews are routinely conducted after major scenarios in EX MG, the results of which are used to inform future training, to date there has been relatively little quantitative assessment of EX MG training, especially from the perspective of the other WoG players.

Because so little is known about the nature and specifics of interagency training, we wanted to begin to understand the degree of interaction that took place between the OGD members, CF personnel and the Afghan role players, both within the exercise scenarios and more informally. We also asked a series of questions tapping perceptions of training effectiveness, specifically the amount learned, the tools and skills that the training provided, the usefulness of the training as preparation for the upcoming deployment, and the impact of the training on ability to work effectively. We then sought to determine the relationships between amount of interaction and training effectiveness and if perceptions of training effectiveness differed depending on the agency for which the OGD members worked. Finally, we asked participants to provide comments on their experience, including any suggestions that might assist in further improving the training experience from their perspective.

The results of this research suggest that the OGD respondents had a great deal of contact with members of the CF during the training scenarios and some degree of more informal contact with them outside of the scenarios proper. More importantly, they found EX MG to be of value to them in terms of what they learned about the CF; the generally usefulness of the training in terms of working with the CF while deployed; the skills and tools that the training provided them to work with members of the CF, and its impact on their ability to work with members of the CF in their upcoming deployment. Participants' comments from the survey indicated that they learned a great deal from the training exercise about the CF's organizational structure, culture and planning processes, and that the training helped them to establish useful relationships with the CF (and other) personnel with whom they would be working in theatre.

Results regarding perceptions of the training experience as it related to working with members of the Afghan population were significantly less positive, however. Specifically, the mean ratings of the degree of contact with the Afghan role players were lower than was the case regarding contact with the CF. Fully half of the comments indicating a lack of interaction, and the potential impact of that lack of interaction were made by members of the Police group. Moreover, from the ratings data, it does not appear that the Police group as a whole already knew a great deal about the Afghan Public prior to EX MG; therefore, the reported lack of learning about the Afghan Public for the Police group is not a reflection of already having a great deal of knowledge in this area.

OGD members' ratings of the perceived training effectiveness of EX MG as it relates to their future work with members of the Afghan population while deployed were similarly significantly lower than was the case for ratings of the training effectiveness with respect to future work with the CF. That is, overall, OGD respondents rated the training as having little effect or impact on their perceived ability to work with members of the Afghan population while deployed, and as having provided few tools/skills for in the upcoming deployment in this respect. Interestingly, and in contrast to the comments made by members of the Police group regarding a desire for more interaction with the Afghan role players, results of quantitative analyses suggested that members of the DFAIT group reported significantly lower in these respects than was the case on average for the CIDA group. Finally, the pattern of correlations among the interaction and training effectiveness variables with respect to member of the Afghan population also differed from that seen for the CF. In particular, although in the predicted direction, the amount of interaction with the Afghan role players was not statistically significantly related to perceptions of training effectiveness.

In addition, respondents recommended several ways to enhance the training from their perspective. In particular, they suggested that they would have benefited from more information concerning the exercise and the military prior to attending EX MG to ensure adequate preparation of OGDs for the training itself. They also felt that incorporating more information about the roles and responsibilities of OGDs as well as Afghan culture into the training exercise would be beneficial for everyone, including members of the CF. Some individuals felt that the training experience would be further improved by engaging OGDs at an earlier stage in the exercise planning process. Finally, a few comments suggested that having functional computers and other technology at the outset of the exercise would have made them more effective contributors to the training as well.

Although informative, the current analyses clearly represent only a first step and more work needs to be done to develop a more complete understanding of the potential of interagency training in facilitating WoG effectiveness. First, as the data were collected over a single EX MG, it is necessary to replicate the study and determine the stability of these findings. Second, future research designs should incorporate longitudinal designs, for instance, by obtaining ratings of training effectiveness from OGD members while deployed, as well as post-deployment. Indeed, arguably deployment and post-deployment ratings would have more validity in terms of addressing the value of interagency training. Third, there are a variety of psychological processes that should be assessed to better inform the underlying question of why interagency training is important. For instance is it simply awareness or knowledge that is the driver, or are other psychological states implicated such as increased trust, or group cohesion – and what are the relevant contributions of these psychological processes to optimal interagency effectiveness within a CA? Fourth, reflecting the WoG approach as well as the comments from these OGD participants that the training should include information for the CF concerning OGD roles and responsibilities, future research in this area should also consider the addition of CF perceptions to further inform and elucidate this aspect of WoG training.

Fifth, while perceptions of training effectiveness represent one marker of training effectiveness, other behavioural measures of training effectiveness, such as performance during scenarios, would also be highly compelling. Measures such as these would certainly be a challenge to obtain within EX MG, as it is conducted based on a "free play" approach; not all scenarios unfold in exactly the same way, but rather often evolve based on the unique decisions and responses of the primary training audience. These decisions and actions in turn can affect the development of the next scenario within the exercise. Moreover, the senior commanders can elect to have specific scenario injects that will be unique to the primary training audience's needs and requirements. While the flexibility inherent in free play maximizes the training benefits, the non-standardized nature of the exercise does limit the extent to which the same set of behavioural outcome measures can be used across exercises and samples. Nonetheless, future work might be devoted to determining what behavioural or performance-associated metrics that address WoG effectiveness can be gleaned from EX MG.

While acknowledging that the current research is only the beginning of what should be a large, coordinated program of research, this work represents among the first research of which we are aware that applies statistical analyses to determine the extent of contact during integrated training, and the degree to which formal and informal interaction during the training is associated with a variety of training effectiveness outcomes, and for whom. From this standpoint, the study indicates the potential of this approach to understanding the dynamics of interagency training. Just as importantly, the results begin to confirm the value of interagency training, despite the substantial financial, planning, logistical and scheduling costs associated with such training exercises. As such, these data also represent a useful starting point for informing senior staff and decision makers within the Canadian WoG enterprise, as well as EX MG personnel, in terms of future CA training requirements and activities.

Chapter 18

THE RELATIONSHIP BETWEEN NON-GOVERNMENTAL ORGANIZATIONS AND THE CANADIAN FORCES

Tara Holton, Angela Febbraro,
Emily-Ana Filardo, Marissa Barnes,
Brenda Fraser, and Rachel Spiece

Introduction

The Canadian Forces (CF) is adopting a more coordinated and comprehensive approach to operations (i.e., joint, interagency, multinational, public, or JIMP). The capacity to be "JIMP-capable" is now cited by the Directorate of Land Concepts and Designs as an important enabler for the Army of Tomorrow, and a key means to ensure mission success in an increasingly complex land environment (Gizewski and Rostek, 2007). Of the JIMP dimensions, the "public" aspect, which includes a variety of civilian organizations, including but not limited to non-governmental organizations (NGOs), may pose some of the greatest challenges for the CF in terms of interacting with non-military players. These challenges relate to the sheer diversity of organizations and other entities included within the public aspect of JIMP; to the often significant differences between the organizational culture and values of the CF and the culture and values of various public organizations and entities; and, from the perspective of NGOs, to the concerns about physical security and neutrality that are raised when contemplating any relationship with the military in general.

Security Operations in the 21st Century: Canadian Perspectives on the Comprehensive Approach, ed. M. Rostek and P. Gizewski. Montreal and Kingston: Queen's Policy Studies Series, McGill-Queen's University Press.

Thus, the challenges of the CF-NGO relationship are daunting and, require further understanding.

As a result of the need to better understand the public aspect of JIMP, a research project entitled "JIMP Essentials in the Public Domain: Implications for the Tactical Commander," was developed at DRDC Toronto. Some of the main objectives of this project include: 1) a conceptual clarification of the public aspect of JIMP capability; 2) identification of individual differences/aptitudes that enable individuals to work effectively and succeed in a JIMP environment, with implications for training, selection and teamwork; and 3) integration of historical and international perspectives on the public aspect of JIMP. The present chapter is based on an interview study which supports this larger project through exploration of the relationship between the CF and NGOs.

The need to better understand the NGO and CF relationship has become apparent in the years since the Cold War, as the changing nature of international conflict has resulted in militaries increasingly taking on roles in humanitarian relief and development, a field traditionally belonging to civilian organizations. Tensions have been noted to arise when civilian and military personnel are concurrently involved in providing humanitarian aid in areas of crisis (Winslow, 2002). For example, research has explored tensions between militaries and NGOs in regard to organizational structure and culture, tasks and ways of accomplishing them, the control of resources, definitions of success and time frames, and information control and sharing (Winslow, 2002). In terms of organizational structure and culture, for instance, militaries tend to adopt hierarchical structures and decision-making cultures, whereas NGOs, although quite heterogeneous, tend to adopt flatter organizational structures and decision-making cultures. In terms of approaches to the accomplishment of tasks, militaries tend to emphasize efficient planning, whereas NGOs tend to emphasize the importance of community participation. Further, militaries tend to establish short-term goals and definitions of success (e.g., civil security), whereas NGOs tend to define success in terms of long-term social and economic development. In regard to control of resources, NGOs are sometimes concerned that the use of military resources will compromise their neutrality, which may be critical to their success and safety. On the other hand, both militaries and NGOs may have security concerns in regard to information sharing. It has also been suggested that these tensions may be exacerbated by stereotypes and assumptions on both sides (e.g., military members might perceive NGO workers as "flaky do-gooders," whereas NGO members might perceive military members as "authoritarian" or "arrogant") (Winslow, 2002). While many theories regarding these tensions exist, few studies have explored the issue thoroughly from a Canadian perspective, and few studies have examined the potentially positive aspects of the military-NGO relationships (i.e., the factors that may lead to more positive or improved relationships, or the strengths that may characterize these relationships). The goal of this research is to contribute to a better understanding of the relationship between the CF and NGOs, in terms of both strengths and challenges, and to find ways to improve these relationships that meet the needs and goals of both groups.

Purpose

The purpose of this chapter is to explore the perspectives of NGO workers and CF members on the relationship between NGOs and the CF, in particular as it pertains to their collaboration in theatre. Although the focus of previous research has been on exploring the tensions, challenges, or negative aspects of the military-NGO relationship, the present study examines potentially positive aspects, or strengths, as well. This chapter will shed light on the current relationship between NGOs and the military from a Canadian perspective, and will aim to provide information and recommendations on "what is working" and "how to make it work" within the requirements of what is needed and acceptable for both parties.

Method

Interviews for this study were conducted with 5 NGO participants, 5 CF participants and one additional Subject Matter Expert (SME) for a total of 11 participants. Each interview was 2 hours in length. Participants ranged in age from 30 to 70 years, and were at varying stages in their careers. Ranks of the CF members included a Sergeant, Lieutenant, Captain, Major and Colonel (Ret.). All were Army. The CF and NGO participants were equal number male (3 CF, 2 NGO) and female (3 NGO, 2CF). The additional SME, an expert in development-military collaboration, was male. Although participants were classified as either CF, NGO, or other SME, it is important to note that some CF participants had also been members of an NGO at one time and some of the NGOs had been members of the military in their past; thus, to some extent, there was overlap among the participant categories in terms of their prior experiences. Reported ethnicity was varied, and in the participants' own words included: Canadian, Asian, Scottish, Irish, English, Hungarian, Russian, Japanese, and Palestinian. All CF participants had interacted with NGOs during their career as a CF member (e.g., as members of Provincial Reconstruction Teams, or PRTs, and as Civil-Military Cooperation [CIMIC] officers or liaison officers) and all of the NGO participants had interacted with the military (the CF and the militaries of other countries) during their career as a member of an NGO. All participants had been deployed internationally over the course of their careers. Participants all reside in Canada, and all interviews took place in person or by phone across Canada, with the exception of one participant, who was in Afghanistan at the time of the interview. In all cases, participants were volunteers acquired through professional contacts and snowball sampling. In order to offset any selection bias that may result from this form of participant selection (e.g., a bias towards negative participant experiences), the interview questions focused on a diversity of both positive and negative participant experiences and perceptions. Interviews were tape-recorded (with consent) using digital recording equipment, and subsequently transcribed.

Content analysis was conducted using conventional qualitative data-analytical tools and techniques to analyze the interview data. Specifically, NVivo8, a qualitative software package, was used to identify and categorize themes and issues pertaining to specific interview questions as well as themes and issues that emerged from the interviews. The coding percent agreement was 98 percent.

Findings

A number of findings emerged from this study that may contribute to a better understanding of the relationship between NGOs and the Canadian Forces, and suggest some directions toward improving their understanding of one another and their interaction in theatre.

First, although some participants, both NGO and CF, expressed reservations at the thought of any type of interaction between NGOs and the CF, in theatre or otherwise, most acknowledged that a relationship is in many cases inevitable, in some cases a necessity, and as these findings reveal, is often already in place. Both groups recognized the importance of the other's role, and agreed that these roles are ultimately interrelated within a broad security mission. However, participant thoughts on what the NGO and CF relationship should look like varied greatly depending on two aspects: (i) the context of the situation in which NGOs and the CF find themselves, and (ii) the mandate of the NGO with whom the CF are interacting. Addressing the first aspect, all participants felt that in a context such as a natural disaster, where the CF are not combatants and may effectively be seen as a neutral party, a relationship between the two organizations was acceptable. Given that in the case of a natural disaster, the goals of both organizations are transparent and in essence the same, it may be that NGO members feel that they can trust the motives of the CF, as well as interact with them, without compromising their neutrality. Addressing the issue of the mandate of the NGO with whom the CF are interacting, in this case, if neutrality is an integral part of the NGO mandate, then partnering with the CF in conflict areas is an impossibility. As one NGO participant suggested, the minute an NGO so much as accepts a CF escort, they've compromised their neutrality. In a conflict area, the CF are considered combatants and hence cannot be neutral parties, but participants suggested that this does not mean that the CF do not have a role to play in the humanitarian mission. Many participants felt that while NGOs and the CF could not interact within a conflict zone, a coordination of roles could be possible and is needed. For example, participants perceived a broader mission, which could be broken down into stages, where in the first stage the CF are responsible for securing and maintaining the peace so that NGOs and other humanitarian and development workers can implement the second stage, humanitarian aid. Some of the CF participants pointed out that communication between NGOs and the CF is necessary in order to achieve this goal, for example, to make certain that the CF does not mistake NGOs for insurgents, to avoid an NGO so that they are not in any way affiliated with the CF, which some feel could affect their security, or to inform NGOs of a rapid change in insurgent activity. Participants even suggested creative ways in which the CF could communicate information to NGOs and others without face-to-face interaction, and hence without compromising neutrality, such as a general information board which could inform on both the humanitarian and security conditions. In situations such as these, participants indicated that reciprocation of security-related information, while welcomed and useful, would not be necessary.

Interestingly, however, despite widespread acknowledgement that NGOs and the CF already do not function separately, and that both groups may benefit from some form of relationship, participants struggled to express what any interaction between the CF and NGOs should look like. There was concern regarding any relationship in which one organization would be in charge of the other, any relationship that compromised the neutrality of NGOs and any relationship that endangered either party or the beneficiaries of aid. Ultimately, most participants felt that the answer may involve flexible coordination that could maintain NGO impartiality and that could be tailored to the diversity of the situation and the organizations and individuals involved. Participants provided examples of "when it has worked," in which successful situations invariably involved individuals with the "right" personalities, who were willing to step outside of the rigid boundaries set by their respective organizations, and while not altering specific mandates, could be flexible in how they interacted with one another and respectful of what the other could bring to the table. Participants suggested that currently, the "right personalities" coming together is a random occurrence, one that the CF in particular feel could be improved upon and formalized through further development of the role of CIMIC within the CF. CIMIC officers are meant to be a bridge between the military and the public, that is, individuals who participants felt could "speak both military and civilian" and who could advise their commanding officer on the best approach to a given civil-military interaction. Participants belonging to the CF felt that while CIMIC has been developing over the years, it is the key to mission success in the increasingly complex environments within which the CF are working. It was suggested that selection for this role is insufficient, and that the primary use of reservists in the role has resulted in individuals who were poorly prepared for their roles as CIMIC officers. Despite the fact that reservists naturally integrate well across the military and civilian cultures, their preparation for the position is short term, often commencing at the same time as pre-deployment training. Currently, there is no full-time career path for CIMIC officers, although one participant mentioned that a pilot study for a full-time program is underway.

Another major theme emerging from the data involved the management of optics. For both the CF and NGOs, the issue of optics was linked to security and mission success. NGO participants felt that an image of neutrality protects them from being associated with the CF and any security risks that this association may have. In addition, NGO participants felt that maintaining that image of neutrality, in combination with one of fulfilling humanitarian goals, increases the trust and maintains the relationships that they have with the local public. Perhaps equally important, the maintenance of this image keeps their donors happy and their funding intact. For the CF, participants felt that the improvement of the CF image, both in theatre and at home, may allow for benefits in terms of security and support from civilians, again both in theatre and at home. Participants, both CF and NGO, reported positive experiences where the CF were able to facilitate the maintenance of NGO optics by communicating in a manner that maintained NGO neutrality. This supports the above finding that in some cases effective communication between the two groups already exists, and suggests that it is possible to facilitate development of a relationship that fulfills the requirements of NGOs but would allow NGOs and the CF to coordinate the broader mission. Although findings suggest that the maintenance of NGO optics could benefit from a delicate balance of communication and avoidance in regard to the CF, while simple avoidance could in fact place them in a position of danger and of compromised neutrality. This coordination may not resemble what most think of as communication. Rather, compromise and flexibility, or the ability to "think outside the box," are characteristics that participants indicated are prerequisites for this unique relationship. Findings also revealed that the media is complicit in promoting sensational, negative stories about the CF rather than positive ones, and that the CF should consider learning from the more media-savvy NGOs in regard to how to manage the media.

Organizational culture and structure also emerged as a major theme within the discourses of the participants. In regard to organizational culture, perhaps surprisingly, all of the participants indicated that the values and end goal of the CF and of NGOs were likely very similar. All felt that both NGOs and the CF wanted to "do good" and protect basic human needs and rights. They suggested, however, that the motivation behind those values, the interpretation of those values, and the means of achieving goals associated with those values, were fundamentally different, and resulted in a strained relationship between the two organizations.

While some participants suggested that this similarity in values allowed for an opportunity to bridge across organizations at a core level, many of the NGO participants felt that this was a case of the end not justifying the means, and were reluctant to see "shared values" as a potential facilitator to the NGO and CF relationship. Gender differences and the competitive nature of NGOs were also cited by participants as a hindrance to forming an effective relationship between the two organizations. In the case of gender differences, one NGO participant expressed how being a young woman was a barrier to having a voice with the CF, while another participant indicated that being female in the CF and working with an NGO from the host country, where women are not regarded in high esteem, was also a challenge. Benefits of women working with women (be they CF, NGOs or the local public) to further mission success, however, offered a possible bridging aspect for the CF and NGO relationship. In the case of the competitive nature of NGOs, some participants suggested that because competition for funding is so fierce amongst NGOs, successful movement toward anything which might hinder their edge in the competition, such as being seen collaborating with the CF, would be a challenge.

In terms of organizational structure, participants felt that even when efforts are made to bridge the gap between NGOs and the CF, the structure of the organization may stall the process. Role clarity was described by many as a key concern, where the CF hierarchy (i.e., the military rank structure) does not allow an NGO to have a voice in the system, even if that NGO member's opinion is solicited and respected. Participants suggested, however, that providing space for an NGO to have voice within the CF was a challenging prospect because it disrupts the chain of command and hence the identity of members of the CF. Timelines were also raised by participants as a potential barrier to an effective relationship. Short rotations limited the CF's ability to sustain projects and build relationships. However, some participants noted that CF short rotations and NGO skill at sustainability and longer mission times could potentially complement one another, with the CF providing security and influx of quick, much needed projects, and NGOs coming in later, to implement and sustain humanitarian work, thus providing a form of exit strategy for the CF.

Another key theme that emerged was the lack of trust that NGOs have for the CF. As mentioned earlier, participants indicated that the formation of a relationship between NGOs and the CF is perceived by NGOs to compromise their neutrality and their reputation with the public, both local and at home in Canada. This in turn can affect their security and their image in the eyes of their donors, but most importantly, may compromise their mandates. The issue of trust has to do with suspicion surrounding CF motivations for forming a relationship, and with the fear that information passed from NGO to CF could be used for reasons which do not align with NGO values. Nonetheless, participants felt that the development of trust was essential for reasons of security, and that efforts should be made by the CF to build trust by developing CIMIC's capability, which would hence allow for the "right" people to bridge and effectively maintain these relationships.

As a means of addressing some of the concerns discussed within the interviews, participants themselves had several recommendations for improvement of the CF and NGO relationship. The main theme that emerged was, not surprisingly, the need for training and education. Participants suggested that at present neither the CF nor many NGOs provide training of significance on civil-military cooperation, and hence do not reflect the reality of what soldiers and humanitarian workers are experiencing on the ground. They felt that education and training may allow for more effective interaction between the two types of organizations and for exposure through joint training, academic conferences, and opportunity for open dialogue. Several of the participants also recommended the development and implementation of a selection system for CIMIC officers and endorsed a full-time career path for CIMIC officers, indicating that the development of CIMIC would improve the capability of the CF to bridge the military-civilian divide. Finally, participants endorsed flexible approaches to forming an effective relationship between the two types of organizations, suggesting that a "thinking outside the box" approach would allow for creative means of communication that did not compromise the values or mandates of either organization.

In short, findings from the interviews would suggest that the ever-changing nature of the complex environment faced by the military and humanitarians alike renders the CF and NGO missions inextricable (albeit often functioning sporadically), despite the seemingly conflicted natures of their respective values and mandates. This is in keeping with the current literature which suggests that the existence of the "humanitarian space" is in question and is shrinking to be replaced by a hybrid, shared space which is uncoordinated, changing, and at times made up of conflicting positions (Monaghan, 2007). Findings from participant interviews indicate that the NGO and CF relationship, although faced with constraints, is something that is already being facilitated through both formal and, most interestingly, informal means. There are instances where without compromising their respective values, mandates or doctrines, the respective players are navigating their own way through the new territory of this shared, hybrid space. While participants echo the oft heard concerns, barriers and stereotypes that one traditionally associates with the NGO and CF relationship, embedded within these interviews were examples of creative solutions, opportunity for dialogue, and recognition of change. While this relationship is still in its infancy, and participants struggled to articulate what the relationship between the military and humanitarians should look like, each participant in different ways acknowledged the importance of such a relationship. Although the description of the interaction discussed by participants is not what one might consider a traditional relationship, and not entirely in keeping with the fully integrated model espoused by the JIMP concept, its development is perhaps the best answer to the growing, diversifying and increasingly complex needs of today's security operations. Several means of "making it work" emerged from the interviews and are presented below.

Making it Work

First, in order to support and develop the capability that CIMIC affords the CF, it is suggested that a full-time career path be considered for CIMIC. CIMIC officers are the bridge between the CF and every civilian organization or group in the "outside world" with whom they wish to interact. They allow a voice within the CF for the other civilian partners in theatre. CIMIC officers have the capacity to build trust, manage relationships and maintain optics among other areas of expertise. While CIMIC officers are already in place and doing what they can with what they have, participants indicated that they would benefit greatly from a proper selection process, from training that reflects the flexibility required of their role, and from a sustainable career path that would allow them to develop the role to its full potential. This would allow the CF to place the importance on the role of CIMIC that it so clearly warrants in the changing and increasingly complex security environment.

Second, as suggested in the interview data, female soldiers may have a unique role to play in bridging the relationship between the CF and NGOs, as well as the local public. Given that the participation of a nation's women is recognized as a key factor in any country's sustainable development (Tamas, 2009) and that NGO participants within this study indicated they felt that they did not have a voice with the CF, in part due to gender differences between the two organizations, it may be a prudent course of action to place emphasis on developing female CIMIC officers within the CF with whom NGOs and the local public might be more likely to make contact. Endorsing and promoting gender equity in operations, and recognizing the advantage that a female CIMIC officer may have in initiating effective communication with NGOs and the local population, depending on the local context, may go a long way in furthering the NGO and CF relationship.

Third, one of the main barriers to an effective relationship between the CF and NGOs is the lack of trust. Participants indicated that this lack of trust stems in part from suspicion regarding the motivations of the CF, particularly fear that any information passed between the two groups would be used by the military for reasons that that did not align with NGO values. This is supported by the fact that trust does not seem to be an issue for participants when the military is performing tasks for which it is known and respected, such as protection. Transparency (in as much as is possible) of CF motivations behind forming a relationship with NGOs could begin to break down this barrier. For example, some participants described instances in theatre where NGOs have been quite surprised to learn that the CF do not want or need to take credit for development or humanitarian projects that they wish to support, be it through financial means, information sharing, or equipment sharing. Through transparency and the airing of "other agendas" (again, in as much as is possible), it may be possible to demonstrate the sincerity of the CF desire to support development and humanitarian aid. Once again, the development of well-trained operators who can have frequent dialogue with the other players in theatre and build that trust is key to a sustainable model of an effective NGO-CF relationship.

Fourth, another problematic issue had to do with a lack of role clarity for NGOs who are attempting to communicate with and advise the CF. The relationship that the CF have with other players in the complex security environment is often about control, jockeying for power, and having voice. Some NGO members indicated that there is not often a space within the CF hierarchy for their voices to be heard, despite the fact that their presence is often requested by the CF, and despite the fact that they do feel valued for their experience and knowledge. This issue was deemed by participants to be particularly problematic, as interfering with the chain of command is too disruptive to the identity of the general CF population and is unlikely to be well received. Yet NGOs have a wealth of information, connections, history and experience that the CF simply do not have in the humanitarian world, and to be stalled by hierarchy is particularly frustrating to both sides. Role clarity within CIMIC, however, which is known for flexibility, may be a possibility. Providing NGOs with a clear role in conjunction with CIMIC officers would allow for a line of communication to the commanding officer, and the possibility of effecting real change.

Fifth, there needs to be recognition that the relationship between the CF and NGOs is one that must be flexible and tailored to each different NGO according to their own unique requirements. While the idea of co-ordination with neutrality was put forth in this chapter, what that looks like would differ according to the needs of each NGO. In some cases this might mean having contact only for the purposes of better avoiding one another. While this is a far cry from the integrated philosophy espoused by JIMP, we do have to walk before we can run. Speaking candidly, the present study suggests that an integrated response that NGOs and other development workers are willing to live with is likely not going to look like the philosophy as originally conceived. It is going to have to be flexible, tailored to the diversity of players in theatre, and able to be modified as per the NGO or other civilian group working with the CF. It will have to be based upon compromise and that requires flexibility from both parties. It will likely be a different kind of integration, one in which the CF will not be "driving the bus," but one of mutual respect and mutual benefit.

Sixth, as mentioned in the recommendations made by the participants themselves, further education and training on the topic of civil-military interaction offers a possible solution to the strained CF and NGO relationship. Education and training needs to better reflect the reality of what soldiers and humanitarian workers are experiencing on the ground. Multifunctional and multi-sector training which promotes operational awareness regarding the roles, mandates and doctrines of other organizations is needed to effect change (Meharg, 2009). Furthermore, joint education and training could not only allow for better awareness and preparedness for civil-military missions, it would also allow for exposure, which, as indicated in the results, is a key component to getting everyone "back to the table," despite their differences, so that they can work together toward a common goal. Drawing on classic social psychology, it may be that constructive, direct personal experience is key for NGOs and CF to begin to develop positive attitudes toward one another.

Seventh, as suggested by one of the participants, it might be fruitful to consider the implementation of an annual national conference on neutral ground, funded by a neutral party (not the CF), examining Canadian involvement in both natural disaster and in conflict situations. The conference could be a window into areas of consensus as well as lack of consensus between the different Canadian players. Participants could include CF, the NGO community, as well as various government departments such as the Department of National Defence (DND), the Canadian International Development Agency (CIDA), the Department of Foreign Affairs and International Trade (DFAIT), the Solicitor General, etc. Among other things, a yearly publication deriving from the proceedings could provide an ongoing yearly measure of what is happening with the evolving relationships in the ever changing complex security environment.

Finally, it is critical to recognize the importance of understanding, assessing and developing CF cultural competence. Cultural competence is a concept that has its origins in the sociological, anthropological and psychological literatures. It differs from other approaches to instilling cultural skills, such as cultural awareness, in that it functions as a process and is not something that can simply be developed overnight, for example, through pre-deployment training. Cultural competence is a practice that is built upon and improved over time, in which knowledge about individuals and groups is integrated and transformed into skills that allow an individual or organization to work effectively in culturally diverse situations (Cross et al., 1989). As one participant indicated, there is a "fundamental issue in organizational culture that your power relationships and your cultural dynamics inside an organization are going to be reflected *at the boundary between the organization and its environment.*" Self-assessment is a necessary characteristic of a culturally competent organization. Understanding the meanings made in CF discourses about culture is an important first step toward developing CF cultural competence. Research which focuses on understanding the discourses within and between the intercultural groups in the NGO and CF relationship can reveal a variety of important information, from the negative, such as disparities in understanding or unintentional prejudice, to the positive, such as potential avenues of communication. CF, or NGO, self-assessment will shed light on what is being reflected at the boundary between the CF or NGO and the complex security environment.

Chapter 19

THE COMPREHENSIVE APPROACH: AN EMERGENT INTERNATIONAL NORM?

MICHAEL ROSTEK

Introduction

Security analysis affirms that not only does the world remain uncertain and unpredictable, in terms of military and security threats, uncertainty and unpredictability have actually increased (Chief of Force Development, 2008, 87) Globalization continues to be a key distinguishing phenomenon of the global security environment. Globalization is a historical process with important consequences for the global environment, for the autonomy of the state and its capacity to provide security (Lebow and Stein, 2002, 63). While globalization proceeds it continues to engender an uneven distribution of prosperity which in turn has created turbulence in both interstate and intrastate affairs – a condition most recently manifested in the failing or failed state phenomenon. Failing and failed states – loss of physical control of territory or of monopoly on the legitimate use of force, erosion of legitimate authority to make collective decisions, an inability to provide reasonable public services and the inability to interact with other states (*Foreign Policy*, 2009) – are often accompanied by bitter communal conflict, violent ethnic nationalism, militarism and possibly endemic regional conflict. Considered by the Canadian government as "[a]mong the greatest contemporary security threats" (Government of Canada, 2005, 13), strategic analyst and think tanks alike, acknowledge that weak and failed states (often regarded today as ungoverned spaces) persist today

Security Operations in the 21st Century: Canadian Perspectives on the Comprehensive Approach, ed. M. Rostek and P. Gizewski. Montreal and Kingston: Queen's Policy Studies Series, McGill-Queen's University Press.

and are likely to continue to threaten international peace and security in the years ahead (*Harvard International Review*, 2008; Farah, 2006).

Perhaps most significantly, weak and failed states have engendered a modern form of conflict articulated by Mary Kaldor as new wars. New wars arise from "...the erosion of the autonomy of the state and in some extreme cases the disintegration of the state" (Kaldor, 2001) further contributing to the weak and failed state phenomenon mentioned above. Often, such wars are particularly brutal as civilians and non-combatants become the targets, to varying degrees, signaling a new strategy of "warfighting." New wars can also encompass conflict based on identity politics (ethnicity, racial, and religious) (Kaldor, 2001, 76 and 138). Western secularism and radical Islam represent the current and most obvious protracted struggle in Afghanistan; however, other identity-based conflicts have also signaled its prominence. Kosovo, Rwanda, and Chechnya each represent the persistence and highly destructive nature of such conflict (Kaldor, 2001, 109 and 155). Of considerable concern to the developed world is the "...tendency on the part of such groups to ignore generally accepted international norms governing the use of force in pursuit of their goals (i.e., ethnic cleansing)" (Department of National Defence, 2003, 13).

The characteristics listed above – globalization, weak and failed states and new wars – are by no means exhaustive. Yet they are ever-more prominent in today's international system. While globalization may offer prospects for greater international cooperation, it also has a darker side. Increasing inequality, weak and failed states and new wars have all emerged to generate a more pervasive sense of insecurity – a condition which not only underlines the continuing importance of security itself but the need to develop new approaches to complex security problems. One such approach, indeed an emergent international norm, is called the Comprehensive Approach.

An Emergent International Norm: The Comprehensive Approach?

Norms make up an integral part of human life and "...are a core part of social systems" (Goetz, 2003, 32). A norm is accepted behaviour that sets standards for daily life defined as "...collective expectations for the proper behaviour of actors within a given identity" (Katzenstein, 1996, 5). Norms delineate boundaries (i.e., spheres of influence of states), serve as sign posts (i.e., warn policymakers of prearranged actions by states), routinize transnational actions (i.e., commercial contracts between states), and serve as tripwires to rule violation (i.e., focus on a transgression that allows for a collective response) (Raymond 1992). Norms are legitimized to the extent that members of the particular society practice the behaviour without question. Norms themselves are intersubjective, by definition, to the extent that they are a social, collective phenomenon whether existing at the domestic, regional or international level (Kacowicz, 2005, 17; Risse, Ropp, and Sikkink 1997, 7). Norms can regulate, they can constitute and they can enable specific actions (Kacowicz, 2005; Raymond, 1992; Finnemore and Sikkink, 1998, 891). But how and where do norms come from and which norms matter at any given point in time? There are several answers to these questions. As Kacowicz (2005) notes:

> New norms are responses to critical changes in the international environment; they are the result of imitation or emulation; they are created through internal processes stimulated by subnational groups; they are the outcome of a given distribution of power within the state system; they derive from the prominence of a potential rule or from the coherence between that rule and the larger, pre-existing normative order; or they are the result of the action of moral (normative) entrepreneurs.

The emergence of the CA, "…a framework within which diverse situationally-aware actors resolve complex issues through the purposeful coordination and de-confliction of their information, actions and effects" (Chief of Force Development, 2010, 1), is primarily a response to a more complex international security environment. Such a security environment and the varied threats and challenges it poses place a range of demands on the military. Externally, it suggests not only an increased need for combat and counter-insurgency operations, but also complex stabilization and reconstruction missions in societies ravaged by man-made and natural disasters. The complexities of contemporary conflict in fact heighten the need to operate across a wide spectrum of conflict. Not only must the CF be capable of effectively conducting a range of operations (i.e., high intensity combat in one area, stabilization operations in another and humanitarian aid or support in a third), but also of quickly and effectively transitioning from one mission to another. And given that missions may even overlap, the CF must also be capable of conducting a variety of operations simultaneously, and increasingly as part of broader, integrated teams.[69]

In addition, it is clear that many of these challenges require a wider range of personnel, skill-sets and resources than ever before. This not only stems from the character of the often multidimensional nature of the challenges themselves, but the wide range of players that could well be involved in such challenges as they unfold. Adversaries, both state and non-state, populations of varying religion and ethnicity, as well as a range of government, non-governmental and international organizations and institutions, allied, adversarial and neutral may all come into play during the course of an operation be it international or domestic in nature.

Accordingly, a capacity to effectively navigate through such diversity ensuring that interactions among a wide array of institutions and organizations are effective will be important to success. In particular, the capacity to harness a range of human assets in a coherent, collaborative and efficient manner will be ever more crucial to achieving lasting solutions to the challenges encountered in the years ahead (Patrick and Brown, 2007, 58). This, in fact, establishes the demand for a new international norm, the Comprehensive Approach.

But how does this new international norm materialize? Many norms emerge through the efforts of "entrepreneurs" (Farrell, 2005, 19) who act out of commitment to empathy (interest in the welfare of others for its own sake), altruism (a shared perception of common humanity) and ideational commitment (belief in the ideals and values embodied in the norm) (Finnemore and Sikkink, 1998, 898). A norm entrepreneur can be an individual or group of individuals, an organization or even a state. The norm entrepreneur is a critical component of the first stage in the "lifecycle" – norm emergence – of norm evolution. Martha Finnemore and Kathryn Sikkink, acclaimed norm researchers, have outlined a generic norm "lifecycle" involving a three stage process:

Norm Emergence. The successful creation of most norms involves norm entrepreneurs and the art of persuasion. Entrepreneurs are critical to the emergence of norms as they call attention to, or even create, issues focused on appropriate behaviour within their community (Finnemore and Sikkink, 1998, 897). Motivated by altruism, empathy or ideational commitment, their advocacy must be underpinned by strong communication skills if they are to convince other actors to adopt the norm. Norm entrepreneurs require an institutional platform from which they can promote their norms. Platforms can either be existing (i.e., International Organizations – United Nations) or they can be created by the norm entrepreneur for the expressed purpose of promoting the norm (Non Governmental Organizations – Greenpeace). Regardless of the type of platform used, "…norm entrepreneurs and the organizations they inhabit usually need to secure support of state actors to endorse their norms and make norm socialization a part of their agenda…" (Finnemore and Sikkink, 1998, 900).

Tipping Point. After the norm entrepreneur has persuaded a critical mass of states to adopt the new international norm, the norm is said to have reached its tipping point. While there is general agreement amongst norm scholars that a tipping point does occur, there is no "…theoretical account for why norm tipping occurs, nor criteria for specifying a priori where, when and how we would expect it" (Finnemore and Sikkink, 1998, 901) However, Finnemore and Sikkink propose two hypotheses about what constitutes a critical mass of states necessary to reach a tipping point:

- About one-third of the total states in the system adopt the international norm; and/or

- "Critical" states adopt the international norm. States are considered critical due to either their moral standing in the international community or by their ability to compromise the goals of the international norm (Finnemore and Sikkink, 1998, 900).

Once the tipping point is achieved, enough states and critical states redefine appropriate behaviour for the international community of states leading to "norm cascade."

Norm Cascade. Up to the tipping point, little normative change occurs without significant domestic support. After the tipping point, domestic influence becomes less influential as a new international socialization process begins. Socialization occurs through emulation (of heroes), praise (for behaviour that conforms to group norms), and ridicule (for deviation) (Waltz, 1979, 75-76). This socialization process is not only undertaken by states; but rather, networks of norm entrepreneurs and international organizations also play a role. Finnemore and Sikkink (1998) note that this socialization process is analogous to "peer pressure" amongst states and states respond to this pressure for three reasons: legitimation (reputation, trust and credibility), conformity (establish sense of belonging), and esteem (leaders want others to think well of them), the leaders also want to think well of themselves.

Norm Internalization. During this stage, norms will become so widely accepted that they eventually achieve a taken-for-granted quality (Finnemore and Sikkink, 1998, 895). States automatically follow the international norm as it has become robust enough to resist challenge and is regarded within the international community of states as standard practice.

Each stage is characterized by different actors, motives and mechanisms of influence (Finnemore and Sikkink, 1998, 895). As a result, we can see that the degree of acceptance for a new norm depends on its location within the lifecycle. For example, the influence of a norm will be significantly less in the norm emergence stage than at the norm cascade stage.

It is proposed here that the Comprehensive Approach is an emergent international norm that is arising from changes to the international security environment; the post-Cold War global security environment characterized by globalization, failed and failing states and new wars. However, not all new international norms attain the desired "taken for granted" status and those that do have followed the general path outlined by Finnemore and Sikkink's lifecycle model (1998). A closer examination of the Comprehensive Approach and how it relates to the norm lifecycle offers insight into the strength of this emergent international norm and also the next steps required to set it on the path towards a "taken for granted" status.

CA and the Norm Lifecycle

Within the CF, interest in the CA and the capacity to practice it reflects a growing belief in the importance of achieving greater interoperability and collaboration among key players in the operational arena as well as in the development of the requisite networking capabilities and skills essential to achieving one's objectives.[70] Properly conceived and implemented, this would offer an effective, efficient means of applying diverse and often disparate assets to a problem and could potentially lead to the creation of synergies in capability that would not otherwise exist.

Even more fundamentally, support for its creation stems from a growing consensus that outward-focused, integrated and multidisciplinary approaches to security threats and challenges must be the norm given the complex problems and challenges posed by a multidimensional security environment. However, the question remains, how do you operationalize such a concept? Analysis of the Comprehensive Approach within the international norm lifecycle may yield results indicating a way ahead.

Norm Emergence. As noted above, norm entrepreneurs and the institutional platforms from which they employ persuasive techniques are the key components of the norm emergence stage. While no one individual within Canada has consistently and explicitly advocated on behalf of the CA, the ideas embedded within the whole-of-government (WoG) or defence, diplomacy, development, and commerce (3D+C), viewed as predecessors to CA, have generated a web of "CA entrepreneurs" extending from academia to the public and private sectors. For example, the Right Honourable Paul Martin was Prime Minister when the International Policy Statement (IPS) combined Foreign, Defence, Development and Commerce polices into a single coherent document. The IPS proclaimed government departments must become better connected with each other, and develop whole-of-government strategies (Government of Canada, 2005). The team of Ms. Elissa Goldberg, first Representative of Canada in Kandahar (RoCK) in Afghanistan, and Brigadier General Denis Thompson, then Joint Task Force Commander in Afghanistan (JTF-A), perhaps best epitomized the collaborative and cooperative nature underpinning WoG and/or CA in a hostile environment. More significantly, both Goldberg and Thompson have moved on to influential positions within their respective government departments – Goldberg: Director START and Thompson: Head of International Policy – where they continue to engage in discussion and debate on WoG and CA. This list is by no means exhaustive and indeed, several authors in this volume as well as a host of diplomats, bureaucrats, scientists, military officers, volunteers, and private military companies can also be considered norm entrepreneurs. This web of entrepreneurs provides a necessary foundation for awareness and debate critical in the norm emergence stage. Norm entrepreneurs are as varied as the institutional platforms they use to communicate their message. From academia to think-tanks and social media, to advocacy groups and government institutional structures, a variety of institutional platforms are being used to articulate this emergent international norm – the Comprehensive Approach. However, while entrepreneurs and the platforms they use to communicate their message are evident and critical for the development of the international norm, considerable research exists postulating that international norms must first work their influence through the filter of domestic structures and norms (Finnemore and Sikkink, 1998, 893; Checkel, 1999; Legro, 1997; Cortell and Davis, 2005). Measurement of new norms is difficult. However, methods have been developed whereby state support for a new norm can be measured through domestic salience using indicators such as state policy, institutions and doctrine.

A key indicator of domestic norm salience – how norms achieve constitutive effects within the state – can be found within state policies (Raymond, 1992, 219). Triggered by the emergent security environment, the earliest vestiges of the CA in Canada emerged in the IPS (Government of Canada, 2005). Here, the GoC sought to bring greater policy coordination to the international operations within Canada through a "3D" or "whole-of-government" (WoG) approach but also fully recognized that this form of engagement extended beyond WoG:

> Canadian officials recognize that in multinational operations, an integrated or 3D approach in the field may actually include representatives from separate donor governments, for example, with development officials from one country collaborating with diplomatic or military actors from another (Patrick and Brown, 2007, 61).

Further, the Canada First Defence Strategy released in 2008 re-emphasized the importance of WoG approaches:

> Today's deployments are far more dangerous, complex and challenging than in the past, and they require more than a purely military solution. In Afghanistan, for example, the Canadian Forces' contribution is only one component, albeit an essential one, of a "whole-of-government" approach. Only by drawing upon a wide range of governmental expertise and resources will Canada be successful in its efforts to confront today's threats (Government of Canada, 2008a, 9).

More explicit articulation of the Comprehensive Approach can be found in Canada's foreign policy surrounding Security Sector Reform SSR:

> Canada promotes a coherent and Comprehensive Approach to security system reform, which recognizes the interconnectedness of the military, policing, justice, corrections, border management, and customs sectors, and the need to enhance civilian and parliamentary oversight of all the security system (DFAIT, 2011a).

Further, in espousing a domestic application, DFAIT stated that a "...
comprehensive approach will lead to greater coherence and co-ordination between federal departments and agencies having a stake in the
development of the circumpolar region" (DFAIT, 2011b). In addition,
the Minister of Foreign Affairs along with the Foreign Ministers of the
G8 have recognized the importance of a Comprehensive Approach the
most recent being Muskoka in 2010. (DFAIT, 2011c) In relation to the war
in Afghanistan, the Minister articulated support for the Comprehensive
Approach in stating that:

> Canada has tried, and I think with some success, to put into practice what
> NATO calls the "Comprehensive Approach." This is something I've been en-
> gaged with as Foreign Minister and, now, as Defence Minister (DFAIT 2011d).

As evidenced above, WoG and CA have been incorporated into state
policy signifying a degree of domestic salience. In addition to policy articulation, salience of the new norm within the Canada can be measured
by the creation of new state institutions:

- In 2005, the GoC created the Stabilization and Reconstruction Task
  Force (START) to help answer the growing international demand for
  Canadian support and involvement in complex crises – conflict or natural disaster related – and to coordinate whole-of-government policy
  and program engagements in fragile states, such as Afghanistan, Haiti
  and Sudan (DFAIT 2011e).
- In order to capture actors beyond the GoC, CANADEM (Canada –
  "Experts Mobilized") was established with assistance and funding
  of the government of Canada, to support Canada's determination
  to advance international organizations, to advance the universal
  principles of the UN Charter, and to advance international peace &
  security, human rights and the responsibility to protect (DFAIT 2011f).
- In recognition of the complex security environment in Afghanistan,
  the GoC established a Representative of Canada in Kandahar (RoCK).
  The RoCK works closely with the Commander of the Canadian
  Forces' Joint Task Force Afghanistan to support the coherent and effective implementation of Canada's objectives in Afghanistan. This
  collaboration aims to ensure that the WoG civilian and military team
  in Afghanistan has successfully synchronized governance, development, and security lines of operation (DFAIT 2011g).
- While not an invention of the GoC, the concept of a Provincial
  Reconstruction Team (PRT) was embraced in Afghanistan to coordinate the development efforts in a failed state – Afghanistan (Manley
  et al., 2008). The PRT perhaps best exemplifies the success of WoG
  diplomats and development specialists, Canadian police officers,

including the RCMP, Canadian corrections experts, and the military work in a collaborative and cooperative manner.

While the above is representative of the WoG achieving salience within Canada, it must be emphasized at this point that the Comprehensive Approach is considered the next logical step beyond WoG. That is, while current practice has brought the joint, interagency and multinational players together under WoG, it is now time to acknowledge the "public" as the next logical step in prosecuting international security crisis. Indeed the success of WoG has laid the foundation for the Comprehensive Approach to take hold.

Further, the Comprehensive Approach has undergone a salience process within other states such as the US (US Department of Defense, 2010), the UK (United Kingdom House of Commons Defence Committee, 2010), Australia (Government of Australia, 2009), and the Netherlands (Hansen, 2009), among others, advocating the necessity of such an approach.[71] More significantly, while the above examples demonstrate a degree of diffusion of the Comprehensive Approach worldwide, it is also important to note "which" states are utilizing this new norm (i.e., US, UK, Canada) as this too impacts on the norm taking hold and moving towards its tipping point.

Institutional platforms which further diffuse this emergent norm also play an important role in the norm emergence stage. Besides the G8 noted above, international organizations such as the UN (integrated approach) (UN, 2008a), the OECD (OECD, 2007), and NATO (NATO, 2011) play a key role in producing and promoting ideas, in providing a venue in which the debate can proceed, and serving as mechanisms for legitimating, and at times implementing changed understandings of the approach to international security operations espoused by the Comprehensive Approach. Based on the analysis above, it is clear that a tipping point has not yet been achieved for this emergent international norm; however, progress within the norm emergence stage is evident. As with the requirement for new entrepreneurs noted above, international platforms – existing or newly created – must continue to endorse and debate the Comprehensive Approach. This is essential to expose a greater number of states to the value of this collaborative and cooperative process.

Conclusion

Peace and security challenges have historically been a primary concern in matters of state and norms and normative considerations have long been part of solutions to the persistence of war in an anarchic world. Today, the uneven effects of globalization and the withdrawal of the Cold War overlay, confront policymakers with more complex and multifaceted challenges best described as failed and failing states and the emergence of new wars. In the last twenty years, the new wars have spawned one crisis after another and the decision on whether and how to intervene, particularly with respect to use of military force, confronts the international society of states. As a result, new approaches are emerging on how to approach armed violence in the 21st century. One such approach is called the Comprehensive Approach.

First articulated as 3D or WoG, the Comprehensive Approach seeks to move to a new level where "…diverse situationally-aware actors resolve complex issues through the purposeful coordination and de-confliction of their information, actions and effects" (Chief of Force Development, 2010, 1). The relationship between WoG and the Comprehensive Approach is significant as it helps decision-makers identify and attach meaning to the emergent international norm. It has been articulated that the Comprehensive Approach allows the forging of a unity of effort and a unity of purpose among the many diverse actors in the security community (Caldwell, 2009, 11). Indeed, the Comprehensive Approach represents a collective expectation about how to deal with complex security situations, in essence a new international norm.

As an international norm, the Comprehensive Approach is clearly in the norm emergence stage of the international norm lifecycle. There are no guarantees that it will move to the tipping point identified as approximately one third of the global community states adopting the new international norm. Therefore, while considerable progress has been made toward the adoption of this new norm, continued advocacy by entrepreneurs through a variety of institutional platforms must continue.

The salience of the Comprehensive Approach is on the rise in Canada. As such Canada is in an ideal position to be a norm entrepreneur for the Comprehensive Approach in its own right. While much of the success of domestic salience of this new norm was borne out of the trial and tribulations in Afghanistan, the shift to a training focus in 2011 should not be cause for hesitation or regression concerning the Comprehensive Approach. Indeed, the time has arrived for Canada to consolidate its gains and take the lead as an international norm entrepreneur for the Comprehensive Approach.

CONCLUSION

CHRISTIAN LEUPRECHT

The comprehensive approach is a bit like a Gregorian chant: Sung over and over as a form of meditation to make us believe and convince us that we are doing the right thing. But how do we know that our beliefs are guiding us well? How do we know that the comprehensive approach is actually working? The challenge is to translate the comprehensive approach from just another ephemeral government buzzword into a strategy and a method with its requisite operational and tactical components. Such is the crux of this conclusion.

The problem at the crux of the comprehensive approach is straightforward economics: compete or cooperate? Yet, the armed forces are quintessentially competitive: After all, their functional imperative is, according to Clausewitz, to fight other militaries and win decisively, to the point that the other side clearly understands that it lost. Similarly, government bureaucracies compete against each other for money, staff, influence, etc. Cooperation, then, does not come naturally. The comprehensive approach seeks to change the game by shifting from competition to cooperation.

Although examples drawn from Canada's Northern Strategy, the 2010 Vancouver Olympics, and the Royal Canadian Mounted Police's Integrated Border Enforcement Teams demonstrate the broad utility of the comprehensive approach, the initial impetus behind the CA has been to create sustainable conditions for peace in security zones, by employing multiple resources, capabilities and expertise in a concerted effort. The focus on the comprehensive approach abroad was driven by a perception that it was an easier problem to solve. Domestic operations were not ignored, rather, the assumption was that, once the expeditionary doctrine was completed, it would be readily applicable at the domestic level.

Security Operations in the 21st Century: Canadian Perspectives on the Comprehensive Approach, ed. M. Rostek and
P. Gizewski. Montreal and Kingston: Queen's Policy Studies Series, McGill-Queen's University Press.
© 2011 Queen's Centre for International Relations, Queen's University at Kingston. All rights reserved.

Initially, Canada's 3D Strategy – Defence, Development and Diplomacy – involved three departments in intergovernmental operations. It now includes PCO, Immigration Canada, Transport Canada, Public Health and a number of others. It has since morphed into "Whole-of-Government," "Joined-Up" or "JIMP" (Joint, Inter-agency, Multi-National, Public). The CA has manifested itself as a process and implementation tool around the world, with growing acknowledgement that security operations cannot be solved by military means alone. The idea of JIMP-capable Land Forces is the military attempt to operationalize the CA. Whereas Joint indicates national military elements, Inter-agency involves other governmental departments (OGDs) and agencies, Multinational includes military allies and coalition partners and Public recognizes that various domestic and international civil elements need to be included. Public elements can be local populations, news media and NGOs. In the belief that attaining greater awareness, coordination and cooperation will ultimately yield actions that have greater strategic effect in operations, agencies seek to facilitate coordination and ideally, cooperation among actors. Those investigating the idea seem to agree that strong leadership and political endorsement from the beginning of operations are key to its success. And mechanisms and processes to structure relationships between actors are also crucial.

Still, these different terms ought not to be substituted uncritically as synonyms for the comprehensive approach. Moreover, the concept itself has different meanings in national and international contexts.

Adapting to the increased complexity of operations necessitates ever closer cooperation. Historically, faith in linear problem-solving was widespread: Every "problem" had a "solution." By the 1980s, however, it became evident that these apparent "solutions" conjured up unintended consequences and triggered problems of their own which then had to be remedied. Part of the reason was the growing complexity of problems that government could no longer solve on its own. "Solving" problems such as acid rain required government to work with the private sector, the public sector, expert knowledge found in universities, NGO's, different levels of government and different countries. This cognizance represented the advent of what Ulrich Beck (2008) and Anthony Giddens (1990) refer to as second modernity. Problems are increasingly systemic and ecological in nature; tweaking any part of the system has ripple effects throughout the rest of the system.

The same process is reflected in the evolution of peacekeeping. Traditionally, peacekeeping involved monitoring some sort of ceasefire between two protagonists, usually countries that committed to a ceasefire, and often under some duress, invited the international community to monitor it. Compare the relative simplicity of that task with today's peace-enforcement and stability operations, which tend to be marked by the absence of state-centric protagonists, absence of a ceasefire, sometimes hostile local populations, the need for militaries actively to "clear, hold, and build" rather than just keep the peace. When the world's mightiest militaries have trouble keeping a few hundred insurgents at bay, when soldiers routinely come home in body bags, when missions involve everything from building institutions of governance to providing basic sanitary infrastructure, then we are observing a new phenomenon. This phenomenon is commonly described as asymmetric warfare. Yet, the term also has a normative connotation, one that refers precisely to the aforementioned complexity and the way apparent "solutions" would appear to spawn more "problems."

This is a distinctly new phenomenon. Since the 17th century, warfare had been about seizing and protecting territory. The military played its role in achieving a state's security objectives by fighting other armies and defending and violating territorial integrity. Writing about the growth of European armies in the late 1600s and early 1700s, John Lynn (1995, 182) concluded that "in a greater Clausewitzian sense, armies are instruments intended to force the enemy to do your will, but in the narrower context of seventeenth-century strategy, armies were instruments to seize and protect territory. Territory was the object of, and the key to, the ruler's will." Asymmetric warfare, by contrast, poses no immediate territorial threat. Conventional warfare had little use for diplomats during a campaign. As depicted by Hans Holbein in his sixteenth-century enigmatic painting "The Ambassadors," diplomats conferred with other diplomats (or rulers to other rulers) with little direct coordination between the spheres of activities other than, in Clausewitz's famous formulation, the threat or use of "military force as diplomacy by other means." At the conclusion of major campaigns or decisive battles, diplomacy would be used to divide up the spoils among the victors and determine the price the losers would pay.

The post-WWII international system was driven by the primacy of the state. The world was also less interconnected and wired. Consequently, opportunities to network quickly and regularly with organizations and individuals were less available. As a result, both the incentives to engage in CA-type actions, as well as the capacity to do so, were limited. The end of the Cold War ushered in new security challenges and introduced a range of important new actors. Transnational threats, intra-state conflicts and complex emergencies became the norm. Human security now competed with national security as an important consideration in global affairs. The realization of security thus meant having to deal with a growing cacophony of actors.

Harold Brown recognized the shift towards the non-linear battlefield in his well-known book *Thinking about National Security* (1983). Yet, militaries remain structured as they were in the days of Carl von Clausewitz and Antoine-Henri Jomini. While the days of denying the enemy when and where the war ends are long gone, militaries do not have the capacity to deal with the complexities inherent to asymmetric warfare.

The comprehensive approach is thus both a means of aligning the armed forces better with operational requirements and a means of aligning them better with government expectations. Owing to demographic, societal, economic and political change, government's expectations are changing: not only with respect to operational effectiveness but also with respect to the resource available to fulfill mandates. On the one hand, these changes intimate more of these ever more complex missions. On the other hand, they translate into fiscal austerity for the armed forces. In short, the armed forces have fit a square peg into a round hole: More heavy lifting with fewer resources (Leuprecht, 2010a, 2010b). From an economic perspective, the way to surmount such a challenge is to harness synergies realized through cooperation. Smaller and middle powers have a comparative advantage in this regard as their bureaucracies are smaller and their global objectives more restrained. Concomitantly, their future contributions to large international missions is in doubt as fiscally-strained governments shun mounting body bags and exorbitant costs, both of which are an electoral liability for them. As a result, a middle power such as Canada is probably more predisposed towards smaller limited-term engagements such as training and capacity-building missions.

In other words, we need to make the comprehensive approach work because working collaboratively is the only way of confronting the compound effect of greater demands, growing complexity, yet austere resources. Concurrently we might confront the geopolitical fall-out of a looming energy and environmental crisis, exacerbated by the cultural clashes and domestic fragmentation brought about by global pressures. The odds are that we may also have to deal with domestic and transnational challenges such as pandemics, earthquakes, and political crises, which will present opportunities for enemies abroad and evil opportunists at home. The comprehensive approach is thus as much about the strategy of overcoming mounting resource constraints as it is a tactic of confronting asymmetric warfare.

Overcoming the collective-action problems inherent to such a strategy, however, is more difficult than it appears, in part because of significant resource, managerial and organizational and functional asymmetries between the armed forces and other government departments. The nomenclature and processes employed by the military and civilians are quite different: Militaries tend to operate deductively, civilian departments inductively. Some of the key differences and implications can be broken down as follows:

- Organizational structure and culture: Decision making is centralized and authoritarian among armed forces, as opposed to decentralized and diffused among NGOs and civilian agencies. This gives rise to the potential for miscommunication and misperception.

- Different types of tasks and means of accomplishing them: The military undertake projects in the community, whereas NGOs undertake projects for the community. Armed forces typically undertake quick impact projects (QIPS) that are designed to win the trust and confidence (hearts and minds) of the local population and gain valuable intelligence. NGOs engage in similar projects but for different purposes. Their projects are long term and founded on community input.
- Definitions and timeframes for success: Militaries tend to have short-term goals and short timelines for success. Success might be a function of extracting information from locals, prompt completion and staying within budget. For NGOs, by contrast, success is often gauged as sustainable long-term economic and social development.
- Competition for media resources: The military tends to use media to exert influence whereas NGOs tend to use media to generate funding for their projects.
- Resources: The military controls resources that can enable delivery of humanitarian assistance. For NGOs this poses a predicament: On the one hand, the military can provide transportation, protection and security; on the other hand, this kind of assistance can compromise neutrality and independence.

Military activities are aligned with a straightforward, hierarchical pyramid with more personnel and other resources at the bottom than at the top. Although mid-level and junior leaders can, and often do, perform activities typically described as "civilian" tasks, such as promoting good governance and economic development at the local level, their primary responsibilities are security related integration via a chain of command that is unambiguous. While horizontal coordination occurs between units at the same echelon, most attention is downwards-directed management. The military process is primarily deductive and designed for a specific set of problems (military missions) under a specific set of circumstances (usually combat or stability operations). The military begins with a problem that has largely been defined by a higher headquarters in the form of orders that assign specific missions to each part of the organization.

While decision making among armed forces tends to be centralized and authoritarian, it is generally more decentralized and diffused among NGOs and civilian agencies. In most cases civilian organizations start from scratch, framing the problem to be solved rather than deducing it from higher guidance which, when it exists at all, is likely to be ambiguous and aspirational rather than precise and directive (Wilson, 1989). Military processes are thus not well suited to civilian purposes. That is, civilian and economic tasks are conceived and executed quite differently from military and security tasks. Economic development and governance tasks tend to be aligned by function rather than geography or a rigid hierarchy of authority. Especially in traditional embassy activities, there is much less management directed downwards. The civilian sector is nearly an inverted pyramid with more staffing and resources at the top than at the bottom. This configuration is not top-heavy in the sense of a high ratio of "management" to "workers," but is a reflection of the fact that most of the political and diplomatic work is being conducted parallel to host governments. In contrast to "command and control" functions, as the military likes to refer to them, an embassy's political and economic sections operate with a high degree of autonomy in day-to-day activities. Most economic development programs are decentralized and diffuse. Programs are not "tied-in" with other programs on their left and right boundaries as is the case with military units. There is no battlefield maneuver conducted between or among the programs and thus no requirement for civilian management to be the equivalent of military command and control. Most military tasks can be synchronized in time and space and (this is the crux of "maneuver"), and given a known correlation of forces, have somewhat predicable outcomes that can be modeled using computer simulations. Yet this is often not true for key aspects of political and economic development. While interdependent, the linkages between activities are not rigid.

Ergo, approaches to planning and management differ between military and civilian organizational cultures. Notwithstanding, problems of cohesion and unity of purpose at the level of national cabinets and ministries (e.g., Said and Holt, 2008), Carafano (2006, 2) redirects attention to less obvious echelons: "Interagency cooperation is not so bad at the policy level and not too bad on the ground where individuals work together." Rather, Carafano (2006) believes that the biggest problem "is at the intermediate level, the operational level [...]." Luck and Findlay (2007) point out that the US military "is structured to operate at the national-strategic level in Washington, DC, theater-strategic level at the combatant commands, and operational and tactical levels at the Joint Task Force (JTF) and below." Civilian agencies, by contrast, lack the same degree of vertical integration because they do not have the equivalent of operational level headquarters to bridge the gap between national-level policy/strategy and tactical actions on the ground. Owing to their smaller size and often greater autonomy at the delivery-end of policy, civilian agencies (and private businesses) rarely have organizational structures and planning functions equivalent to the military concept of an operational-level headquarters. Nor is it clear they would benefit from adding such an additional layer in most circumstances. The purpose of civilian mid-level management is usually to reduce the span of control rather than develop plans to link strategy to "tactical" activity by multiple offices or business units (Kelman et al., 2003).

The military component of the CA is a highly visible commitment of national interest in any operation. For better or worse, then, the CA is dominated by defence. The reason is simple: The military will expand to fill gaps as necessary. However, it is not always the best suited organization for the job. In Afghanistan, much of Canadian Overseas Development Aid has been delivered by the military or Civil-Military Cooperation (CIMIC) through projects such as those run by Provincial Reconstruction Teams. But the military use of force is about deterrence, coercion and persuasion. Ergo, aid is allocated with the intention of winning the hearts and minds of the local people. Yet, hearts and minds must be won for the host government, and not for foreign troops or foreign NGOs. But has the CA improved security for the people (or for that matter, perceptions of it)? Perhaps one of the comprehensive approach's greatest liabilities is that its actions get lost in the shuffle. In the "Clear, Hold, Build" approach, the gray area between "Hold" and "Build" is the most challenging. There are competing concepts and metrics for determining what makes an area secure. Whereas the military feels secure if soldiers are able to dismount and walk in an area, some civilian perspectives view any uniformed presence as an indication that the area must be "insecure." Development agencies cannot create an effect if its partners are not able to work in an area. Similarly if an area is "secure," locals are more engaged and inclined to participate (a process leading to sustainability).

Is there any evidence to suggest that the CA has increased the legitimacy of the central government or contributed to winning the hearts and minds for counter-terrorism or to COIN objectives? To these ends, the evidence seems to suggest that the sort of quick impact projects (QIPs) on which the military tends to focus, does little to win the hearts and minds in the long-term. The reason is that when development and assistance in security zones is based on counter-insurgency objectives, then humanitarian space becomes compromised. Imperatives can be conflicting when there is pressure to create an effect in one's area of operation (COIN objective) in a small period (for instance, during a CF rotation of duty). The department or agency that frames a security problem frequently ends up defining the objectives and agenda. A functional CA in the COIN context will acknowledge the different paradigms at play, bridging the gap between "Hold" and "Build" and between short-term gains and long-term sustainability.

This necessitates having civilians in the field and integrating them early on, at the planning level. But how is one to prepare civilians who might be subject-matter experts, but who have no practical experience operating in theatre? Each department operates and learns differently; so each department has to train differently. Moreover, few opportunities exist to hone interagency training as significant costs are associated with executing these sorts of activities. Training can also side-track people from their already overburdened day jobs.

Civilian agencies lack the sort of comprehensive continuing professional education programs for mid-career and senior managers that are a staple in the military. Although some mid-career managers from other departments attend professional education programs run by the military, most have no formal education in strategy or planning. Militaries tend to have a large organization, headed by a senior general, whose "sole" job it is to recruit, train, and educate soldiers, develop leaders, support training in units, develop doctrine and to establish standards. No other organization in government devotes nearly as many resources to such tasks as the armed forces. The disparity is equally striking at the level of management and/or senior leadership experience: A company commander is in charge of more people than most ambassadors. Similarly, most infantry battalions have more soldiers assigned to them than the number of staff found at most embassies.

Furthermore, arguments implying that civilian agencies are not doing their fair share gloss over the fact that defence departments tend to have many more people and a much larger budget than any other agency with national-security responsibilities. As David Kilcullen (2007) has pointed out: "There are substantially more people employed as musicians in Defense bands than in the entire foreign service." Canada's regular force is mandated around 65,000 personnel; Canada's entire Department of Foreign Affairs consists of 3,000 people, a difference in magnitude of about 22:1. The military has the single largest budget within the federal government. At over 100,000 people, it is almost as large as all other federal departments combined. The Canadian Forces' Afghanistan budget alone is larger than the budget allocation received by just about any other government department. The armed forces thus enjoy a significant comparative advantage that allows them to do things no other government department can. But, as observed above, size can also be an obstacle as it gives rise to collective-action problems and hierarchies associated with the administration of larger organizations.

The sheer difference in numbers aside, unlike the military, civilian agencies do not have a large pool of non-deployed personnel who can readily act as a surge capacity to support contingency operations. Ergo, demand for civilian support for stabilization and reconstruction efforts, vastly outstrips supply. Indeed, much has been made of the availability and deployability of civilian components from government departments. Yet blanket statements which imply that civilian departments of government are unwilling to endure hardship and danger, discount the reality that individuals who sign-up for the military do so fully expecting the possibility of being deployed as part of their job. From a civilian perspective, the military is better prepared to live and work in a place with frequent mortar and rocket attacks and ambushes by improvised explosive devices (IEDs) along the roads. The complaint that employees from other departments do not expect to be sent abroad misses the point; sending them away would detract from their primary mission which is confined to activities that are almost exclusively conducted inside their own country.

The military is akin to the fire brigade: Only a relatively small portion of its total number is engaged in operations at any particular time. The remainder is in reserve waiting for a call to action, or in training, or undergoing a "re-set" to prepare for a specific future operation. Civilian agencies, by contrast, are more like the police: Nearly all of their personnel are engaged in current operations with almost no float for training and virtually none being held in reserve. Far from having bodies to spare, owing to the austerity measures of late, departments routinely lack enough staff to meet their own requirements. Since more resources are unlikely to be forthcoming as fiscal constraints prevail, these disparities are unlikely to change.

The Dahla Dam Project is just one example. The nature of the Canadian International Development Agency's (CIDA) structure has meant that there were only two officers assigned to the project, a stark contrast to the way the CF does business. Furthermore, unlike some of its CA counterparts, CIDA has multiple reporting lines to follow. CIDA is accountable to individual directors, PRT directors, RoCK, PCO, etc. which results in greater potential for conflict and micro-management. These civilian command chains are coupled with the military command chains that need to be briefed, updated and approved as well.

Given these asymmetries, what must civil-military relations look like if the comprehensive approach is to succeed? First, the armed forces will have to reorient themselves away from seeing themselves as managers of violence and towards a more comprehensive understanding of managing security writ large. The military is the only department that is in the business of managing violence; but plenty of other departments are in the business of managing security. That translates into a paradigm shift from an input-based to an output-based approach. Violence is a function of inputs. Militaries, one might notice, are almost obsessed about the number, size, and sophistication of their weaponry. By contrast, security is an output-based metric. It is a public good which all citizens consume.

In the jargon of "military transformation" one might say that the comprehensive approach requires the armed forces to shift from command and control to effect-based thinking. That is, thinking about both the effect to be achieved and the means by which that particular effect is best achieved. That means prioritizing security, political, economic, and psycho-social effects. But let us not kid ourselves: Security is the priority. DDR – disarmament, development and reconstruction – is really Ddr: The primary concern is disarmament of which development and reconstruction are an integral yet secondary dimension. The military focus may be on protecting the general population, but the campaign as a whole will only be effective if political control and good governance are established and an effective political process is enabled.

General Sir Frank Kitson, whose experience includes the Mau Mau uprising, the Malayan insurgency, and Northern Ireland, stresses the interplay of political, security and economic measures to restore peace and order. The military was but one part of the campaign, and very much subordinate to the political imperative. There can be no solely military solution to an activity that is not primarily military. Treating the symptoms may be necessary but that alone will not produce security and stability, and that is one of the principal reasons why security operations have to be interwoven with wider government measures and initiatives that may fall outside the central theme of a campaign. As Kitson (1977, 283) noted, "those who turn with relief towards the subject of Security Force operations expecting to find easily-defined problems and clear-cut solutions will be disappointed." Kitson (1971, 58) offered some guidelines to follow for the comprehensive approach to prevail and forestall the appearance of military action taking precedent. First, "the ally always [takes] second place to the host country." Second, and mirroring his call for co-ordinated government machinery, "no arrangement will work unless that host country itself has a properly ordered system for prosecuting the war." He suggests the supreme council or committee as the focal point. Third, the ally, or allies, should co-ordinate aid through one individual who sits on the host country's supreme council to help formulate overall policy. Finally, the ally must be represented at every level of government but always in a subordinate role to the host country, and in an advisory capacity.

Middle and smaller powers with open economies that rely on free trade such as Canada, have few realist interests in the world – other than to safeguard international stability and keep trade routes safe, secure, and open. Make no mistake: Canada benefits from the liberal international order of the Empire of the day – first *pax Brittannica* then *pax Americana*. This liberal international order sustains what some perceive to be the inequities of market forces and the iniquities of mercenary forces. This was Canada's motivation for getting involved in peacekeeping in the first place. In that sense, the objectives that inform Canadian national interest have not changed. Only the means have changed. Neither peacekeeping then, nor peace enforcement and stability operations now, are about "making the world a better place." The comprehensive approach is, first and foremost, about providing, re-establishing, and sustaining security and stability. It is not, in the first instance, about telling the locals how to live their lives or run their affairs. It is all too tempting to work on the patronizing assumption that the locals are stupid or inept; so, "we" need to show "them." As if they had lived without any ability to govern themselves until "we" arrived on the scene. Neither can the comprehensive approach be implemented effectively nor can it work as long as there is mission creep and targets keep on shifting. In the example of Afghanistan, the lack of a centralized strategy left the impression that individual projects had no connection to the Afghan National Development Strategy which reflected a disregard for Afghanistan's sovereignty. Issues that transcend provincial boundaries were difficult to solve and ended up competing for resources and funds from Kabul instead of cooperating.

The problem with mapping a civilizing mission onto a stability operation is that it essentially becomes a form of imperial high policing with a vague mission and vague objectives, other than to domesticate the local savages. Ergo, the comprehensive approach can work only if constructivist ideologues are kept at bay: Otherwise, the operation is likely to degenerate into a form of coercive *realpolitik* at best, or cultural and normative imperialism at worst, that is bound to get the locals' backs up (Last, 2010). By contrast, a genuinely comprehensive approach must be bottom-up, not top-down. Instead of cherry picking, it must be open to collaborating with whoever is prepared to step up to the plate: Making sure that comprehensive approach suits the interests of smaller powers may mean strategic cooperation not only between liberal democracies, but also with other states outside the ambit of superpowers, whose cooperation is necessary for stability.

In sum, the comprehensive approach is about strategy and method. Strategically, it means working together to overcome collective-action problems, harness economies of scale, and use cooperation to mitigate growing resource constraints in an ever more demanding and complex operating environment. Methodologically, it means using an effects-based framework with clear and attainable objectives that make progress measurable. Operationally, it means good civil-military relations, not only by following the strategy and objectives as determined by the government to which actors and agencies are ultimately accountable but also by taking directions from the government and people with respect to their priorities. Reconciling those competing pressures will not always be easy; but it will only be complicated further if distracted by idiosyncratic ideological agendas. Tactically, it means being cognizant of the differences in resources, capacities, and motivations of the different actors and agencies deployed in the field while not falling into the trap of the fallacy of composition: Summing the parts misses the point of the comprehensive approach. The litmus test for the comprehensive approach is simple: The whole must be greater than the sum of the parts.

NOTES

Chapter 1

1. To be sure, other issues can also impede effective inter-organizational co-ordination and collaboration. Such efforts are not only time consuming, but can also have profound resource implications both in financial and human terms. Often, organizations have vastly unequal capabilities for supporting such approaches. Yet it is also clear that such interaction can be perceived as threatening organizational identities, interests and agendas. Indeed, not only does such practice by its very nature require considerable inter-agency dialogue, but at times a willingness to compromise and thus dilute key aspects of one's own agenda. As such, it can pose a challenge to organizational visibility and status. Not surprisingly, in the absence of forces compelling inter-agency interaction and collaboration such practice has tended to be more the exception than the rule.

2. This is not to imply a desire on the part of all private organizations to work with, or influence, government. In some cases, the mandates of such organizations may demand that cooperation and collaboration with government organizations be carefully avoided so as to ensure strict neutrality and organizational credibility in addressing the challenges confronted. Yet among nongovernmental organizations in which this was not the case, it is still fair to say that neither government interest in such players nor the capabilities for gaining influence within official circles available to them was generally as strong as it has become in more recent times.

3. The fact that existing mechanisms failed to adequately address the challenges of security, governance and development in war-torn regions such as the Balkans and in Africa only served to underline the need for the development and institutionalization of a broader, more holistic approach.

4. Indeed, one need only consider the widespread international fallout surrounding the U.S. response to Hurricane Katrina in 2005, and US President George W. Bush's declaration in 2003 proclaiming the end of major combat operations in Iraq to appreciate the degree to which global communications can work to magnify issues of government legitimacy. For the text of President Bush's speech, see Jarrett Murphy (2003), President Declares End to Major Combat in Iraq, Associated Press. At http://www.cbsnews.com/stories/2003/05/01/iraq/main551946.shtml (accessed 4 January 2011).

5. From a bureaucratic standpoint, the idea has roots in the private sector management theory of re-engineering and aims at streamlining processes from input to output in order to maximize efficiency and remove overlap and duplication. In a theoretical sense, re-engineering seeks to create an end-to-end process that cuts across traditional "stovepipes" leading to an organization that runs more smoothly and efficiently.

6. The attitudinal change is clear when one compares how a CA would differ from CIMIC. As one observer (Djik, 2010) notes in the case of CIMIC, "[m]ilitary members are used to being 'in the lead' and calling the shots – playing the military card whereby all activity is directed towards the military objective." Under (the) old philosophy, when planned activities were executed, all means, military and civilian, were used to reach the militarily defined objective, as clearly defined in NATO's definition of CIMIC: The co-ordination and co-operation, in support of the mission, between the NATO Commander and civil actors, including national population and local authorities, as well as international, national and non-governmental organizations and agencies. (North Atlantic Treaty Organization, 2003, 1-1, Art 102). With this definition, the commander's intent always prevailed in planning and executing the mission. The most significant change in adopting CA is the understanding that the mission is not only a military objective but can be an objective used to integrate a broader approach, leading to an end state that is not simply military in character. By the incorporation of CA, the planning of operations would mean that we would not look to the use of civilian organizations as a means of supporting a military mission, but recognizing that we have to share the planning table with other actors; actors who want to achieve their own objectives! See Djik (2010).

Chapter 2

7. This date changes, depending on the source. In the winter of 1989 George Bush, Sr., and Mikhail Gorbachev declared an end to the decades-long conflict; that same year saw the fall of the Berlin Wall. In the winter of 1991 the Soviet Union was officially dissolved, thus ending any possibility of continued conflict.

8. The Joint aspect of JIMP involves national military elements (e.g., Army, Navy, Air Force); the Interagency aspect involves other government departments and agencies, both domestic and international; the Multinational military aspect involves allies or international coalition partners; and the Public aspect involves a variety of domestic and international civilian elements, including local populations, media agencies, and non-governmental organizations (NGOs), as well as a variety of other "public" entities (see Gizewski and Rostek, 2007, and Leslie, Gizewski, and Rostek, 2008).

9. Throughout this chapter, the term "NGOs" will be used to refer to a broad and heterogeneous category of civilian private organizations, whether domestic or international, engaged in humanitarian aid, humanitarian development, or human rights activities, as a discussion of the differences among these organizations is beyond the present scope.

10. A number of NGOs, such as Médecins sans Frontières/Doctors without Borders, seek to avoid contact with the military on the basis of the principles of neutrality and impartiality.

11. To date, relatively little empirical research has been conducted on the NGO-military relationship. Winslow's (2002) research is based on (i) unstructured interviews and focus groups carried out with Canadian soldiers in Bosnia in 1998 and in the Golan Heights in 1999; (ii) archival research carried out at Canada's National Defence Headquarters on the crisis in the Great Lakes region of Central Africa, which involved Canadian troops; and (iii) documentary sources, particularly the work of US sociologists Laura Miller and Charles Moskos. In addition to interviews with Canadian military personnel, Winslow conducted interviews at NATO headquarters and with European battalion commanders deployed to the former Yugoslavia, and consulted with members of large international relief agencies such as the UNHCR and the International Committee of the Red Cross (ICRC). A more recent study on the NGO-CF relationship (Holton et al., 2010; Holton et al., this volume) echoes some of Winslow's earlier findings, particularly with respect to how differences in organizational culture and structure may pose challenges in this relationship.

Chapter 3

12. See NATO Multi-National Experiment 5 (2009).
13. There are great dimensions of assumed linearity in this approach that do not match the complexity of the problems faced. See Dorner (1998) and Sowell (2007). Both authors point to the error in assuming such linear predictabilities.
14. See publications from the Special Inspector General for Iraq Reconstruction (SIGIR) at www.sigir.mil/publications/index.html. In particular, *Hard Lessons: The Iraq Reconstruction Experience and Applying Iraq's Hard Lessons to the Reform of Stabilization and Reconstruction Operation* (SIGIR, 2010). The theatres are sufficiently different that the lessons do not easily migrate across.
15. Based on briefing of former SRSG/Force Commander of UNFIL, to Multi-National Interoperability Council, March 2010.
16. See www.stabilisationunit.gov.uk. Examples of this include documents such as the unit's *Quick Guide to Stabilisation and Planning, The UK Approach to Stabilisation,* and *The Quick Impact Project Handbook.*
17. See http://www.dtic.mil/doctrine/doctrine/jwfc_pam.htm (Joint Warfighting Center (JWFC). 2005. JWFC Pamphlet. *Draft Planning Framework for Reconstruction, Stabilization, and Conflict Transformation.* 1 December. United States Department of Defense, Defense Technical Information Centre, Joint Electronic Library).
18. See http://www.southcom.mil/AppsSC/pages/staff.php?id=32&flag=1 (United States Southern Command. 2008. Partnering Directorate. Washington, DC. Accessed 17 February 11).

Chapter 4

19. Certain NGOs claim that taking government funds implies picking a side in war. This violates NGO project impartially. Yet others argue that receipt of funding does not translate to control. For instance, Oxfam receives donor government funds, yet such funding does not translate to control or even

influence over the day-to-day work NGOs carry out. Those NGOs receiving funds are not deterred from openly criticizing the conduct of international military forces and the broader international community. Oxfam argues that it sides with Afghan civilians in the conflict state. Donors sometimes impose burdensome reporting requirements on NGO recipients, but they generally do not micro-manage nor impose projects on NGOs. While donors do have preferences for sector financing, NGOs are given the liberty to select projects/programs through the submission of unsolicited proposals within donors' preferred sectors. Complete financial independence from government is difficult for non-profit organizations because NGOs have very little financing of their own. To assume that NGOs would be automatically corrupted by their official funding sources, and written off as pawns of warring parties, would short suit the value that NGOs can offer within fragile states.

Chapter 5

20. The views expressed are those of the author and not those of the United States Institute of Peace.
21. Beth Ellen Cole, testimony to the House Armed Services Committee, Oversight and Investigations Sub-Committee (2 November 2010).

Chapter 7

22. Email from LCol MB Boswell, Senior Staff Officer Capability Development, Land Staff on 6 February 2008. This definition has been endorsed by the Army Terminology Panel (ATP) and submitted to the Defence Terminology Standardization Board (DTSB) for approval.
23. Discussion Colonel Simms and Robert Derouin Director General Stabilization and Reconstruction Task Force (START) Secretariat, Ottawa, Ontario, 12 March 2008.
24. JIMP as a doctrinal or conceptual term has not been accepted by all our key partner nations. The US uses JIM and has not embraced the P or public element.
25. In fact on 29 April 2008 a high level team designated "Rolling Start" of government officials went to Kandahar for an extended technical assistance visit. This team included high ranking officials from the PCO along DFAIT, CIDA, DND (IS Pol), RCMP and others. The team was accompanied and advised by DCOMD CEFCOM. The team will back brief the Clerk of the Privy Council Office in Kandahar during the week of 5 May 2008 on options to further "civilianize" the mission including commanding the PRT, taking over the Strategic Advisory Team (SAT) and appointing a civilian equivalent (or even higher) to the Commander Task Force Afghanistan. Information provided by numerous conversations with these government officials 29 April to 2 May and in office call with Comd TFA in Kandahar on 1 May 2008.
26. The US has continually provided both tactical forces and key enablers to RC (S) under the ISAF mission besides the forces (mainly special forces) operating in the area as part of US Operation Enduring Freedom (OEF). In early Spring 2008 the US surged in considerable ground tactical forces including 24 Marine Expeditionary Unit and has a renewed focus in the SOUTH.

Chapter 8

27. Drafted: IRP/Howard/Therrien; Consulted: IRP, IRG, IRC, IRG, FTAG, FGCE, IDR, MIS, PRMNY; Approved: IRD, IFM, O/USS.

Chapter 9

28. I will use RCMP and Civilian Police (CivPol) interchangeably in this paper, because while there were personnel from other civilian police forces represented in Kandahar, the RCMP was the agency responsible for command and control.
29. The personnel numbers in this paragraph, and the assessments that follow, are based on personal records kept by the author during his assignment as Political Director at the Kandahar PRT, July 2006 to July 2007, and as Director of NATO Policy and Afghanistan Policy with the Department of National Defence from October 2007 to February 2009.
30. An assessment based on discussion between the author and the CO PRT for much of this period, LCol Bob Chamberlain.
31. The issues highlighted here were raised during the "Rolling Start" mission to Kandahar in May 2008, which was mandated to develop a proposal to restructure and enhance Canada's civilian presence in Kandahar; the author of this paper was the Department of National Defence civilian member of that mission.
32. Transforming the Mission, final report of the Rolling Start mission, May 2008. The RoCK, Elissa Golberg, cited a final total of 63 in her June 4 testimony to Parliament, which suggests not all positions envisaged were actually filled.
33. Interview with Elissa Golberg, Government of Canada Afghanistan website, Canada's Engagement in Afghanistan, http://www.afghanistan.gc.ca/canada-afghanistan/speeches-discours/yir-2.aspx?lang=en, 1 December 2009.

Chapter 10

34. Working as policy analysts at CIDA, the authors have benefitted immensely from the work and thinking of their Canadian and international colleagues in preparing this paper. While it is virtually impossible to credit the contribution of other individuals, the authors do take responsibility for all the faults in the final product – all views expressed are personal, and do not necessarily represent the official positions of CIDA or the Government of Canada.
35. This terminology was coined by the OECD Development Assistance Committee (2007) when it endorsed ten "Principles for Good International Engagement in Fragile States and Situations."
36. "The end of the Cold War not only removed a major source of conflict from the international system, it also allowed the UN to begin to play the security-enhancing role that its founders had intended, but which the organisation had long been prevented from pursuing. With the Security Council no longer paralysed by Cold War politics, the UN spearheaded a veritable explosion of conflict prevention, peacemaking and post-conflict peacebuilding activities in the early 1990s" (Human Security Centre, 2005, 8-9).

37. For example: UN Security Council Resolutions 1325 and 1820 on women, peace, and security, the Convention on the Elimination of all Forms of Discrimination Against Women (CEDAW), the UN Convention on the Rights of the Child (CRC) (at http://www.un.org/documents/scres.htm) and the Millennium Development Goals (at http://www.undp.org/mdg/basics.shtml).
38. See, for example, North, Wallis, and Weingast (2009).

Chapter 11

39. See Jones (2003) for a fuller explanation of CAS. Also, see Yaneer (2004) and Gharajedaghi (2006).
40. Various Organisation for Economic Co-operation and Development (OECD) publications like *Whole of Government Approaches to Fragile States* or the *DAC Handbook on Security Sector Reform* fall into this category.
41. For details, see United Nations, Office for the Coordination of Humanitarian Affairs, *One Response* (New York: United Nations), at http://oneresponse.info/Coordination/ClusterApproach/Pages/Cluster%20Approach.aspx.
42. For an outline of the Clear Build Hold process, see Kellerman (2003).

Chapter 12

43. Section 7(1)(d) of the *RCMP Act* (Department of Justice 2010) states the following: The Commissioner may: (d) designate any member, any supernumerary special constable appointed under this section or any temporary employee employed under subsection 10(2) as a peace officer.
44. Title 19 USC 1401 (US Treasury Department, 2004) states: The terms "officer of the customs" and "customs officer" mean any officer of the United States Customs Service of the Treasury Department. Also referred to as the "Customs Service" or any commission, warranted or petty of the Coast Guard, or any agent or other persons, including foreign law enforcement officers, authorized by the law or designated by the Secretary of the Treasury to perform any duties of an officer of the Customs Service. See: http://vlex.com/vid/sec-miscellaneous-19194215 (accessed 7 July 2010).
45. On the BEST program: see US Immigration and Customs Enforcement (2010). Also, CBC News: "Canada – US join forces at Detroit/Windsor border" at http://www.cbc.ca/canada/windsor/story/2009/10/28/windsor-border-task-force-091028.html (accessed 7 July 2010).
46. Consistent with the work of Onuf, Kubalkova, and Kowert (1998, 59-60), in this paper, agency refers not only to individuals, but also to groups of individuals who act on behalf of others. Agents, Onuf et al. claim, are defined by their participation in society, to the extent that rules exist that allow for that participation. Thus, individuals, and groups of individuals, such as policy makers, participate as social actors within the bounds and limits set by rules. Scott (2001, 76) takes the definition one step further by arguing that agents have the capacity to effect some change on the social world around them either through altering the rules or the distribution of resources. In short, agents have the capacity to take action.

47. The War of 1812, the Canadian Rebellion of 1837, the Civil War, illegal immigration at the beginning of the 20th century, prohibition and the war on drugs all represent focusing events that served to strengthen the resource and ideological commitment to the security function of the border.
48. Laitinen (2003, 22) defines a security border as "the border between two or several political unites containing the dimension of security in a traditional sense... the notion of security border is primarily understood in the context of security."

Chapter 13

49. The terms "Arctic" and "North" are used interchangeably here, although three definitions are used at any one time: a people definition which spans the three territories but also the people of Nunavik and Nunatsiavut; a political-geographic definition which only includes the three territories of the Yukon, Northwest Territories and Nunavut; and, the science definition which is used for the International Polar Year which includes anything north of the southern limit of discontinuous permafrost, a definition which skirts the Northern geography of our larger provinces.
50. Ayles Ice Shelf: about 4,500 years old and 15 km long by 5 km wide by 35 meters thick
51. The member states are Canada, Denmark/Greenland/Faroe Islands, Finland, Iceland, Norway, Sweden, The Russian Federation, and USA. Permanent participants are Aleut International Association, Athabaskan Council, Gwich'in Council International, Inuit Circumpolar Council, Raipon, and the Saami Council.
52 More recently, the European Union appears to be moving away from a call for an Arctic multilateral governance regime but is seeking a larger role in Arctic matters, including permanent observer status at the Arctic Council.
53. Arctic Forces Training Centre in Resolute and a deepwater berthing and refuelling facility in Nanisivik.

Chapter 14

54. The core problem actually had two components, one of which was the competition between government agencies and their lack of willingness to cede power or authority in any substantive way. The other was that while PS had a well-developed policy formulation capability, they had little or no skills or capability in the area of the coordination or execution of actual operations.
55. Establishing a common process/understanding for the classification and handling of classified information throughout government and between levels of government. PS Canada is the lead agency for this task. Establishment of a physical system that permits the passage of classified information to all users in government at every level. (Interview with Mercer, 2010.)

Chapter 15

56. The ministry of military chaplains among religious leaders and their communities is an emerging domain in operations for a number of countries,

Canada being among them. American chaplains, in particular, testify to an increasing incidence of chaplains' engaging religious communities on a number of levels. As a result, additional training in the form of Religious Area Assessment and Analysis (RAA) and Religious Leader Liaison (RLL) have been introduced to better equip deploying chaplains to conduct analysis and engage religious leaders, thus benefiting Commanders with a greater capacity to understand and communicate with the religious element in their Area of Responsibility (AoR). The Canadian Forces (CF) Chaplain Branch is following suit. With respect to engaging the religious *other*, the terms RLL and RLE are often used interchangeably in American parlance – both in training and in the literature – to describe such encounters and subsequent activities. Due to its congruence with such doctrinal themes as Key Leader Engagement and civic engagement – critical components of today's expanding operations within the space of indigenous populations – the CF Chaplain Branch has adopted RLE as the descriptor of such operational ministry.

57. "[In addition] they have contact with top-level leaders, but are not bound by the political calculations that govern every move and decision made at that level. Similarly, they vicariously know the context and experience of people living at the grassroots, yet they are not encumbered by the survival demands facing many at this level. Second, the position of middle-range leaders is not based on political or military power, nor are such leaders necessarily seeking to capture power of that sort. Their status and influence in the setting derives from ongoing relations – some professional, some institutional, some formal, others matters of friendship and acquaintance. Third, middle-range actors tend to have pre-existing relations with counterparts that cut across the lines of conflict within the setting. They may, for example belong to a professional association or have built a network or relation that cut across the identity divisions within the society" (Lederach, 1997, 41-42). See also Douglas Johnston and Cynthia Sampson, eds., *Religion, The Missing Dimension of Statecraft* (New York: Oxford University Press, 1994); Douglas Johnston, ed., *Faith-Based Diplomacy: Trumping Realpolitik* (New York: Oxford University Press, 2003); Marc Gopin, *Between Eden and Armageddon: the Future of World Religions, Violence, and Peacemaking* (New York: Oxford University Press, 2000).

58. Again, the authors reinforce the strategic import of local populations to COIN operations: "Generally, within a COIN campaign, strategic centres of gravity are populations and their support of the campaign. The population of the region or nation in question is a centre of gravity over which the insurgents and the COIN elements will fight for support" (Land Force, 2008, 508.6 b. (3), 5-11.

59. For additional information regarding the JIMP concept, see (i) P. Gizewski &and LCol M. Rostek. 2007. Toward a Comprehensive Approach to CF Operations: The Land Force JIMP Concept. In *Defence R&D Canada: Centre for Operational Research and Analysis*, DRCD CORA TM 2007-60; (ii) Major A.B. Godefroy, ed. 2007. *Land Operations 2021 Adaptive Dispersed Operations: The force Employment Concept for Canada's Army of Tomorrow.* (Kingston, Canada: Directorate of Land Concept and Design), 25-27.

60. A number of programs bringing youth and families together from both sides of the Israeli/Palestinian conflict have proven effective. See Kids 4 Peace USA www.kids4peace.org and Landau (2003).

Chapter 16

61. http://www.dfait-maeci.gc.ca/cip-pic/discussions/fragile/official_response-reponse_officiel.aspx?lang=eng, viewed 22 Feb 2010
62. There are other models such as Johnson's cultural web (Johnson, 1988), which identifies a number of elements (The Paradigm, Control Systems, Organizational Structures, Power Structures, Symbols, Rituals and Routines, and Stories and Myths) that can be used to describe or influence Organizational Culture.
63. Most of the material on 7-S in this section came directly from an article published by Dagmar Recklies (2001). Some rewording was done to better align it for application by the military.

Chapter 17

64. This Police group includes members from civilian police forces, the Royal Canadian Mounted Police (RCMP), and the Correctional Service of Canada (CSC).
65. Our thanks to Mr. Roger Roy and Ms. Caroline LePrince for their valuable assistance in data collection.
66. We conducted both Kruskal-Wallis non-parametric and parametric one-way ANOVAs.
67. $F(2, 22.50) = 6.99., MSE = 0.84, p = .004, \eta_p^2 = .17$ and $F(2, 36) = 4.87., MSE = 0.69, p = .013, \eta_p^2 = .21$.
68. Post-hoc (i.e., both parametric and nonparametric) tests showed that members of CIDA ($n = 14, M = 2.84, SD = 0.85$) perceived a significantly greater impact of the EX MG training on their ability to work effectively with members of the Afghan public than did members of DFAIT ($n = 11, M = 1.85, SD = 0.43$), $t(23) = 3.49, p = .002, d = 1.41$. Means for the Police group were not significantly different from either the CIDA or the DFAIT groups. Similarly, members of CIDA ($n = 14, M = 2.44, SD = 0.75$) and of the Police group ($n = 14, M = 2.29, SD = 1.20$) perceived EX MG as having provided them with a significantly greater degree of effective tools/skills to work with members of the Afghan public than did members of DFAIT ($n = 11, M = 1.45, SD = 0.52$), $t(23) = 3.73, p = .001, d = 1.50$ and $t(23) = 2.36, p = .027, d = 0.95$ (note that nonparametric Wilcoxon-Mann-Whitney tests resulted in the same findings.)

Chapter 19

69. Afghanistan and Iraq are especially illustrative of new realities. In fact the former case may represent a template or model of things to come, not necessarily in the sense that future conflict will resemble it entirely – but in the sense that it encompasses many of the operations that could be required. Indeed, Afghanistan illustrates the demands of the three-block war – with combat occurring at the same time that humanitarian and reconstruction efforts are being undertaken. At the very least, this suggests that future war will look more like Afghanistan and Iraq than the Second World War.
70. Interoperability will occur in three broad domains: information interoperability (the way we share information including technological and procedural

aspects); cognitive interoperability (the way we perceive and think reflected in doctrine and decision processes); and behavioural interoperability (the way we carry out the selected course of action). See Canadian Forces Warfare Centre Glossary of Terms (Joint Terminology Panel) website at http://www.cfd-cdf.forces.gc.ca/sites/page-eng.asp?page=7492.

71. Measurement of the respective degree of success of the salience process within these states is beyond the scope of this chapter.

REFERENCES

Allison, G. 1971. *Essence of Decision: Explaining the Cuban Missile Crisis.* Boston: Littlefield and Brown.

American, British, Canadian, Australian, New Zealand Armies Program (ABCA). 2006. *Future Concept.* Rosslyn, Virginia: ABCA Program Office.

Anderson, D. 2006. *Histories of the Hanged: The Dirty War in Kenya and the End of Empire.* London: Phoenix Books, Orion Publishing Group.

Ankerson, C. 2004. *Coordination, Cooperation, or Something Else: A Framework for Assessing Power Relations in the Discourse of Civil-Military Cooperation in Peace Support Operations.* Unpublished document. Ottawa, Carleton University.

Apostolov, M. 2001. *Religious Minorities, Nation States, and Security: Five Cases from the Balkans and Eastern Mediterranean.* Aldershot, Hampshire, England: Ashgate Publishing Ltd.

Appleby, R.S. 2000. *The Ambivalence of the Sacred: Religion, Violence, and Reconciliation.* Lanham, Maryland: Rowman and Littlefield Publishers.

Appleby, R.S., and R. Cizik. 2010. *Engaging Religious Communities Abroad: A New Imperative for US Foreign Policy.* Report of the Task Force on Religion and the Making of Foreign Policy. Chicago: The Chicago Council on Global Affairs.

Army Lessons Learned Centre (ALLC). 2010. *Lessons Synopsis Report (09-018): Expansion of the Stability Zone.* Kingston, Ontario: ALLC. At http://www.crs-csex.forces.gc.ca/reports-rapports/2007/pdf/138P077-eng.pdf.

Aronson, E., D.L. Bridgeman, and R. Geffner. 1978. Interdependent Interactions and Prosocial Behaviour. *Journal of Research and Development in Education* 12:16-27.

Atlantic Council of the United States. 2008. *Saving Afghanistan: An Appeal and Plan for Urgent Action.* Washington, DC: Atlantic Council of the United States.

Australian Public Service Commission. 2004. *Connecting Government: Whole-of-Government Responses to Australia's Priority Challenges.* Canberra: Australian Public Service Commission. At http://www.apsc.gov.au/mac/connecting-government1.htm.

Baron, R.M. 2008. Reconciliation, Trust, and Cooperation: Using Bottom-Up and Top-Down Strategies to Achieve Peace in Israeli-Palestinian Conflict. In *The Social Psychology of Intergroup Reconciliation,* ed. A. Nadler, T.E. Malloy, and J.D. Fisher. New York: Oxford University Press.

Barr, Col D. 2010. The Vancouver 2010 Olympic Games Security. Presentation to conference on Canadian Perspectives on the Comprehensive Approach. Kingston, Ontario: Queen's University.

Beck, Ulrich. 2008. *World at Risk*. Cambridge: Polity Press.

Benthall, J. 1993. *Disasters, Relief, and the Media*. London: I. B. Tauris.

Boutros-Ghali, B. 1992. *An Agenda for Peace: Preventative Diplomacy, Peacemaking and Peacebuilding*. Report of the Secretary-General United Nations, A/47/277-S/24111. At www.un.org/docs/SG/agpeace.html (accessed 3 January 2011).

Brown, A.L., and B.D. Adams. 2010. *Exploring the JIMP Concept: Literature Review*. DRDC Toronto Contract Report (DRDC No. CR 2010-021). Toronto: DRDC.

Brown, Harold. 1983. *Thinking about National Security: Defence and Foreign Policy in a Dangerous World*. Boulder, Colorado: Westview Press.

Byman, D.L. 2001. Uncertain Partners: NGOs and the Military. *Survival* 43:97-114.

Caldwell IV, Lt. General Wm., Commander Combined Arms Centre. 2009. *Fm3-07 Stability Operations: A Comprehensive Approach to the 21st Century*. Official Conference Transcript. Washington, DC: Brookings Institute.

Campbell, J. 2004. *Institutional Change and Globalization*. Princeton: Princeton University Press.

Canadian Forces Development. 2010. *The Comprehensive Approach: Road Map*. Unpublished document. Ottawa, Chief of Force Development.

Canadian Forces Leadership Institute (CFLI). 2005. *Leadership in the Canadian Forces: Doctrine*. Kingston, Ontario: Canadian Defence Academy.

CFLI. 2008. *Broadsword or Rapier? The Canadian Forces' Involvement in 21st Century Coalition Operations*. CFLI Technical Report 2008-01. Kingston, Ontario: Canadian Defence Academy. At http://www.cda-acd.forces.gc.ca/cfli-ilfc/doc/cds-eng.pdf.

Canadian Forces Operations. 2000. B-GG-005-004/AF-000 (18 Dec.), 3-2. Cited by Colonel Craig King in Effects-Based Operations: Buzzword or Blueprint, *The Operational Art: Canadian Perspectives—Context and Concepts*, ed. Allan English et al. Kingston, Ontario: Canadian Defence Academy Press, 2005, 318.

Carafano, James Jay. 2006. Principles for Stability Operations and State Building. Heritage Lecture, 13 February. Washington, DC: The Heritage Foundation. At http://www.heritage.org/Research/NationalSecurity/hl1067.cfm.

CARE Canada. 2009. *CARE Canada History*. Ottawa: CARE Canada. At http://care.ca/main/index.php?en&history (accessed 29 April 2009).

CARE International. 2009. *CARE History*. Chatelaine, Switzerland: CARE International. At http://www.care.org/about/history.asp (accessed 29 April 2009).

Carment, D., S. Lel-Achkar, S. Prest, and Y. Samy. 2006. The 2006 Country Indicators for Foreign Policy: Opportunities and Challenges for Canada. *Canadian Foreign Policy* 13(1):27.

Center on International Cooperation. 2010. *Annual Review of Global Peace Operations*. Press Release. New York: Center on International Cooperation. At http://www.cic.nyu.edu/Lead%20Page%20PDF/ARGPO2010_press_advisory_25Feb.pdf.

Chauvet, L., P. Collier, and A. Hoeffler. 2007. *The Cost of Failing States and the Limits of Sovereignty*. Rep. no. 2007/30. Helsinki: United Nations University, World Institute for Development Economics Research.

Checkel, Jeffrey T. 1999. Norms, Institutions, and National Identity in Contemporary Europe. *International Studies Quarterly* 1999:83-114.

Chief of Force Development. 2008. *The Future Security Environment 2008-2030.* Ottawa: National Defence.

Chief of Force Development. 2010. *The Comprehensive Approach Concept.* Ottawa: National Defence.

Chief of Review Services. 2007. *Evaluation of CF/DND participation in the Kandahar Provincial Reconstruction Team.* 1258-156 CRS. Ottawa: Chief of Review Services.

Clingendael Institute. 2005. *The Stability Assessment Framework.* The Hague: The Netherlands Ministry of Foreign Affairs. At www.clingendael.nl/ publications/2005/20050200_cru_paper_stability.pdf (accessed 28 June 2010).

Community Policing Advisory Council (CPAC) of Ontario. 1996. *CPAC Leading the Revisions of Ontario's Community Policing Model.* At http://www.communitypolicing.ca (accessed 1 July 2010).

Comprehensive Approach: Trends, Challenges, and Possibilities for Cooperation in Crisis Prevention and Management. 2008. Articles from International Actors and from National Delegations. Work of the CAS Research Team and Expertise of the Crisis Management Initiative. Helsinki, Finland: Ministry of Defence.

Cook, S.W. 1985. Experimenting on Social Issues: The Case of School Desegregation. *American Psychologist* 40:452-460.

Cortell, Andrew P., and James W. Davis. 2005. When Norms Clash: International Norms, Domestic Practices, and Japan's Internalization of the GATT/WHO. *Review of International Studies* 2005:3-25.

Cross, T., B. Bazron, K. Dennis, and M. Isaacs. 1989. *Toward a Culturally Competent System of Care.* Volume 1. Washington, DC: Georgetown University.

Czerwinski, Thomas J. 1996. Command and Control at the Crossroads. *Parameters* autumn 26(3):121-132.

Dallaire, R. 2003. *Shake Hands with the Devil: The Failure of Humanity in Rwanda.* Toronto: Random House Canada.

Danan, L., and A. Hunt. 2007. *Mixed Blessings: US Government Engagement with Religion in Conflict-Prone Settings.* A Report of the Post-Conflict Reconstruction Project. Washington, DC: Center for Strategic and International Studies Press. http://csis.org/files/media/csis/pubs/070820_religion.pdf.

DCDC. Policy Statement. www.mod.uk/DefenceInternet/Microsite/DCDC/ OurTeam/Doctrine.htm.

de Coning, C. 2008. *The United Nations and the Comprehensive Approach. DIIS Report. 2008.* 14. Copenhagen, Denmark: Danish Institute for International Studies (DIIS).

Department of Foreign Affairs and International Trade (DFAIT). 2010. *The Global Peace and Security Program (GPSP).* Ottawa: DFAIT. At http://www.international.gc.ca/START-GTSR/gpsp-ppsm.aspx (accessed 10 August 2010).

DFAIT. 2011a. *Security System Reform and International Law.* Ottawa: DFAIT. At http://www.international.gc.ca/glynberry/reform-reforme.aspx?lang=eng (accessed 19 March 2011).

DFAIT. 2011b. *Northern Policy.* Ottawa: DFAIT. At http://www.international. gc.ca/polar-polaire/ndfp-vnpe2.aspx?lang=en (viewed 6 February 2011).

DFAIT. 2011c. *G8 Muskoka Declaration Recovery and New Beginnings.* Ottawa: DFAIT. At http://canadainternational.gc.ca/g8/summit-sommet/2010/muskoka-declaration-muskoka.aspx?lang=eng (accessed 6 February 2011).

DFAIT. 2011d. *Afghanistan: The Comprehensive Approach in Action.* Ottawa: DFAIT. At http://www.afghanistan.gc.ca/canada-afghanistan/speeches-discours/2009/2009_02_07.aspx (accessed 6 February 2011).

DFAIT. 2011e. *START*. Ottawa: DFAIT. At http://www.international.gc.ca/start-gtsr/index.aspx (accessed 2 February 2011).

DFAIT. 2011f. *National Governments: Canada's Role*. Ottawa: DFAIT. At http://www.international.gc.ca/peace-paix/act_gov.aspx?lang=eng and http://www.canadem.ca/home (both accessed 2 February 2011).

DFAIT. 2011g. *Representative of Canada in Kandahar*. Ottawa: DFAIT. At http://www.afghanistan.gc.ca/canada-afghanistan/kandahar/represent.aspx (accessed 2 February 2011).

Department of Justice. 2010. *The Royal Canadian Mounted Police Act*. R.S., 1985, c. R-10. Ottawa: Department of Justice. At http://laws.justice.gc.ca/eng/R-10/page-2.html#anchorbo-ga:l_I (accessed 7 July 2010).

Department of National Defence. 2003. *Future Force: Concepts for Future Army Capabilities*. Kingston, Ontario: Directorate of Land Strategic Concepts, 2003.

Department of National Defence. 2008a. *Counter-Insurgency Operations*, B-GL-323-004/FP-003. Ottawa: Department of National Defence.

Department of National Defence. 2008b. *Land Operations*. B-GL-300-001/FP-001 (209-01-01). Ottawa: Department of National Defence.

Deputy Commandant for Combat Development and Integration. 2009. Concept for Unified Action Through Civil-Military Integration. Quantico, Virginia: US Marine Corps, Marine Corps Combat Development Command. At http://www.dtic.mil/cgi--bin/GetTRDoc?AD=ADA499588&Location=U2&doc=GetTRDoc.pdf (accessed 23 December 2009).

Diani, M., and D. McAdam. 2003. *Social Movements and Networks: Relational Approaches to Collective Action*. New York: Oxford University Press.

Director General Joint Doctrine and Concepts. 2006. *The Comprehensive Approach*. Joint Discussion Note 4/05. London, UK: Ministry of Defence, Joint Doctrine and Concepts Centre. At http://www.mod.uk/NR/rdonlyres/BEE7F0A4-C1DA-45F8-9FDC-7FBD25750EE3/0/dcdc21_jdn4_05.pdf.

Director Land Concepts and Designs. 2009. *Toward Land Operations 2021: Studies in Support of the Army-of-Tomorrow Force Employment Concept*. Kingston, Ontario: Army Publishing Office.

Director Land Concepts and Designs. 2010. *Army Experiment 10 (AE 10) Report*. Kingston, Ontario: Army Publishing Office.

Directorate of Land Concepts and Designs. 2007. *Land Operations 2021: Adaptive Dispersed Operations*. Kingston, Ontario: Army Publishing Office.

Directorate of Land Concepts and Designs. Forthcoming. *Army 2040: First Look*. Kingston, Ontario, Directorate of Land Concepts and Designs.

Djik, G. 2010. *Comprehensive Approach ...and Why It's a Big NATO Issue*. Paper presented to CIOR Symposium on NATO's Comprehensive Approach and the Role of Reservists, 11 August 2010, Stavanger, Norway. At http://www.cior.net/News/2010/COMPREHENSIVE-APPROACH-...--and-why-it-is-a-big-NATO.aspx (accessed 15 November 2010).

Dorman A. 2007. *The Comprehensive Approach: Nice Idea but Is It Real?* Unpublished paper presented to the Inter-University Seminar on Armed Forces and Society International Biennial Conference, Loyola University, Chicago, Ill.

Dorner, D. 1998. *The Logic of Failure: Recognizing and Avoiding Complex Situations*. New York: Basic Books.

Duffey, T. 2002. Cultural Issues in Contemporary Peacekeeping. In *Peacekeeping and Conflict Resolution*, ed. T. Woodhouse and O. Ramsbotham, 142-168. Portland, Oregon: Frank Cass and Co. Ltd.

English, A. 2005. The Operational Art: Theory, Practice, and Implications for the Future. In *The Operational Art: Canadian Perspectives—Context and Concepts*, ed. Allan English, Daniel Gosselin, Howard Coombs, and Laurence M. Hickey. Kingston, Ontario: Canadian Defence Academy Press.

Eriksson, P. 2000. Civil-Military Coordination in Peace Support Operations – An Impossible Necessity? [Electronic Version] *Journal of Humanitarian Assistance* September:1-35. At http://jha.ac/articles/a061.htm (accessed 30 October 2008).

Eyre, D.P. 1998. Working with NGOs: What Every SOF Soldier Should Know. *Special Warfare* 11:14-23.

Farah, Douglas. 2006. *The Strategic Challenge of Failed States*. Alexandria, Virginia: International Assessment and Strategy Center. At http://www.strategycenter.net/research/pubID.120/pub_detail.asp (accessed 21 August 2009).

Farrell, Theo. 2005. *The Norms of War: Cultural Beliefs and Modern Conflict*. Boulder, Colorado: Lynne Rienner Publishers.

Farrell, Theo, and Stuart Gordon. 2009. COIN Machine: The British Military in Afghanistan. *Orbis* 53(4):665-83.

Ferguson, N. 2010. Complex Adaptive Systems: A Blueprint to Analyze Imperial Collapse. *Harvard International Review* 32(2). At http://hir.harvard.edu/law-of-the-land/complex-adaptive-systems (accessed 15 December 2010).

Finnemore, Martha, and Kathryn Sikkink. 1998. International Norm Dynamics and Political Change. *International Organization* 52(4):887-917.

Foreign Policy. 2009. Failed State Index. At http://www.foreignpolicy.com/articles/2009/06/22/2009_failed_states_index_faq_methodology (accessed 21 February 2010).

Forseberg, Carl. 2009. *The Taliban Campaign for Kandahar, Afghanistan*. Report No. 3. Washington, DC: Institute for the Study of War.

Francois, I. 1995. *Civil-Military Cooperation in Humanitarian Emergencies*. Ottawa: Department of National Defence.

Friis, K., and P. Jarmyr. 2008. *Comprehensive Approach: Challenges and Opportunities in Complex Crisis Management*. NUPI Report, Security in Practice No. 11. Oslo: Norwegian Institute of International Affairs.

Fulton, W.J. 2003. *Capabilities Required of DND: Asymmetric Threats and Mass Destruction*, 4th draft, 18 March 01, 2/22.

Gabriëlse, Robert, 2007. A 3D Approach to Security and Development. *PfP Consortium Quarterly Journal* summer 6(2):67-73.

Gallant, B., D. Reding, and P. Gizewski. 2010. Assessment of the TTCP Ad Hoc Study Group: Science and Technology for the Comprehensive Approach. Final Report, Briefing Note.

Gauster, Markus. 2008. *Provincial Reconstruction Teams in Afghanistan*. The Marshall Center Occasional Paper Series No. 16. Germany: The Marshall Center.

Gharajedaghi, Jamshid. 2006. *Managing Complexity: A Platform for Designing Business Architecture*, 2nd ed. Boston: Elsevier.

Giddens, Anthony. 1990. *The Consequences of Modernity*. Cambridge: Polity Press.

Gizewski, P., and LCol M. Rostek. 2007. Toward a Comprehensive Approach to CF Operations: The Land Force JIMP Concept. Ottawa: *DRDC CORA TM 2007-60*.

Gizewski, P., and LCol M. Rostek. 2009. The Canada First Defence Strategy: The Need for a Comprehensive Approach. In *Canada and the Changing Strategic Environment: The Canada First Strategy and Beyond*, ed. Phil Orchard. Proceedings of the Annual Conference of the Security and Defence Forum Centres. Vancouver: Centre for International Relations, University of British Columbia.

Gladwell, Malcolm. 2002. *The Tipping Point: How Little Things Can Make a Big Difference*. New York: Little, Brown and Company.

Gladwell, Malcolm. 2005. *Blink: The Power of Thinking Without Thinking*. New York: Little, Brown and Company.

Gladwell, Malcolm. 2008. *Outliers: The Story of Success* New York: Little, Brown and Company.

Godefroy, Andrew, ed. 2007. *Adaptive Dispersed Operations: A Force Employment Concept for Canada's Land Forces*. Kingston, Ontario: Directorate of Land Concepts and Designs.

Goetz, Gary. 2003. *International Norms and Decision Making: A Punctuate Equilibrium Model*. Lanham, Maryland: Rowman and Littlefield Publishers, Inc.

Goldstone, J., et al. 2005. A Global Forecasting Model of Political Instability. *American Political Science Review* 91(7):57-73).

Gopin, M. 2009. *To Make the Earth Whole: The Art of Citizen Diplomacy in an Age of Religious Militancy*. Lanham, Maryland: Rowan and Littlefield Publishers.

Gordenker, L., and T.G. Weiss. 1996. Pluralizing Global Governance: Analytical Approaches and Dimensions. In *NGOs, the UN, and global governance*, ed. T.G. Weiss and L. Gordenker, 17-47. Boulder, Colorado: Lynne Rienner Publishers.

Gosselin, BGen Daniel. 2006. The Loss of Mission Command for Canadian Expeditionary Operations: A Casualty of Modern Conflict?" In *The Operational Art: Canadian Perspectives - Leadership and Command*, ed. Allan English, 193-228. Kingston. Ontario: Canadian Defence Academy Press.

Government of Australia. 2009. *Defending Australia in the Asia-Pacific Century: Force 2030*. Defence White Paper. Canberra: Department of Defence.

Government of Canada. 2005. *Canada's International Policy Statement: A Role of Pride and Influence in the World*. Ottawa: Department of Foreign Affairs and International Trade.

Government of Canada. 2008a. *Canada First Defence Strategy*. At http://www.forces.gc.ca/site/focus/firts/defstra_e.asp (accessed 17 September 2008).

Government of Canada. 2008b. Independent Panel on Canada's Future Role in Afghanistan. Ottawa: Government of Canada.

Government of Canada. 2008d. *Representative of Canada in Kandahar — Terms of Reference*. Ottawa: Government of Canada.

Government of Canada. 2009a. *Canada's Engagement in Afghanistan*. Ottawa: Government of Canada.

Government of Canada. 2009b. *Sustaining Canada's Engagement in Acutely Fragile and Conflict-Affected Situations*. Ottawa: Government of Canada.

Government of Canada. 2010. Muskoka 2010 G-8 Canada. Ottawa: Supply and Services Canada. At http://g8.gc.ca/wp-content/uploads/2010/06/mar_annex58.pdf (accessed 29 June 2010).

Government of Canada, Department of National Defence. 2004. *CF Strategic Operations Concept*, Draft 4.4 (For CDS Review).

Government of Canada, Department of National Defence. 2006. B-GJ-307/FP-030. *Peace Support Operations*. Ottawa: Supply and Services Canada.

Government of Canada, House of Commons. 2007. *Speech from the Throne, 16 October 2007*. At http://www.sft-ddt.gc.ca/eng/media.asp?id=1364 (accessed 12 March 2008).

Grafstein, R. 1988. The Problem of Institutional Constraint. *The Journal of Politics* 50:577-599.

Gray, C. 2007. *War, Peace, and International Relations: An Introduction to Strategic History*. Abingdon, Oxon: Routledge.

Gray, C. 2008. Designing Government Strategies and Drawing them Together. Remarks presented to the Conference Sustaining the Force-Soldier First RUSI/DEM Future Land Warfare 08, Banqueting House, Royal Palace at Whitehall and Royal United Services Institute, United Kingdom 12-13 June.

Hack, K. 2009. The Malayan Emergency as a Counter-Insurgency Paradigm. *Journal of Strategic Studies* 32(3):383-414.

Hall, P.A., and C.R. Taylor. 1996. Political Science and the Three New Institutionalisms. *Political Studies* 44:936-957.

Halperin, M. 1974. *Bureaucratic Politics and Foreign Policy*. Washington, DC: Brookings Institution.

Hamblet, W., and J. Kline. 2000. Interagency Cooperation: PDD 56 and Complex Contingency Operations. *Joint Force Quarterly* Spring:92-97.

Hansen, Flemming Splidsboel, ed. 2009. *The Comprehensive Approach: Challenges and Prospects*. Copenhagen: Royal Dutch Defense College.

Harvard International Review. 2008. Failed States: Picking Up the Pieces, winter 9(4). At http://www.harvardir.org/symposia/78/ (accessed 21 August 2009).

Hataley, Inspector T. 2010. Comments to conference on Canadian Perspectives on the Comprehensive Approach, 15-16 April. Kingston, Ontario: Queen's University.

Holton, T.L., A.R. Febbraro, M. Barnes, E.-A. Filardo, B. Fraser, and R. Spiece. 2009. *The Relationship between Non-governmental Organizations and the Canadian Forces: A Pilot Study*. DRDC Toronto TR 2009-198. Toronto: Defence R&D Canada (DRDC).

Horn, B. 2006. Outside the Wire—Some Leadership Challenges in Afghanistan. *Canadian Military Journal* Autumn:6-14.

House of Commons. 2009. Special Committee on the Canadian Mission in Afghanistan. At http://www2.parl.gc.ca/HousePublications/Publication.aspx?DocId=3955406&Language=E&Mode=1&Parl=40&Ses=2.

Hrychuk, H., and P. Gizewski. 2008. *The Comprehensive Approach: Historical Antecedents: Annotated Bibliography, Part 1*. Toronto: DRDC CORA TN 2008-037 October.

Human Security Centre, Liu Institute for Global Issues. 2005. Human Security Report 2005. Vancouver: University of British Columbia.

Immergut, E.M. 1998. Theoretical Core of the New Institutionalism. *Politics and Society* 26(1): 5-34.

Ink, D.A. 2008. *The 1964 Alaskan Earthquake: Case Study for the Project on National Security Reform*. Washington, DC: Project on National Security Reform and the Centre for the Study of the Presidency. At http://www.pnsr.org/web/page/653/sectionid/579/pagelevel/3/parentid/590/interior.asp (accessed 15 November 2010).

International Committee of the Red Cross (ICRC). 2007. *ICRC Strategy 2007-2010*. Geneva: ICRC. At http://www.icrc.org/web/eng/siteeng0.nsf/html/stragegy-2007-2010.

ICRC. 2010. *ICRC Mandate and Missions*. Geneva: ICRC. At http://www.icrc.org/web/eng/siteeng0.nsf/htmlall/section_mandate?OpenDocument.

Interview with Assistant Commissioner Bud Mercer, Chief Operating Officer – Integrated Security Unit, Vancouver 2010 Olympic Games, by author (Brister), Surrey, BC, 1 October 2010.

Interview with Integrated Security Unit Emergency Measures Coordinator, by author (Brister), Victoria, BC, 27 September 2010.

Interview with Integrated Security Unit Planner, by author (Brister), Vancouver, BC, 30 September 2010.

Interview with Senior Games Operations Officer, by author (Brister), Richmond, BC, 15 May 2008, and Canada Privy Council Office at http://www.pco-bcp.gc.ca/docs/Org/2009-03-eng.pdf.

Interview with Senior Games Security Liaison and Coordinator, by author (Brister), Richmond, BC, 15 May 2008.

Interview with Senior Official, Department of National Defence, by author (Brister), Ottawa, 5 May 2008.

Interview with Senior Provincial Manager, by author (Brister), Surrey, BC, 30 September 2010.

Interview with W.P.D. Elcock, Coordinator, 2010 Olympics and G8 Security, by author (Brister), Ottawa, 20 July 2009.

Iribarnegaray, D. 2002. Peacekeeping's New Partnerships [Electronic Version]. *Peace, Conflict and Development: An Interdisciplinary Journal* 2:1-21. At http://www.peacestudiesjournal.org.uk/ (accessed 30 October 2008).

Jakobsen, P.V. 2008. NATO's Comprehensive Approach to Crisis Response Operations: A Work in Slow Progress. Danish Institute for International Affairs (DIIS) Report No. 15. At http://www.diis.dk/sw69155 (accessed 3 January 2011).

Jan Potgieter. 2007. *Commercial Deal Based Negotiation Strategy.* The Negotiation Academy. At http://www.negotiations.gr/Articles/tabid/71/ctl/Details/mid/533/ItemID/10/Default.aspx (accessed 22 November 2008).

Jenny, J. 2001. Civil-Military Cooperation in Complex Emergencies: Making It Work. *European Security* 10:23-22.

Johnson, G. 1988. Rethinking Incrementalism. *Strategic Management Journal* 9:75-91.

Joiner, Carl. 1967. The Ubiquity of the Administrative Role in Counterinsurgency. *Asian Survey* 7(8):540-554.

Joint Task Force Afghanistan (JTFA). 2009. *Preliminary Report. Application of the Whole of Government (WoG) Approach: Afghanistan.* Theatre Lessons Learned Report (TLR) 03/09. Headquarters, Joint Task Force Afghanistan.

Jones, Wendel. 2003. Complex Adaptive Systems. In *Beyond Intractability,* ed. Guy Burgess and Heidi Burgess. Boulder: Conflict Research Consortium, University of Colorado, At http://www.beyondintractability.org/essay/complex_adaptive_systems/.

Kacowicz, Arie M. 2005. *The Impact of Norms in International Society—The Latin American Experience 1881-2001.* Notre Dame, Indiana: University of Notre Dame Press.

Kaldor, Mary. 2001. *New and Old Wars: Organized Violence in the Global Era.* Stanford: Stanford University Press.

Kapstein, E.B. 2010. Do Three Ds Make an F? The Limits of Defense, Diplomacy, and Development. *Prism* 1(3):21-26. At http://www.ndu.edu/press/prism1-3.html (accessed 1 December 2010).

Katz, J.E., and M. Aakhus 2002. *Perpetual Contact : Mobile Communication, Private Talk, Public Performance.* New York: Cambridge University Press.

Katzenstein, P.J., ed. 1996. *The Culture of National Security.* New York: Columbia University Press.

Keck, Margaret E., and Kathryn Sikkink, 1998. *Activists Beyond Borders : Advocacy Networks in International Politics*. Ithaca, NY: Cornell University Press.

Kellerman, Captain Jennifer. 2003. *Operation KALAY: Moving on to Build in the South*. Ottawa: Department of National Defence. At http://www.comfec.forces. gc.ca/pa-ap/fs-ev/2009/09/18-eng.asp.

Kelman, H.W. 2008. Reconciliation from a Social-Psychological Perspective. In *The Social Psychology of Intergroup Reconciliation*, ed. A. Nadler, T.E. Malloy, and J.D. Fisher. New York: Oxford University Press.

Kelman, Steven, Fred Thompson, L.R. Jones, and Kuno Schedler. 2003. Dialogue on the Definition and Evolution of the Field of Public Management. *International Public Management Review* 4(2):1-19.

Kilcullen, David. 2007. New Paradigms for 21ˢᵗ Century Conflict *Small Wars Journal*, 23 June. At: http://smallwarsjournal.com/blog/2007/06/new-paradigms-for-21st-century/.

Kitson, Frank. 1971. *Low Intensity Operations: Subversion, Insurgency, Peacekeeping*. London: Faber and Faber.

Kitson, Frank. 1977. *Bunch of Five*. London: Faber and Faber.

Koslowski, R., and F.V. Kratochwil. 1994. Understanding Change in International Politics: The Soviet Empire's Demise and the International System. *International Organization* 48(2):215-247.

Kozij, J. 2010. Comments to Conference, Canadian Perspectives on the Comprehensive Approach. 15-16 April. Kingston: Queen's University.

Krishnasamy, Kabilan. 2003. The Paradox of India's Peacekeeping. *Contemporary South Asia* 12(2):263-280.

Kuhn, T. 1996. *The Structure of Scientific Revolutions*. Chicago: University of Chicago Press.

Laitinen, K. 2003. Geopolitics of the Northern Dimension: A Critical View on Security Borders. *Geopolitics* 8(1):22.

Land Force. 2008. *Counter-Insurgency Operations*. B-GL-323-004/FP-003. Kingston, Ontario: Army Publishing Office.

Land Force. 2009. Doctrine Note 2-09. Key Leader Engagement (KLE)—Approval Draft.

Land Forces Western Area (LFWA). 2009. Training Website for Exercise Maple Guardian. Edmonton, Alberta: Land Forces Western Area. At http://www. army.gc.ca/lfwa/tf309/feature_ex_maple_guardian.asp (accessed 22 December 2009).Landau, Yehezkel. 2003. Healing the Holy Land: Interreligious Peacebuilding in Israel/Palestine. *Peaceworks* 51.

Last, David. 2010. Respectful Collaborative Stabilization Operations and Rule of Law. In *Mission Critical: The Role of Smaller Democracies in Global Stability Operations*, ed. Christian Leuprecht, Jodok Troy, and David Last, 275-296. Montreal and Kingston: McGill-Queen's University Press.

Lawner, D., B. Kaster, and N. Matthews. 2010. Recipes for Failure and Keys to Success in Interagency Cooperation: Two Case Studies. *Defense Concepts* 4(4):22-31.

LeBlanc, G. 2007. *The Challenges of Military Humanitarian Operations*. Toronto, Ontario: Canadian Forces College.

Lebow, Richard Ned, and Janice Gross Stein. 2002. Globalization and Security: An Alternative World History. In *Transformative Change and Global Order*, ed. Doris A. Fuchs and Friedrich Kratochwil, 63-83. Piscataway, New Jersey: Transactions Publishers.

Lederach, J.P. 1997. *Building Peace: Sustainable Reconciliation in Divided Societies.* Washington, D.C.: United Institute of Peace Press.

Legro, Jeffrey W. 1997. Which Norms Matter? Revisiting the "Failure" of Internationalism. *International Organization* 51(1):31-63.

Leslie, A., P. Gizewski, and M. Rostek. 2008. Developing a Comprehensive Approach to Canadian Forces operations. *Canadian Military Journal* 9(1):11-20.

Leuprecht, Christian. 2010a. At the Demographic Crossroads: International Security Strategy for the 21st century. In *Mission Critical: The Role of Smaller Democracies in Global Stability Operations,* ed. Christian Leuprecht, Jodok Troy, and David Last, 13-47. Montreal and Kingston: McGill-Queen's University Press.

Leuprecht, Christian. 2010b. International Security Strategy in the Age of Population Aging. *Journal of Strategic Security* winter 3(4):27-48.

Locher III, James R. 2009. National Security Reform: A Prerequisite for Successful Complex Operations. *Prism^* 1(1):77-86. At http://www.ndu.edu/press/prism1-1.html (accessed 1 December 2010).

Longhurst, G.M. 2007. The Evolution of Canadian Civil-Military Cooperation (CIMIC). *Canadian Military Journal* winter 7():55-64.

Luck, Gary, and Michael Findlay. 2007. *Insights and Best Practices: Interagency, Intergovernmental and Nongovernmental Cooperation (A Joint Force Operational Perspective).* Focus Paper #3. Norfolk. Virginia: Joint Warfighting Center, United States Joint Forces Command. At http://jko.cmil.org/f ile/109/view.

Lynn, John. 1995. The trace italienne and the Growth of Armies. In *The Military Revolution Debate,* ed. Clifford J. Rogers. Boulder, Colorado: Westview Press.

MacDonald, N. 2007. Losing Hearts and Minds: The Empty Shell of Human Security in Southern Afghanistan. *The Human Security Bulletin* Jan/Feb:8-10.

Magnuson, S. 2009. Playing Nice: Integrating Civilians into Military Operations Remains Difficult. *National Defense* December:36-38.

Manley, The Honourable John, P.C., Derek H. Burney, O.C., The Honourable Jake Epp, P.C., The Honourable Paul Tellier, P.C., C.C., Q.C., and Pamela Wallin, O.C. S.O.M. 2008. *Independent Panel on Canada's Future Role in Afghanistan.* At http://www.afghanistan.gc.ca/canada-afghanistan/assets/pdfs/Afghan_Report_web_e.pdf (accessed 2 February 2011).

Mantle, C.L. 2008. *How Do We Go about Building Peace While We're Still at War? Canada, Afghanistan, and the Whole-of-Government Concept.* Canadian Forces Leadership Institute Technical Report 2008-02. Kingston, Ontario: Canadian Defence Academy.

March, J.G., and J.P. Olsen. 1998. The Institutional Dynamics of International Political Orders. *International Organization* 52(4):948.

Meharg, S.J. 2009. *Measuring What Matters in Peace Operations and Crisis Management.* School of Policy Studies. Kingston, Ontario: Queen's University, McGill-Queen's University Press.

Meisel, N., and J.O. Aoudia. 2008. Is "Good Governance" a Good Development Strategy? Working Paper 58. Paris: Agence France de développement.

Melkert, Ad. 2009. Opening Statement by Under-Secretary General and Administrator *a.i.,* United Nations Development Programme, *3C Conference,* Geneva, 19 March. At http://content.undp.org/go/newsroom/2009/march/ad-melkert-3c-conference-in-geneva.en?src=print.

Metz, Stephen. 2008. American Grand Strategy: Concepts, Theory, History, and Futures. Presentation at the US Army War College Strategic Studies Institute.

Carlisle, Pennsylvania: Army War College. At http://www.scribd.com/doc/2419351/Grand-Strategy (accessed January 05, 2011).

Miller, L.L. 1999. From Adversaries to Allies: Relief Workers' Attitudes toward the US Military. *Qualitative Sociology* 22(3):181-197.

Mockaitis, Thomas R. 2004. *Civil-Military Cooperation in Peace Operations: The Case of Kosovo.* Carlisle, Pennsylvania: US Army War College, Strategic Studies Institute.

Moir, J.S. 1962. *History of the Royal Canadian Corps of Signals, 1903-1961.* Ottawa: Corps Committee of the Royal Canadian Corps of Signals.

Monaghan, S. 2007. Conclusion: Connecting Theory and Practice. In *Helping Hands and Loaded Arms: Navigating the Military and Humanitarian Space,* ed. S.J. Meharg. Clementsport, Nova Scotia: The Canadian Peacekeeping Press.

Morcos, K. 2005. *Principles for Good International Engagement in Fragile States.* Paris: Organisation for Economic Co-operation and Development. DCD (2005)8/REV2. At http://www.oecd.org/dataoecd/61/45/38368714.pdf.

Nadler, A., and N. Shnabel. 2008. Instrumental and Socioemotional Paths to Intergroup Reconciliation and the Needs-Based Model of Socioemotional Reconciliation. In *The Social Psychology of Intergroup Reconciliation,* ed. A. Nadler, T.E. Malloy, and J.D. Fisher. New York: Oxford University Press.

Nagl, John. 2002. *Counterinsurgency Lessons from Malaya and Vietnam: Learning to Eat Soup with a Knife.* Westport, Connecticut: Praeger Publishers.

National Post. 2008. Manley Report invokes the spirit of Pearson. At http://www.nationalpost.com/news/story.html?id=256093 (accessed 23 January 2008).

Natsios, A.S. 1996. NGOs and the UN System in Complex Humanitarian Emergencies: Conflict or Cooperation? In *NGOs, the UN, and Global Governance,* ed. T.G. Weiss and L. Gordenker, 67-81. Boulder, Colorado: Lynne Rienner Publishers.

Newman, D. 2003. On Borders and Power: A Theoretical Framework. *Journal of Borderland Studies* 18(1):14.

North Atlantic Council. 2008. Bucharest Summit Declaration. Brussels: North Atlantic Council. At http://www.nato.int/cps/en/natolive/official_texts_8443.htm?mode=pressrelease.

North Atlantic Treaty Organization (NATO). 2003. NATO Civil-Military Cooperation, Allied Joint Publication 9. Brussels: North Atlantic Treaty Organization. At http://www.nato.int/ims/docu/AJP-9.pdf (accessed 13 December 2010).

NATO. 2007. *Future Comprehensive Civil-Military Interaction Concept (FCCMIC).* Version 1.1. Brussels: NATO. At https://transnet.act.nato.int/WISE/EnhancedCi/Documents/copy_of_FCCMIC/file/_WFS/FCCMIC%20V%201.%201%20%20%40%2017%20May%2007.doc (accessed 12 February 2011).

NATO. 2009. *Chief of Transformation Conference. Final Analysis Report.* December, pp. 7-13.

NATO. 2010. *NATO's Role in Afghanistan.* Brussels: NATO. At http://www.nato.int/cps/en/natolive/topics_8189.htm (accessed 1 July 2010).

NATO. 2011. *A Comprehensive Approach.* Brussels, NATO. At http://www.nato.int/cps/en/natolive/topics_51633.htm (accessed 5 February 2011).

NATO Bucharest Summit. 2008. Declaration Issued by the Heads of State and Government Participating in the Meeting of the North Atlantic Council in Bucharest, 3 April. NATO. http://www.summitbucharest.ro/en/doc_201.html.

NATO Multi-National Experiment 5. 2009. *Multinational Interagency Strategic Planning.* Version 8. In *Key Elements of a Comprehensive Approach: A Compendium of Solutions.* Helsinki: Finnish Ministry of Defence. At http://www.uscrest.org/files/MNE5.pdf.

NATO Public Policy Division. 2006. *Prevailing in Afghanistan, Improving Capabilities, Enhancing Cooperation*. Brussels: NATO Public Policy Division. At http://www. nato.int/docu/nato_after_riga/nato_after_riga_en.pdf.

North, D.C., J.J. Wallis, and B.R. Weingast. 2009. *Violence and Social Orders: A Conceptual Framework for Interpreting Recorded Human History*. Cambridge: Cambridge University Press.

Northrup, T.A. 1989. The Dynamic of Identity in Personal and Social Conflict. In *Intractable Conflicts and Their Transformation*, ed. L. Kriesburg, T.A. Northrup, and S.J. Thornson. Syracuse, New York: Syracuse University Press.

O'Connell, Thomas W. 2007. An Interview with Thomas W. O'Connell, Assistant Secretary of Defense for Special Operations and Low-Intensity Conflict. *Joint Force Quarterly* 44(1):9.

O'Connor, Maura R. 2011. The UN "Cluster System" Is as Bad as It Sounds. Posted Friday, Jan. 7, 2011, at 7:11 a.m. At http://www.slate.com/id/2279858/entry/0.

Okros, A. 2008. *Cultural Complexity vs. Cultural Conflict: Considering the Inter-Relations amongst Cultures and Military Operations*. Paper presented at the 10th Asia-Pacific Programme for Senior Military Officers, Singapore.

Oliver, J. 2009. Speaking Notes of Chief Superintendent Director General Border Integrity, RCMP. Northern Border Security Challenges and Cross-Border Cooperation. Yale Club, New York City, 8 October 2009. At http://www.public-safety.gc.ca/prg/le/_fl/int-cross-brdr-martime-eng.pdf (accessed 7 July 2010).

Olson, L., and H. Gregorian. 2007. *Side by Side or Together? Working for Security, Development, and Peace in Afghanistan and Liberia*. Calgary: The Peace-building, Development, and Security Program (PDSP), Centre for Military and Strategic Studies, University of Calgary. At http://cmss.ucalgary.ca/pdsp/files/pdsp/sidebysideortogether_oct2007.pdf.

Onuf, N., V. Kubalkova, and P. Kowert, eds. 1998. *International Relations in a Con-structed World*. London: M.E. Sharpe.

Organisation for Economic Co-operation and Development (OECD). 2001. *OECD DAC Guidelines: Helping Prevent Violent Conflict*. Ministerial Statement on Help-ing Prevent Violent Conflict: Orientations for External Actors. Paris: Centre français d'exploitation de droits de copie (CFC). At http://www.oecd.org/dataoecd/15541886146.pdf.

OECD. 2005. *Paris Declaration on Aid Effectiveness*. Paris: OECD. At http://www. oecd.org/dataoecd/30/63/43911948.pdf.

OECD. 2006. *Whole-of-Government Approaches to Fragile States*. Paris: Organisation for Economic Co-operation and Development.

OECD. 2007. *The OECD Handbook on Security System Reform*. Paris: OECD. At http://www.oecd.org/dataoecd/43/25/38406485.pdf.

OECD. 2008. *Accra Agenda for Action*. Paris: OECD. At http://www.oecd.org/dataoecd/30/63/43911948.pdf.

OECD. 2010. *Dili Declaration. A New Vision for Peacebuilding and Statebuilding*. Dili, Timor-Leste. At http://www.c-r.org/our-work/influencing-policy/Dili%20 Declaration_FINAL_12042010.pdf.

OECD Development Assistance Committee (DAC). 1997. *Policy Statement on Conflict, Peace, and Development Cooperation on the Threshold of the 21st Century*. Paris: OECD. At http://www.oecd.org/dataoecd/15541886146.pdf.

OECD DAC. 2007. *Principles for Good International Engagement in Fragile States and Situations*. Paris: OECD DAC, High Level Forum. At http://www.oecd.org/dataoecd/61/45/38368714.pdf.

OECD DAC. 2010. *Ensuring fragile states are not left behind*. Paris: OECD. At http://www.oecd.org/dataoecd/38/33/44822042.pdf.

OECD Development Cooperation Directorate (DCD)-DAC. 2007. *Principles for Good International Engagement in Fragile States*. Paris: OECD. At http://www.oecd.org/document/48/0,3343,en_2649_33693550_35233262_1_1_1_1,00.html.

Ostrom, Elinor, and Nives Dolesak. 2003. *The Commons in the New Millennium: Challenges and Adaptation (Politics, Science, and the Environment)*. Cambridge, Mass.: MIT Press.

Otis, P. 2004. Religion and War in the Twenty-first Century. In *Religion and Security: The New Nexus in International Relations*, ed. R.A. Seiple and D.R. Hoover. Lanham, Maryland: Rowan and Littlefield Publishers.

Paasi, A. 1996. *Territories, Boundaries and Consciousness: The Changing Geographies of the Finnish-Russian Border*. New York: John Wiley and Sons, Ltd.

Patrick, Stewart, and Kaysie Brown. 2007. *Greater Than the Sum of Its Parts? Assessing Whole-of-Government Approaches to Fragile States*. New York: United Nations International Peace Academy.

Permanent Mission of Canada to the United Nations. 2008. Research Resources: CANADEM. Ottawa: DFAIT. At http://www.canadainternational.gc.ca/prmny-mponu/resources-ressources/civil_society-societe-civile/resources-ressources.aspx?lang=eng (accessed 28 February 2011) and http://www.canadem.ca/home (accessed 2 February 2011).

Peters, T., and R.H. Waterman, Jr. 1982. *In Search of Excellence: Lessons from America's Best-Run Companies*. New York: Harper and Row Publishers Inc.

Peters, G.B., J. Pierre, and D.S. King. 2005. The Politics of Path Dependency: Political Conflict in Historical Institutionalism. *The Journal of Politics* 67(4):1275-1300.

Petersen, Friis Arne, and Hans Binnendijk. 2007. The Comprehensive Approach Initiative: Future Options for NATO. *Defense Horizons* 58.

Pettigrew, T.F. 1998. Intergroup Contact Theory. *Annual Review of Psychology* 49:65-85.

Pierson, P. 2000. Not Just What, but When: Timing and Sequence in Political Processes. *Studies in American Political Development* 14:72-92.

Pierson, P. 2004. *Politics in Time: History, Institutions and Social Analysis*. Princeton: Princeton University Press.

Pollick, S. 2000. Civil-Military Cooperation: A New Tool for Peacekeepers. *Canadian Military Journal* 1:57-63.

Potgieter, Jan. 2007. *Commercial Deal Based Negotiation Strategy*. The Negotiation Academy. At http://www.negotiations.gr/Articles/tabid/71/ctl/Details/mid/533/ItemID/10/Default.aspx (accessed 22 November 2008).

Project on National Security Reform. 2008. *Preliminary Findings Report*. Washington, DC: Project on National Security Reform and the Centre for the Study of the Presidency. At http://www.pnsr.org/data/images/pnsr%20preliminary%20findings%20july%202008.pdf (accessed November 15, 2010).

Public Safety Canada. 2009. *Framework Agreement on Integrated Cross-Border Maritime Law Enforcement Operations between the Government of Canada and the Government of the United States of America*. Ottawa: Public Safety Canada. At http://www.publicsafety.gc.ca/prg/le/_fl/int-cross-brdr-martime-eng.pdf (accessed 7 July 2010).

QSR International. 2009. *NVivo*. Doncaster, Australia: QSR International. At http://www.qsrinternational.com/products_nvivo.aspx (accessed 22 December 2009).

Ramo, Joshua Cooper. 2009. *The Age of the Unthinkable*. New York: Little and Brown.

Raymond, Gregory A. 1992. Problems and Prospects in the Study of International Norms. *Mershon International Studies Review* 41(2 November):205-245.

Recklies, D. 2001. *Recklies Management Project GmbH*. Magdeburg, Germany: Recklies Management Project GmbH.

Rietjens, S.J.H. 2008. Managing Civil-Military Cooperation: Experiences from the Dutch Provincial Reconstruction Team in Afghanistan. *Armed Forces and Society* 34:173-207.

Rintakoski, Kristiina, and Mikko Autti, eds. 2008. *Comprehensive Approach: Trends, Challenges, and Possibilities in Crisis Prevention and Management*. Based on Comprehensive Approach Seminar, 17 June. Helsinki: Ministry of Defence.

Risse, Thomas, Stephen C. Ropp, and Kathryn Sikkink, eds. 1997. *The Power of Human Rights: International Norms and Domestic Change*. Cambridge: Cambridge University Press.

Roy, LCol Richard. 2009. All in: Developing the Comprehensive Approach. *Vanguard*. Aurora, Ontario: John Jones. At http://www.vanguardcanada.com/ExplainingTheComprehensiveApproachRoy.

Roy, LCol R. 2010. Comments to Conference, Canadian Perspectives on the Comprehensive Approach. 15-16 April. Kingston, Ontario: Queen's University.

Royal Canadian Mounted Police. 2006. *Mission, Vision, and Values*. Ottawa: RCMP. At http://www.rcmp-grc.gc.ca/about-ausujet/mission-eng.htm (accessed 1 July 2010).

Royal Canadian Mounted Police. 2009a. *Cadet Training Program Overview*. Ottawa: RCMP. At http://www.rcmp-grc.gc.ca/depot/ctp-pfc/index-eng.htm (accessed 1 July 2010).

Royal Canadian Mounted Police. 2009b. *Proceeds of Crime Program*. Ottawa: RCMP. At http://www.rcmp-grc.gc.ca/poc-pdc/pro-crim-eng.htm (accessed 1 July 2010).

Said, Sami, and Cameron Holt. 2008. A Time for Action: The Case of Interagency Deliberate Planning. *Strategic Studies Quarterly* fall 2(3):30-71.

Schaefer, P.S., S.B. Shadrick, J. Beaubien, and B.T. Crabb. 2008. *Training Effectiveness Assessment of Red Cape: Crisis Action Planning and Execution*. Research Report 1885. Arlington, VA: US Army Research Institute for the Behavioral and Social Sciences.

Schaefer, Peter F., and P. Clayton Schaefer. 2008. *Japan after WWII: Case Study for the Project on National Security Reform*. Washington, DC: Project on National Security Reform and the Centre for the Study of the Presidency. At http://www.pnsr.org/web/page/659/sectionid/579/pagelevel/3/parentid/590/interior.asp (accessed 15 November 2010).

Schelling, Thomas. 1966. *Arms and Influence* New Haven, Connecticut: Yale University Press.

Scheltinga, T.A.M., S.J.H. Rietjens, S.J. de Boer, and C.P.M Wilderom. 2005. Cultural Conflict within Civil-Military Cooperation: A Case Study in Bosnia. *Low Intensity Conflict and Law Enforcement* 13:54-69.

Schreiter, R. J. 1992. *Reconciliation: Mission and Ministry in a Changing Social Order*. Maryknoll, New York: Orbis Books.

Scott, James W. 2001. *Institutions and Organizations*. Thousand Oaks, CA: Sage.

Sowell, T. 2007. *Basic Economics: A Common Sense Guide to the Economy*, 3rd ed. New York: Basic Books.

Simms, J. 2008. *The Joint, Interagency, Multi-National, and Public (JIMP) Environment: Making Sense of a Crowded Battlespace.* Toronto: Canadian Forces College. At http://wps.cfc.forces.gc.ca/papers/nssc/nssc10/simms.doc.

Special Inspector General for Iraq Reconstruction (SIGIR). 2010. *Hard Lessons: The Iraq Reconstruction Experience and Applying Iraq's Hard Lessons to the Reform of Stabilization and Reconstruction Operation.* Arlington, Virginia: US Government Printing Office.

Spence, N. 2002. Civil-Military Cooperation in Complex Emergencies: More than a Field Application. *Journal of Peacekeeping* 9:165-171.

Sphere Project. 2004. *Humanitarian Charter and Minimum Standards in Disaster Response.* Geneva: The Sphere Project. At www.sphereproject.org.

Stein, J.G. 2001. In the Eye of the Storm: Humanitarian NGOs, Complex Emergencies, and Conflict Resolution. *Peace and Conflict Studies Journal* 8:17-41.

Stephenson, M., and M.H. Schnitzer. 2006. Interorganizational Trust, Boundary Spanning, and Humanitarian Relief Coordination. *Nonprofit Management and Leadership* 17:211-233.

Stepputat, Finn. 2009 Integrated National Approaches to International Operations: The Cases of Denmark, UK, and The Netherlands. *Danish Institute of International Studies Report* 14:15.

Stewart, K.G., C.M. Macklin, A.C. Proud, N.G. Verrall, and M. Widdowson. 2004. *Organisational and Sociological Factors of Multinational Forces: Baseline Studies Final Report.* Farnborough, UK: Centre for Human Sciences, QinetiQ.

Sweeney, J.K. 1996. *A Handbook of American Military History: From the Revolutionary War to the Present.* Boulder, Colorado: Westview Press, Inc.

Swiss Agency for Development and Cooperation. 2009. *3C Roadmap.* Geneva: Swiss Agency for Development and Cooperation. At http://www.reliefweb.int/rw/RWFiles2009.nsf/FilesByRWDocUnidFilename/ASHU-7UK4SX-full_report.pdf/$File/full_report.pdf.

Tamas, A. 2009. *Warriors and Nation Builders: Development and the Military in Afghanistan.* Kingston, Ontario: Canadian Defence Academy Press.

The Office of the Executive Director Conflict Management. 2001. *Interest-Based Negotiation and Alternative Dispute Resolution Course Participant's Manual.* Interest-Based Negotiation Presentation. Ottawa: Department of National Defence.

The Prime Minister's Strategy Unit. 2006. *Countries at Risk of Instability.* London: UK Prime Minister's Strategy Unit. At http://webarchive.nationalarchives.gov.uk/20070101092320/http://cabinetoffice.gov.uk/strategy/work_areas/countries_at_risk/index.asp (accessed 28 June 2010).

Thompson, M.M., and R. Gill. 2010. The Role of Trust in Whole-of-Government Missions. In *Mission Critical: Smaller Democracies' Role in Global Stability Operations*, ed. C. Leuprecht, T. Jodok, and D. Last. Montreal and Kingston: McGill-Queen's University Press.

Thompson, Robert. 1966. *Defeating Communist Insurgency: The Lessons from Malaya and Vietnam.* New York: Praeger Publishers.

Thomson, M.H., C.D.T. Hall, and B.A. Adams. 2010. *Canadian Forces Education and Training for Interagency Operational Contexts.* DRDC Toronto Contract Report (DRDC No. CR 2010-013). Toronto: DRDC.

Toronto Police Service. 1999. *Mission Statement.* Toronto: Toronto Police Service. At http://www.torontopolice.on.ca/mission-values.php (accessed 1 July 2010).

Towards Comprehensive Development Policies. The OECD Development Centre's 2005-2006 Programme of Work. 2005. Paris: The Organisation for Economic Cooperation and Development (OECD) Development Centre, July. http://www.oecd.org/dataoecd/57/62/35005392.pdf.

Trofimov, Y. 2010. Risky Ally in War on Polio: The Taliban. *Wall Street Journal*, 15 January. At http://online.wsj.com/article/SB126298998237022117.html (accessed 23 March 2010).

United Kingdom (UK) Cabinet Office. 1999. *Modernising Government*. London: Modernising Government Secretariat. At *http://archive.cabinetoffice.gov.uk/moderngov/download/modgov.pdf.

UK Development, Concepts, and Doctrine Centre. 2010. *Global Strategic Trends — Out to 2040*. United Kingdom, Ministry of Defence. At http://www.mod.uk/NR/rdonlyres/D70F2CC7-5673-43AE-BA73-1F887801266C/0/20100202GST_4_Global_Strategic_Trends_Out_to_2040UDCDCStrat_Trends_4.pdf (accessed 5 January 2011).

UK Foreign and Commonwealth Office. 2003. *The Global Conflict Prevention Pool: A Joint UK Government Approach to Reducing Conflict*. London: United Kingdom Foreign and Commonwealth Office.

UK House of Commons Defence Committee. 2010. *The Point of War Is Not Just to Win but Make a Better Peace*. Government's Response to the Committee's Seventh Report of Session 2009–10. London: Stationary Office.

UK Ministry of Defence. 2010. Ministry of Defence Home Page. London: Ministry of Defence. At http://www.mod.uk/DefenceInternet/Home/ (accessed 12 February 2011).

UK Ministry of Defence, Assistant Chief of Defence Staff (Development, Concepts, and Doctrine). 2009. Joint Doctrine Publication 3-40. *Security and Stabilisation: The Military Contribution*. United Kingdom: Ministry of Defence.

United Nations (UN). 2003. *Principles and Good Practice of Humanitarian Donorship*. Stockholm: UN. At http://www.reliefweb.int/ghd/a%2023%20Principles%20EN-GHD19.10.04%20RED.doc.

UN. 2006. *Integrated Missions Planning Process (IMPP)*. Guidelines endorsed by the Secretary-General. New York: United Nations. At http://www.undg.org/docs/9907/IMPP-Revised-Guidelines-130606.pdf (accessed 5 February 2011).

UN. 2008a. *Decision Number 2008/24: Integration*. Decisions of the Secretary-General, Meeting of the Policy Committee. New York: United Nations. At http://www.undg.org/docs/9898/Integration-decision-SG-25-jun-08.pdf (accessed 5 February 2011).

UN. 2008b. *United Nations Peacekeeping Operations, Principles and Guidelines*. New York: United Nations Department of Peacekeeping Operations. At www.pbpu.unlb.org/pbps/Library/Capstone_Doctrine_ENG.pdf.

UN. 2009. *United Nations Peacekeeping*. Geneva: UN. At http://www.un.org/Depts/dpko/dpko/index.asp (accessed 23 February 2009).

UN Department of Economic and Social Affairs (DESA). 2008. State Building in Post-Conflict Countries Requires a Different Approach. Policy Brief No. 7. New York: UN-DESA.

UN Departments of Peacekeeping Operations (DPKO) and Field Support (DFS). 2006. *DPKO Policy Directive: Joint Operations Centres and Joint Mission Analysis Centres* (Ref. POL/2006/3000/04), 1 July. New York: United Nations DPKO.

UN Departments of Peacekeeping Operations (DPKO) and Field Support (DFS) 2010. *DPKO Policy Directive: Civil-Military Coordination in UN Integrated Peace-keeping Missions* (Ref. 2010.2), January. New York: United Nations DPKO.

United Nations Development Program (UNDP). 1994. *Human Development Report.* (New York: Oxford University Press).

UN General Assembly. 2000. Verbatim Report, Meeting 85, Session 55. New York: UN. At http://www.undp.org/mdg/basics.shtml.

UN General Assembly. 2004. *A More Secure World: Our Shared Responsibility. Report of the High-Level Panel on Threats, Challenges, and Change.* A/59/565. Geneva: UN General Assembly.

UN Integrated Missions Planning Process (IMPP). 2008. Guidelines Endorsed by the Secretary-General on 13 June 2006. *International Peacekeeping* Volume 15(4):588-607. At http://www.informaworld.com/smpp/491498813-628694/title~db=all~content=t713635493~tab=issueslist~branches=15 - v15.

UN Interoffice Memorandum. 2008. *Decisions of the Secretary General, 25th Meeting of the Policy Committee.* New York: United Nations.

United States (US) Army. 2008. *Marine Corps Counterinsurgency Field Manual* 3-24 MCWP 3-33-5. Washington, DC: Government Printing Office.

US Department of Defense. 2010. *Quadrennial Defense Review Report 2010.* Washington, DC: Department of Defense.

US Department of Justice. 2009. *Community Policing Defined.* Washington, DC: US Government Printing Office.At http://www.cops.usdoj.gov/default.asp?item=36 (accessed 1 July 2010).

US Department of State. 2009. *US Government Counterinsurgency Guide.* Washington, DC: Department of State. At http://www.state.gov/documents/organization/119629.pdf (accessed 12 February 2011).

US Department of State. 2010. *Diplomacy in Action.* Washington, DC: Department of State. At http://www.state.gov/s/crs/civilianresponsecorps/index.htm(accessed 12 February 2011).

US Geological Survey (USGS). 2009. *Circum-Arctic Resource Appraisal.* Colorado: USGS Information Services. At http://energy.usgs.gov/arctic/.

US Immigration and Customs Enforcement. 2010. *Border Enforcement Security Task Forces.* Washington, DC: US Department of Homeland Security. At http://www.ice.gov/pi/news/factsheets/080226best_fact_sheet.htm (accessed 7 July 2010).

United States Institute of Peace (USIP). 2007. *Guide for Participants in Peace, Stability, and Relief Operations.* Washington, DC: United States Institute of Peace.

USIP. 2009. USIP, US Army Unveil First Civilian Doctrine for Peace Operations. Washington, DC: USIP. At http://www.usip.org/print/newsroom/news/usip-us-army-unveil-first-civilian-doctrine-peace-operations (accessed 18 March 2011).

USIP. 2010. *Guiding Principles for Stabilization and Reconstruction.* Washington, DC: US Institute of Peace. At http://www.usip.org/newsroom/news/usip-us-army-unveil-first-civilian-doctrine-peace-operations (accessed 12 February 2011).

US Institute of Peace and US Peacekeeping and Stability Operations Institute. 2009. *Guiding Principles for Reconstruction and Stabilization.* Washington, DC: US Institute of Peace Press. At http://www.usip.org/resources/guiding-principles-stabilization-and-reconstruction.

US Marine Corps. 2006. *Counter-insurgency.* Field Manual No. 3-24. Marine Corps Warfighting Publication No. 3-33.5. Washington DC: Headquarters, Department of the Army.

US Marine Corps Combat Development Command. 2009. *Concept for Unified Action Through Civil-Military Integration.* Quantico, Virginia: Deputy Commandant for Combat Development and Integration, US Marine Corps. At http://www.dtic. mil/cgi--bin/GetTRDoc?AD=ADA499588&Location=U2&doc= GetTRDoc.pdf (accessed 23 December 2009).

US National Intelligence Council, Office of the Director of National Intelligence. 2008. *Global Trends 2025: A Transformed World.* Washington, DC: US Government Printing Office. At http://www.dni.gov/nic/PDF_2025/2025_Global_Trends_ Final_Report.pdf (accessed 23 October 2010).

US Reconstruction and Stabilization Policy Coordinating Committee. 2008. *Interagency Conflict Assessment Framework,* Washington, DC: United States Reconstruction and Stabilization Policy Coordinating Committee.

US Treasury Department. 2004. USC 19-US CODE 19-US Code Title 19 Customs Duties. Washington, DC: US Government Printing Office. At http://vlex.com/ vid/sec-miscellaneous-19194215.

USAID. 2010. *Religion, Conflict and Peacebuilding: An Introductory Programming Guide.* Washington, DC: US Agency for International Development. At http:// www.usaid.gov/our_work/cross-cutting_programs/conflict/publications/ docs/Religion_Conflict_and_Peacebuilding_Toolkit.pdf.

van der Kloet, I. 2006. Building Trust in the Mission Area. *Small Wars and Insurgencies* 17:421–436.

Varshney, A. 2002. *Ethnic Conflict and Civic Life: Hindus and Muslims in India.* New Haven, CN: Yale University Press.

Waltz, Kenneth. 1979. *Theory of International Politics.* Reading, Massachusetts: Addison-Wesley.

Ward, Olivia. 2008. Canada confusing political, aid relief goals in Afghanistan, MD says. *Toronto Star,* 22 April. At http://www.thestar.com/News/World/ article/416888 (accessed 10 February 2011).

Waterman, R.H., T. Peters, and J.R. Phillips. 1980. Structure Is Not Organization. *Business Horizons* 23(3):14-26.

Watkin, Kenneth. 2004. Controlling the Use of Force: A Role for Human Rights Norms in Contemporary Armed Conflict. *The American Journal of International Law* 98(1):1-34.

Watts, Duncan J. 2003. *Six Degrees: The Science of a Connected Age,* 1st ed. New York: WW Norton.

Wendt, A. 1992. Anarchy Is What States Make of It: The Social Construction of Power Politics. *International Organization* 46(2):398.

Whitfield, Teresa. 2007. *Friends Indeed? The United Nations, Groups of Friends, and the Resolutions of Conflict.* Washington, DC: United States Institute of Peace Press.

Williams, M.C. 1998. *Civil-Military Relations and Peacekeeping.* Adelphi Paper, Vol. 321. London: Oxford University Press.

Wilson, G.I., J.P. Sullivan, and H. Kempfer. 2003. *4GW Tactics of the Weak Confound the Strong.* Washington, DC: Project on Government Oversight (POGO). At http://www.dnipogo.org/fcs/comments/c490.htm.

Wilson, James Q. 1989. *Bureaucracy.* New York: Basic Books.

Winslow, D. 2002. Strange Bedfellows: NGOs and the Military in Humanitarian Crises. *The International Journal of Peace Studies* 7(2):35-56. At http://www.gmu. edu/academic/ijps/vol7_2/cover7_2.htm (accessed 2 April 2009).

Winslow, D., and J. Dunn. 2002. Women in the Canadian Forces: Between Legal and Social Integration. *Current Sociology* 50:647-667.

World Bank. 2001. *Voices of the Poor*. Washington, DC: World Bank. At http://publications.worldbank.org/index.php?main_page=product_info&cPath=&products_id=23221.

Yaneer, Bar-Yam. 2004. *Making Things Work: Solving Complex Problems in a Complex World*. New York: Knowledge Press.

Zegart, Amy. 1999. *Flawed by Design: The Evolution of the CIA, JCS, and NSC*. Palo Alto, California: Stanford University Press.

CONTRIBUTORS

Laura C. **Ball**, PhD Candidate. History & Theory of Psychology Program, Department of Psychology, York University. Toronto, Ontario.

Nipa **Banerjee**, PhD. School of International Development & Globalization & Associate-Graduate School of Public and International Affairs University of Ottawa. Ottawa, Canada.

Marissa **Barnes**, PhD Candidate. History & Theory of Psychology Program, Department of Psychology, York University. Toronto, Ontario.

Anne-Renée **Blais**. Research Psychologist, Collaborative Performance and Learning Section, Defence Research and Development Canada. Toronto, Ontario.

Sylvia **Bogusis**. Senior Policy Analyst, Strategic Policy and Integration, Indian and Northern Affairs Canada. Ottawa, Canada.

Major Bernard **Brister**, CD, PhD. Assistant Professor, Royal Military College of Canada. Kingston, Ontario.

Gavin **Buchan**. Director, Afghanistan Policy, Department of National Defence. Ottawa, Canada.

Beth Ellen **Cole**. Director of Intergovernmental Affairs, US Institute of Peace.Washington, DC 20036.

Kevin **Coppock**. Humanitarian Affairs Liaison, Médecins Sans Frontières. Toronto, Canada.

Angela **Febbraro**, PhD. Defence Scientist, Organizational Behaviour Group Leader, Collaborative Performance and Learning Section, Defence Research & Development Canada. Toronto, Ontario.

Emily-Ana **Filardo**, PhD. Visiting Fellow, Collaborative Performance and Learning Section, Defence Research & Development Canada. Toronto, Ontario.

Brenda M. **Fraser** B.A. Research Technologist, Technical Group, Collaborative Performance and Learning Section, Defence Research & Development Canada. Toronto, Ontario.

Steve **Fritz-Millett** (Lieutenant-Colonel Retired), CD, BEng. Calian Technologies Limited. Kingston, Ontario.

Peter **Gizewski**. Defence Scientist/Strategic Analyst, Land Capability Development Operational Research Team (LCDORT). Kingston, Ontario.

Todd **Hataley**, PhD. Adjunct Professor Royal Military College of Canada. Kingston, Ontario.

Xiang **He**. Policy Analyst, Peace, Conflict and State Resilience, Policy Development Division, Strategic Policy and Performance Branch, Canadian International Development Agency. Ottawa, Canada.

Tara **Holton**, PhD. Defence Scientist, Organizational Behaviour Group, Collaborative Performance and Learning Section, Defence Research and Development Canada. Toronto, Ontario.

Michael **Koros**. Team Leader and Senior Analyst, Peace, Conflict and State Resilience, Policy Development Division, Strategic Policy and Performance Branch, Canadian International Development Agency. Ottawa, Canada.

John W. **Kozij**. Director Strategic Policy & Integration Division Strategic Policy & Devolution Branch Indian and Northern Affairs Canada. Ottawa, Canada.

Christian **Leuprecht**, PhD. Associate Professor, Department of Political Science and Economics Royal Military College of Canada. Kingston, Ontario.

Marilyn **McHarg**. Executive Director, Médecins Sans Frontières. Toronto, Canada.

Major/Padre S.K. **Moore**, CD, PhD. Canadian Forces Chaplain & Visiting Research Fellow Saint Paul University (Conflict Studies). Ottawa, Ontario.

Kim Richard **Nossal**. Sir Edward Peacock Professor of International Relations and Director, Queen's Centre for International and Defence Policy, Queen's University. Kingston, Ontario.

Michel **Rentenaar**. Civil Military Interface Advisor, NATO's Supreme Headquarters Allied Powers in Europe. Casteau, Belgium.

Lieutenant-Colonel Michael A. **Rostek**, CD, PhD. Concepts Team Leader, Directorate of Land Concepts and Designs. Kingston, Ontario.

Lieutenant-Colonel Richard C. **Roy**, CD. Comprehensive Approach Special Advisor, Chief of Force Development. Ottawa, Ontario.

Colonel Jim **Simms**, CD. Commander, Combat Training Centre, CFB Gagetown, Gagetown, New Brunswick.

Rachel **Spiece**. B.A. Research Technologist, Technical Group, Collaborative Performance and Learning Section, Defence Research & Development Canada. Toronto, Ontario.

START Secretariat. Department of Foreign Affairs and International Trade. Ottawa, Canada.

Megan **Thompson**, PhD. Section Scientific Advisor, Collaborative Performance and Learning Section, Defence Research and Development Canada. Toronto Ontario.

Caroline **Vavro, MA.** Comprehensive Approach Research Assistant, Chief of Force Development. Ottawa, Ontario.

Queen's Policy Studies
Recent Publications

The Queen's Policy Studies Series is dedicated to the exploration of major public policy issues that confront governments and society in Canada and other nations.

Manuscript submission. We are pleased to consider new book proposals and manuscripts. Preliminary enquiries are welcome. A subvention is normally required for the publication of an academic book. Please direct questions or proposals to the Publications Unit by email at spspress@queensu.ca, or visit our website at: www.queensu.ca/sps/books, or contact us by phone at (613) 533-2192.

Our books are available from good bookstores everywhere, including the Queen's University bookstore (http://www.campusbookstore.com/). McGill-Queen's University Press is the exclusive world representative and distributor of books in the series. A full catalogue and ordering information may be found on their web site (http://mqup.mcgill.ca/).

School of Policy Studies

Making the Case: Using Case Studies for Teaching and Knowledge Management in Public Administration, Andrew Graham, 2011. Paper ISBN 978-1-55339-302-3

Canada's Isotope Crisis: What Next? Jatin Nathwani and Donald Wallace (eds.), 2010. Paper ISBN 978-1-55339-283-5 Cloth ISBN 978-1-55339-284-2

Pursuing Higher Education in Canada: Economic, Social, and Policy Dimensions, Ross Finnie, Marc Frenette, Richard E. Mueller, and Arthur Sweetman (eds.), 2010. Paper ISBN 978-1-55339-277-4 Cloth ISBN 978-1-55339-278-1

Canadian Immigration: Economic Evidence for a Dynamic Policy Environment, Ted McDonald, Elizabeth Ruddick, Arthur Sweetman, and Christopher Worswick (eds.), 2010. Paper ISBN 978-1-55339-281-1 Cloth ISBN 978-1-55339-282-8

Taking Stock: Research on Teaching and Learning in Higher Education, Julia Christensen Hughes and Joy Mighty (eds.), 2010. Paper ISBN 978-1-55339-271-2 Cloth ISBN 978-1-55339-272-9

Architects and Innovators: Building the Department of Foreign Affairs and International Trade, 1909–2009/Architectes et innovateurs : le développement du ministère des Affaires étrangères et du Commerce international,de 1909 à 2009, Greg Donaghy and Kim Richard Nossal (eds.), 2009. Paper ISBN 978-1-55339-269-9 Cloth ISBN 978-1-55339-270-5

Academic Transformation: The Forces Reshaping Higher Education in Ontario, Ian D. Clark, Greg Moran, Michael L. Skolnik, and David Trick, 2009. Paper ISBN 978-1-55339-238-5 Cloth ISBN 978-1-55339-265-1

The New Federal Policy Agenda and the Voluntary Sector: On the Cutting Edge, Rachel Laforest (ed.), 2009. Paper ISBN 978-1-55339-132-6

Measuring What Matters in Peace Operations and Crisis Management, Sarah Jane Meharg, 2009. Paper ISBN 978-1-55339-228-6 Cloth ISBN 978-1-55339-229-3

International Migration and the Governance of Religious Diversity, Paul Bramadat and Matthias Koenig (eds.), 2009. Paper ISBN 978-1-55339-266-8 Cloth ISBN 978-1-55339-267-5

Who Goes? Who Stays? What Matters? Accessing and Persisting in Post-Secondary Education in Canada, Ross Finnie, Richard E. Mueller, Arthur Sweetman, and Alex Usher (eds.), 2008. Paper ISBN 978-1-55339-221-7 Cloth ISBN 978-1-55339-222-4

Economic Transitions with Chinese Characteristics: Thirty Years of Reform and Opening Up,
Arthur Sweetman and Jun Zhang (eds.), 2009.
Paper ISBN 978-1-55339-225-5 Cloth ISBN 978-1-55339-226-2

*Economic Transitions with Chinese Characteristics: Social Change During Thirty Years of
Reform*, Arthur Sweetman and Jun Zhang (eds.), 2009.
Paper ISBN 978-1-55339-234-7 Cloth ISBN 978-1-55339-235-4

Dear Gladys: Letters from Over There, Gladys Osmond (Gilbert Penney ed.), 2009.
Paper ISBN 978-1-55339-223-1

Immigration and Integration in Canada in the Twenty-first Century, John Biles,
Meyer Burstein, and James Frideres (eds.), 2008.
Paper ISBN 978-1-55339-216-3 Cloth ISBN 978-1-55339-217-0

Robert Stanfield's Canada, Richard Clippingdale, 2008. Cloth ISBN 978-1-55339-218-7

Exploring Social Insurance: Can a Dose of Europe Cure Canadian Health Care Finance?
Colleen Flood, Mark Stabile, and Carolyn Tuohy (eds.), 2008.
Paper ISBN 978-1-55339-136-4 Cloth ISBN 978-1-55339-213-2

Canada in NORAD, 1957–2007: A History, Joseph T. Jockel, 2007.
Paper ISBN 978-1-55339-134-0 Cloth ISBN 978-1-55339-135-7

Canadian Public-Sector Financial Management, Andrew Graham, 2007.
Paper ISBN 978-1-55339-120-3 Cloth ISBN 978-1-55339-121-0

Emerging Approaches to Chronic Disease Management in Primary Health Care,
John Dorland and Mary Ann McColl (eds.), 2007.
Paper ISBN 978-1-55339-130-2 Cloth ISBN 978-1-55339-131-9

Fulfilling Potential, Creating Success: Perspectives on Human Capital Development,
Garnett Picot, Ron Saunders and Arthur Sweetman (eds.), 2007.
Paper ISBN 978-1-55339-127-2 Cloth ISBN 978-1-55339-128-9

Reinventing Canadian Defence Procurement: A View from the Inside, Alan S. Williams, 2006.
Paper ISBN 0-9781693-0-1 (Published in association with Breakout Educational Network)

SARS in Context: Memory, History, Policy, Jacalyn Duffin and Arthur Sweetman (eds.),
2006. Paper ISBN 978-0-7735-3194-9 Cloth ISBN 978-0-7735-3193-2
(Published in association with McGill-Queen's University Press)

Dreamland: How Canada's Pretend Foreign Policy has Undermined Sovereignty,
Roy Rempel, 2006. Paper ISBN 1-55339-118-7 Cloth ISBN 1-55339-119-5
(Published in association with Breakout Educational Network)

Canadian and Mexican Security in the New North America: Challenges and Prospects,
Jordi Díez (ed.), 2006. Paper ISBN 978-1-55339-123-4 Cloth ISBN 978-1-55339-122-7

*Global Networks and Local Linkages: The Paradox of Cluster Development in an Open
Economy*, David A. Wolfe and Matthew Lucas (eds.), 2005.
Paper ISBN 1-55339-047-4 Cloth ISBN 1-55339-048-2

Choice of Force: Special Operations for Canada, David Last and Bernd Horn (eds.), 2005.
Paper ISBN 1-55339-044-X Cloth ISBN 1-55339-045-8

Centre for the Study of Democracy

Jimmy and Rosalynn Carter: A Canadian Tribute, Arthur Milnes (ed.), 2011.
Paper ISBN 978-1-55339-300-9 Cloth ISBN 978-1-55339-301-6

*Unrevised and Unrepented II: Debating Speeches and Others By the Right Honourable Arthur
Meighen*, Arthur Milnes (ed.), 2011. Paper ISBN 978-1-55339-296-5
Cloth ISBN 978-1-55339-297-2

The Authentic Voice of Canada: R.B. Bennett's Speeches in the House of Lords, 1941-1947, Christopher McCreery and Arthur Milnes (eds.), 2009.
Paper ISBN 978-1-55339-275-0 Cloth ISBN 978-1-55339-276-7

Age of the Offered Hand: The Cross-Border Partnership Between President George H.W. Bush and Prime-Minister Brian Mulroney, A Documentary History, James McGrath and Arthur Milnes (eds.), 2009. Paper ISBN 978-1-55339-232-3
Cloth ISBN 978-1-55339-233-0

In Roosevelt's Bright Shadow: Presidential Addresses About Canada from Taft to Obama in Honour of FDR's 1938 Speech at Queen's University, Christopher McCreery and Arthur Milnes (eds.), 2009. Paper ISBN 978-1-55339-230-9 Cloth ISBN 978-1-55339-231-6

Politics of Purpose, 40th Anniversary Edition, The Right Honourable John N. Turner 17th Prime Minister of Canada, Elizabeth McIninch and Arthur Milnes (eds.), 2009.
Paper ISBN 978-1-55339-227-9 Cloth ISBN 978-1-55339-224-8

Bridging the Divide: Religious Dialogue and Universal Ethics, Papers for The InterAction Council, Thomas S. Axworthy (ed.), 2008. Paper ISBN 978-1-55339-219-4
Cloth ISBN 978-1-55339-220-0

Institute of Intergovernmental Relations

Canada: The State of the Federation 2009, vol. 22, *Carbon Pricing and Environmental Federalism*, Thomas J. Courchene and John R. Allan (eds.), 2010.
Paper ISBN 978-1-55339-196-8 Cloth ISBN 978-1-55339-197-5

Canada: The State of the Federation 2008, vol. 21, *Open Federalism and the Spending Power*, Thomas J. Courchene, John R. Allan, and Hoi Kong (eds.), forthcoming.
Paper ISBN 978-1-55339-194-4

The Democratic Dilemma: Reforming the Canadian Senate, Jennifer Smith (ed.), 2009.
Paper ISBN 978-1-55339-190-6

Canada: The State of the Federation 2006/07, vol. 20, *Transitions – Fiscal and Political Federalism in an Era of Change*, John R. Allan, Thomas J. Courchene, and Christian Leuprecht (eds.), 2009. Paper ISBN 978-1-55339-189-0 Cloth ISBN 978-1-55339-191-3

Comparing Federal Systems, Third Edition, Ronald L. Watts, 2008.
Paper ISBN 978-1-55339-188-3

Canada: The State of the Federation 2005, vol. 19, *Quebec and Canada in the New Century – New Dynamics, New Opportunities*, Michael Murphy (ed.), 2007.
Paper ISBN 978-1-55339-018-3 Cloth ISBN 978-1-55339-017-6

Spheres of Governance: Comparative Studies of Cities in Multilevel Governance Systems, Harvey Lazar and Christian Leuprecht (eds.), 2007. Paper ISBN 978-1-55339-019-0
Cloth ISBN 978-1-55339-129-6

Canada: The State of the Federation 2004, vol. 18, *Municipal-Federal-Provincial Relations in Canada*, Robert Young and Christian Leuprecht (eds.), 2006.
Paper ISBN 1-55339-015-6 Cloth ISBN 1-55339-016-4

Canadian Fiscal Arrangements: What Works, What Might Work Better, Harvey Lazar (ed.), 2005. Paper ISBN 1-55339-012-1 Cloth ISBN 1-55339-013-X

Canada: The State of the Federation 2003, vol. 17, *Reconfiguring Aboriginal-State Relations*, Michael Murphy (ed.), 2005. Paper ISBN 1-55339-010-5 Cloth ISBN 1-55339-011-3

Queen's Centre for International Relations

Europe Without Soldiers? Recruitment and Retention across the Armed Forces of Europe, Tibor Szvircsev Tresch and Christian Leuprecht (eds.), 2010.
Paper ISBN 978-1-55339-246-0 Cloth ISBN 978-1-55339-247-7

Mission Critical: Smaller Democracies' Role in Global Stability Operations, Christian Leuprecht, Jodok Troy, and David Last (eds.), 2010. Paper ISBN 978-1-55339-244-6

The Afghanistan Challenge: Hard Realities and Strategic Choices, Hans-Georg Ehrhart and Charles Pentland (eds.), 2009. Paper ISBN 978-1-55339-241-5

John Deutsch Institute for the Study of Economic Policy

The 2009 Federal Budget: Challenge, Response and Retrospect, Charles M. Beach, Bev Dahlby and Paul A.R. Hobson (eds.), 2010. Paper ISBN 978-1-55339-165-4
Cloth ISBN 978-1-55339-166-1

Discount Rates for the Evaluation of Public Private Partnerships, David F. Burgess and Glenn P. Jenkins (eds.), 2010. Paper ISBN 978-1-55339-163-0 Cloth ISBN 978-1-55339-164-7

Retirement Policy Issues in Canada, Michael G. Abbott, Charles M. Beach, Robin W. Boadway, and James G. MacKinnon (eds.), 2009.
Paper ISBN 978-1-55339-161-6 Cloth ISBN 978-1-55339-162-3

The 2006 Federal Budget: Rethinking Fiscal Priorities, Charles M. Beach, Michael Smart, and Thomas A. Wilson (eds.), 2007. Paper ISBN 978-1-55339-125-8
Cloth ISBN 978-1-55339-126-6

Health Services Restructuring in Canada: New Evidence and New Directions, Charles M. Beach, Richard P. Chaykowksi, Sam Shortt, France St-Hilaire, and Arthur Sweetman (eds.), 2006. Paper ISBN 978-1-55339-076-3
Cloth ISBN 978-1-55339-075-6

A Challenge for Higher Education in Ontario, Charles M. Beach (ed.), 2005.
Paper ISBN 1-55339-074-1 Cloth ISBN 1-55339-073-3

Current Directions in Financial Regulation, Frank Milne and Edwin H. Neave (eds.), Policy Forum Series no. 40, 2005. Paper ISBN 1-55339-072-5 Cloth ISBN 1-55339-071-7

Higher Education in Canada, Charles M. Beach, Robin W. Boadway, and R. Marvin McInnis (eds.), 2005. Paper ISBN 1-55339-070-9 Cloth ISBN 1-55339-069-5

Our publications may be purchased at leading bookstores, including the Queen's University Bookstore (http://www.campusbookstore.com/) or can be ordered online from: McGill-Queen's University Press, at **http://mqup.mcgill.ca/ordering.php**

For more information about new and backlist titles from Queen's Policy Studies, visit http://www.queensu.ca/sps/books or visit the McGill-Queen's University Press web site at: **http://mqup.mcgill.ca/**